Knowledge Management in Healthcare

For those who share and seek knowledge.

Knowledge Management in Healthcare

Edited by
LORRI ZIPPERER

Routledge
Taylor & Francis Group

LONDON AND NEW YORK

First published 2014 by Gower Publishing

Published 2016 by Routledge
2 Park Square, Milton Park, Abingdon, Oxfordshire OX14 4RN
711 Third Avenue, New York, NY 10017, USA

First issued in paperback 2016

Routledge is an imprint of the Taylor & Francis Group, an informa business

British Library Cataloguing in Publication Data
A catalogue record for this book is available from the British Library

Library of Congress Cataloging-in-Publication Data
Knowledge management in healthcare / by Lorri Zipperer.
    pages cm
  Includes bibliographical references and index.
  ISBN 978-1-4094-3883-0 (hbk)
  1. Health services administration. 2. Knowledge management. I. Zipperer, Lorri
  A., 1959- editor of compilation.
  RA971.K56 2013
  362.1068--dc23

                                                                    2013028768

ISBN 13: 978-1-138-27141-8 (pbk)
ISBN 13: 978-1-4094-3883-0 (hbk)

Contents

List of Figures and Tables

Figures

Tables

About the Editor

Lorri Zipperer, Cybrarian is the principal at Zipperer Project Management, in Albuquerque, NM. Lorri has been in the information and knowledge management field for over two decades, over half of which have been focused on patient safety. She was a founding staff member of the National Patient Safety Foundation as the information project manager. Lorri currently works with clients to provide patient safety information, knowledge sharing, project management and strategic development guidance. Lorri has recently led projects in patient safety educational tool development, publication evidence identification and organizational knowledge access improvement. She currently serves as the Cybrarian for AHRQ's Patient Safety Network collaborating with the multidisciplinary editorial and production team since the launch of the site in 2005. She was recognized that same year with a 2005 Institute for Safe Medication Practices 'Cheers' award for her work with librarians, libraries and their involvement in patient safety. She has initiated and published two national surveys of librarians on their role in patient safety work to map the evolution of that role over time. Ms. Zipperer's expertise was highlighted in the June 2009 Medical Library Association policy on the role of librarians in patient safety. She has launched blogs, online groups and communities of practice to support sharing of information and knowledge to facilitate safety and quality improvement amongst her peers.

Ms. Zipperer was a 2004–2005 Patient Safety Leadership Fellow where she explored how information and knowledge transfer behaviors affect a learning culture. She has participated in research to explore the process of knowledge sharing both at the bedside and with clinical teams. In 2007 and 2009, she was funded by regional offices of the National Network of Libraries of medicine to work with her colleagues in acute care environments to facilitate avenues for implementation of knowledge sharing initiatives. In 2008, Ms. Zipperer worked with the WHO Patient Safety to envision an effective knowledge sharing role for that organization. More recently Lorri has participated in a series of workshops looking at systematic and cognitive impacts that evidence, information and knowledge can have on decision making the diagnostic error. She has designed and co-facilitates an interprofessional workshop on knowledge sharing in hospitals which has been noted as being "transformational."

Lorri earned her MA in library and information studies from Northern Illinois University. She has served as an adjunct professor for library management at the university level. Lorri has received honors from the library and information science community and has been published on topics such as alternative roles for librarians, patient safety, collaboration, systems thinking and knowledge management.

About the Contributors

Geraldine Amori, PhD, ARM, CPHRM, DFASHRM   Geri is the Vice President for Academic Affairs for Coverys based in Boston, MA. In that role, Dr. Amori develops, analyzes and coordinates professional development/ education programs for a variety of healthcare organizations. In addition, she presents, teaches, coaches, and facilitates educational programs about Risk Management and Patient Safety issues. Dr. Amori has served as Vice President for the Education Center of the Risk Management and Patient Safety Institute, Principal of Communicating HealthCare, and as Risk Manager for Fletcher Allen Health Care in Burlington, Vermont. Dr. Amori received a Ph.D. in Counselor Education from the University of Florida and an MS in Counseling and Human Systems from Florida State University. She is an active member of the American Society for Healthcare Risk Management (ASHRM) and is a past president of the society. She is the 2004 recipient of the ASHRM Distinguished Service Award and three time recipient of the ASHRM Journal Author Excellence Award. A CPHRM and Distinguished Fellow in the American Society for Healthcare Risk Management, Dr. Amori is also the past president of the Northern New England Society for Healthcare Risk Management. Dr. Amori has been published often, recently developing a chapter on communicating with patients and families for the 6th edition of the *Risk Management Handbook for Healthcare Organizations* (ASHRM, 2010).

Barbara Balik, RN, EdD   Barbara is the Co-Founder of Aefina Partners, Senior Faculty at the Institute of Healthcare Improvement, and member of the National Patient Safety Foundation Board of Governors. She works with healthcare leaders and physicians to build systems and culture for quality, safety, patient-family experience, and staff-provider engagement. Recent partnerships involved developing skills and processes for patient-and-family centered care, excellent patient experience, reliable transitions in care, and quality infrastructures. Her recent publications include: *The Heart of Leadership: Inspiration and Practical Guidance for Transforming Your Health Care Organization* (AHA, 2010) and *Achieving an Exceptional Patient and Family Experience of*

Impatient Hospital Care (Institute for Healthcare Improvement, 2011). Barbara has a BS and MS in nursing and a doctorate in educational leadership. Her previous roles include: Allina Hospitals and Clinics, MN – EVP of Quality, Safety, and Technology; CEO at United Hospital and Clinics; VP of Patient Care/ CNO at United Hospital; System CNO Council Chair; Minneapolis Children's Medical Center – VP of Patient Care/CNO.

Margaret Moyan Bandy, MALS, AHIP, FMLA   Margaret is Medical Librarian and Manager of Library and Knowledge Services at Exempla Saint Joseph Hospital in Denver, CO. She served on the Medical Library Association (MLA) Board of Directors from 2005–2008. Bandy co-edited the *Medical Library Association Guide to Managing Health Care Libraries*, 2nd edition (MLA, 2011), which received the Ida and George Eliot Prize in 2012. In 2009 she collaborated in the development of the MLA Position Statement *Role of Health Sciences Librarians in Patient Safety*. Bandy received an MALS from Dominican University, River Forest, Illinois in 1972 and an MA in English from Loyola University, Chicago, IL in 1976. Since 1990 she has been a Distinguished Member of the Academy of Health Information Professionals (AHIP) of the Medical Library Association, becoming a Fellow of MLA in 2010. She has received a number of awards including the MLA Lois Ann Colaianni Award for Excellence and Achievement in Hospital Librarianship in 2002 and the Marla M. Graber Award for Excellence and Achievement in Health Sciences Librarianship from the Colorado Council of Medical Librarians in 2005.

Pamela Barnard, MSLS   Pamela supports the patient care, performance improvement, professional development and research needs of employees and affiliated providers in her work as a Knowledge Consultant at Allina Health Library Services. Pamela received her Master's in Library and Information Science from the University of North Carolina at Chapel Hill.

Margaret H. Burnette, MLIS   Peg is an Assistant Professor and Biomedical Sciences Librarian at the University of Illinois at Urbana-Champaign. She is liaison to biomedical programs and research across multiple departments, institutes, and programs and guest lecturer at the University of Illinois Graduate School of Library and Information Science. Peg's current research adapts knowledge management principles to dispersed interdisciplinary biomedical research initiatives spanning areas as diverse as basic science, genomic research, and clinical and applied health research. Prior to joining the University of Illinois at Urbana-Champaign in October 2012, Peg was an Assistant Professor and Information Services Librarian at the Library of the

Health Sciences, University of Illinois at Chicago, College of Medicine-Peoria. Peg's areas of interest include knowledge sharing, e-science, biomedical informatics and health literacy.

Christine Chastain-Warheit, MLS, AHIP   Christine served as Director, Medical Libraries, Christiana Care Health System, for 25 years, from March, 1987 to retirement in March, 2012. The libraries grew from two sites to five, the staff size doubled, transitioning the libraries from print to digital collections and services, serving over 10,000 employees and 300 residents, adding teaching services, medical informationist services and consumer health services. Unique contributions included co-writing the original Class B Internet license grant for the health system, serving on health-system-wide patient safety, videoconferencing, intranet web advisory committees and as a faculty member of the health system graduate level quality and performance improvement team skills, nationally-recognized course (Achieving Competency Today). Professionally Christine has had several publications and national presentations, most notably as a co-author of "Hospital Librarianship in the United States: At the Crossroads," *Journal of the American Medical Association*, in January 2002 and as an invited speaker for the Transformational Change in Health Sciences Libraries Symposium at Penn State Hersey Medical School in 2009. She received the Lois Ann Colaianni Award for Excellence and Achievement in Hospital Librarianship in 2004, an NLM Medical Informatics Fellowship at Woods Hole in 1994, and served as Chair, Hospital Libraries Section of the Medical Library Association, 2008–2009. Christine has been a Distinguished member of the Academy of Health Information Professionals since 1995.

Jan Chindlund, MBA, MLS   Jan is Library Dean at Columbia College Chicago. Prior to joining Columbia College Chicago in 2007, Jan managed two special libraries in the Chicago metropolitan area: the Research Library of Duff & Phelps and the McDonald's Corporation Global Business & Consumer Insight Information Center where she was honored with the President's Award. Jan holds a Master of Library and Information Science from Dominican University and a Master of Business Administration from Benedictine University. Active in Special Libraries Association (SLA) at the chapter, division and association levels since 1987, she served as SLA Illinois Chapter president (2003–2004) and as B&F secretary (1994–1996) and director (1998–2000). Jan received the SLA Dow Jones Leadership Award in 2000, was named an SLA Fellow in 2006, and was the 2010 recipient of SLA Rose L. Vormelker Award.

Michael G. Dieter, Ph.D., MLIS, MBA   Michael has worked at the University of Illinois at Chicago (UIC) for over 20 years in a number of roles that include teaching, research, and administration. He is a long-standing faculty member in the UIC Department of Biomedical and Health Information Sciences' graduate Health Informatics program. Over the years, Dr. Dieter has contributed significantly to the program's transformation from onsite classroom to fully online course delivery and has served as the Program Director since 2011. Currently, his efforts are focused on expanding the program's research curriculum track, instituting high quality synchronous online instructor training for adjunct faculty, and adapting the curriculum to respond to rapidly evolving professional learning needs in the field of Health Informatics. He teaches the program's "Knowledge Management in Healthcare Organizations" course. Michael's additional areas of academic interest include Consumer Health Informatics, Information and Health Literacy, eLearning, curriculum studies, and discourse studies.

Heidi A. Heilemann, MLS, MLA, AHIP   Heidi is Associate Dean for Knowledge Management and Director of the Lane Medical Library and Knowledge Management Center at Stanford University Medical Center where she has worked in various library positions since 1993. She received her Master of Librarianship from the University of Washington in 1993, a Master of Liberal Arts from Stanford University in 2003, and a Bachelor of Arts degree in Art History & Criticism in 1989. Heilemann has held several leadership positions at the Medical Library Association and is a Distinguished member of the Academy of Health Information Professionals (AHIP). Heidi was a 2007–2008 NLM/AAHSL Leadership fellow and is currently serving as a mentor in the program.

Michael Leonard, MD   Michael is the founder of Safe & Reliable Healthcare, a Faculty member of the Institute for Healthcare Improvement (IHI), and Adjunct Professor of Medicine at Duke University. An honors graduate of the University of Missouri School of Medicine, Dr. Leonard did his postgraduate training in Internal Medicine and Anesthesiology at Harvard's Beth Israel Hospital in Boston, with fellowship training in cardiac anesthesia. A practicing anesthesiologist for 21 years, he spent 14 years with the Colorado Permanente Medical Group, where he was Chief of Anesthesia, Chief of Surgical Services, and Chairman of the Board of Directors. He spent 10 years as the National Physician Leader for Patient Safety for Kaiser Permanente. In 1999, he helped Kaiser forge a collaborative relationship with Dr. Robert Helmreich's Human Factors Research Project to work on the application of human factors teamwork and communication training within medicine. For the past several years, he has taught extensively throughout the Kaiser system and outside organizations in high-risk areas such as surgery, obstetrics, critical care and others to enhance safety. At the IHI, he has been active in several domains in safety and care transformation both in the US and the United Kingdom. In addition to teaching and lecturing widely, Dr. Leonard has co-authored two books on patient safety: *The Essential Guide for Patient Safety Officers* (Joint Commission, 2013), and *Achieving Safe and Reliable Healthcare* (Health Administration Press, 2004).

Michael F. Moore, MLS   Michael is a Senior Information Analyst at the MITRE Corporation in Bedford, MA, working with their Systems Engineering Practice Office. He works as an embedded librarian, and has published on embedded librarianship in *Information Outlook*. Michael is also 2013 Chair of the Military Libraries Division of the Special Libraries Association, and active in his local Toastmasters club. Michael received his Bachelor of Arts in Music and English from St. Olaf College, Northfield, MN, and his Master in Library and Information Science from Dominican University through the College of St. Catherine, St. Paul, MN. Michael enjoys using Peter Senge's causal loop diagram techniques in the *Fifth Discipline* to better understand systems. Michael met Lorri when she taught about Systems Thinking at Special Libraries Association conferences.

Julianne M. Morath, RN, MS   Julie is a recognized expert in healthcare quality and patient safety is CEO of the Hospital Quality Institute (HQI), a collaboration of the California Hospital Association and the three Regional Associations. Prior to joining HQI, Morath served as chief quality and patient safety officer for Vanderbilt University Medical Center. She is a founding and current member of the Lucian Leape Institute of the National Patient Safety Foundation and serves on the Board of Commissioners of The Joint Commission and Board of the Virginia Mason Medical Center and Health System. Morath is also a distinguished advisor to the National Patient Safety Foundation. In addition, she is a past member of the National Quality Forum Best Practices Committee. Morath has more than three decades of executive and academic experience in healthcare that includes the University of Cincinnati, Brown University, University of Rhode Island, University of Minnesota and Vanderbilt University. Her work is distinguished through translating research into practice and building cultures of safety and excellence. Before joining Vanderbilt, Morath served as COO at Children's Hospitals and Clinics of Minnesota. She has authored two books on quality and safety and is widely published on topics of quality, patient safety, leadership, and patient/family engagement. Among her many awards, Morath was the inaugural recipient of the John Eisenberg Award for Individual Lifetime Achievement in Patient

Safety, awarded through The Joint Commission and National Quality Forum; and received the Industry Leader Award from the Minnesota Business Community in 2007.

Judith Napier, RN   Judith is the Vice President for Risk Services for Allina Health in Minnesota. Before joining Allina Health, Napier was a Sr. Director for Patient Safety and Risk Management for Children's Hospitals and Clinics of Minnesota. Napier has held past positions of Senior Vice President for MMI Companies, an international healthcare risk management company where she was a Sr. Consultant and Healthcare leader working with domestic and international hospitals and healthcare systems on risk management tools and patient safety techniques for clinical and administrative performance improvements. Before her work with MMI Companies, Napier held positions in perinatal clinical care and academics where she led the maternal child nursing curriculum for the associate nursing degree program in a community college setting. Napier is a Registered Nurse with a Bachelors of Science in Nursing from Niagara University in New York State, and a Masters in Nursing from California State University at Los Angeles. She has a certificate of completion from HRET and the Health Forum/National Patient Safety Foundation Patient Safety Leadership Fellowship 2004–2005 and completion of the Institute for Healthcare Improvement's "Patient Safety Executive Development Program." Judith has been a national and international speaker in the areas of patient safety, quality, and risk management.

Becky A. Steward, BSN, RN   Becky works with hospitals, health systems, professional associations, and software companies to integrate best practices in quality and patient safety into the daily work of healthcare organizations. Ms. Steward is a former co-instructor in the master's program in patient safety leadership at University of Illinois at Chicago, IL, and the master's program in patient safety at Northwestern University in Chicago, IL.

Cathy Tokarski   Cathy is health policy writer and editor in the Chicago office of RTI International, a nonprofit health and research institute based in Research Triangle Park, NC. Her clients include the Agency for Healthcare Research and Quality, the Centers for Disease Control and Prevention, and other federal health agencies. Prior to joining RTI, Cathy worked as an editor and writer for Medscape/WebMD, the American Medical Association and *Modern Healthcare*. Cathy is skilled in translating and communicating complex concepts and research findings, including patient safety and quality improvement, to multiple audiences, including physicians, health professionals, consumers, and media.

Kathryn Eblen Townsend, RN, JD, ARM, CPHRM, LHRM   Kathryn is a nurse attorney with over 30 years in healthcare. She is the Director of Client Insurance Programs for PeriGen, an innovative provider of advanced technology systems designed to augment obstetrical decision-making and improve communication at the point of care. Ms. Townsend's prior experience includes serving as hospital in-house counsel, healthcare system corporate risk manager, and executive with a medical malpractice risk retention group insuring several leading academic medical centers. She received her law degree and her nursing degree from the University of Kentucky. Ms. Townsend has been an active member of the American Society for Healthcare Risk Management (ASHRM) for many years, serving on multiple committees and taskforces, and contributed to the creation of ASHRM's inaugural exam for healthcare risk management certification. She also helped develop ASHRM's patient safety certificate program, serving as curriculum team leader and faculty since inception. Ms. Townsend has served on the Board of Directors for the Florida Society of Healthcare Risk Management and was selected as a Fellow of the Salzburg Seminar on Patient Safety and Medical Error in Austria.

Annette L. Valenta, DrPH   Annette is Professor, Biomedical and Health Information Sciences, College of Applied Health Sciences at University of Illinois at Chicago (UIC). She was recruited by her alma mater in 1991 to develop, with funding through the Health Resources and Services Administration, UIC's model curriculum in health informatics and information management, the first national graduate-level specialization in the discipline. Participating on the grant were faculty from UIC's Library of the Health Sciences. One of the founding members of UIC's Institute for Patient Safety Excellence, Dr. Valenta is Academic Director of UIC's Patient Safety Leadership educational programs (Master's degree and Certificate) in the Department of Medical Education, College of Medicine. With funding through Agency for Healthcare Research and Quality (AHRQ), Department of Health and Human Services (HHS), and Department of Defense (DOD), Dr. Valenta's research focuses on the study of human subjectivity within and organizational issues surrounding the adoption of health technology. Dr. Valenta's publications have appeared in the *Journal of the American Medical Informatics Association, Academic Medicine, JALN: Journal of Asynchronous Learning Networks, Journal of Medical Systems, Journal of Healthcare Information Management, Proceedings of the 1st ACM International Health Informatics Symposium*, and *Aviation, Space and Environmental Medicine*. She has served as Review Board Member, *Journal of Biomedical Informatics*, and is a member of the Delta Omega Society (a public health honorary fraternity).

Albert W. Wu, MD, MPH   Albert is a practicing internist and Professor of Health Policy and Management and Medicine at the Johns Hopkins Bloomberg School of Public Health, with joint appointments in Epidemiology, International Health, Medicine and Surgery. He is director of the Johns Hopkins Center for Health Service and Outcomes Research, of the AHRQ-funded Hopkins DEcIDE center for comparative effectiveness research. He received BA and MD degrees from Cornell University, completed Internal Medicine residency at the Mount Sinai Hospital and UC San Diego, and received an MPH from UC Berkeley. His research and teaching focus on patient outcomes and quality of care. He has studied the handling of medical errors since 1988, and has published influential papers including "Do House Officers Learn from Their Mistakes" (JAMA, 1991) and "Medical Error: The Second Victim" (BMJ, 2000). He has over 350 published papers and was a member of the Institute of Medicine committee on identifying and preventing medication errors, and was Senior Adviser for Patient Safety to the World Health Organization in Geneva. He is editor of the book *The Value of Close Calls in Improving Patient Safety* (Joint Commission, 2011). He directs the PhD program in health services research, and the certificate program in "Quality, Patient Safety and Outcomes Research" at Johns Hopkins.

Foreword

Julianne M. Morath

"Learners will inherit the future" is a prophetic statement that rings more true each day in healthcare. As healthcare transitions from volume to value; episode to continuum; and individual autonomy to team accountability, the ability to generate and apply new knowledge in accelerated time is a critical success factor. Donald Berwick is quoted, "Transition of medicine from 'contact producing' to a 'knowledge producing' enterprise is at the heart of medicine for the year 2020" (Berwick 1999: n.p.).

Healthcare is in the throws of this transition. The editor, Lorri Zipperer, clearly asserts:

> *Knowledge ignites passion for goals. Knowledge bolsters the hard work of improvement. Knowledge provides context for effort. Knowledge feeds creativity and innovation. Enhancing the use of knowledge to render its reliable use however, is a challenge yet to be recognized fully in healthcare.*

She however, does not leave the reader on this note. Rather she creates a pathway and offers practical advice to move forward and harness the power of knowledge in healthcare.

The editor and her contributing colleagues have made an important contribution to healthcare in writing this book. It is a practical book that is clearly written by individuals at the frontlines of improving healthcare delivery. They each emphasize the skills to create collective understanding and shared meaning; create context; and build the foundations for informed decision making are all prerequisites to successful navigation into the future of healthcare.

Lorri Zipperer is a pioneer and leader in the field of managing information and using that information to create knowledge. We are awash in a tsunami of data, but live in a paucity of information – much less knowledge about making healthcare safer, better, and more enriching to those who have dedicated their careers to solving the complex problems of care. While knowledge management sounds deceptively simple, the reader will soon appreciate the emerging science of this field. Reading the glossary alone introduces new concepts and possibilities, such as "After Action Reviews," the roles of "Boundary Spanners," and the advantages of "Collaboration Software." The power of "Deep Tacit" provides a window into why individuals and organizations behave and perform as they do. The expanding role of clinical librarians to "Informationist" and "Special Librarianship" are introduced along with processes and technologies, such as "Ontologies" to capture, organize, display, and archive knowledge. That is only the glossary of this volume, aimed to generate pathways to collaborate and explore ways to create, transfer, and use knowledge to advance and improve healthcare.

Each contributor has credibility and experience that is generously shared with the reader. As the healthcare industry is often known to do, there is a call for reduced and simplified information. The contributors would disagree, calling instead for organizations to expand and deepen internal capabilities in knowledge management and learning, including the cultural context necessary for such competencies to emerge. They explore Russell Ackoff's hierarchy of knowledge from *Data to Wisdom* through a concise logic cascade of learning, incorporating patient and family systems.

The book emphasizes that knowledge is a holistic and dynamic process requiring humility and authenticity. Knowledge is, in fact, the foundation to success in highly complex systems – a message clearly sprinkled throughout the book. Leadership lessons to create conditions for transparency and learning is given it's fair attention. Creating a knowledge sharing culture is explored as a pre-condition to successful change and performance. There are recommendations for leaders who aspire to move into the future; and an articulation of leadership characteristics to do so, starting with curiosity and ability to bring the future forward. What if an organization fails to manage or mismanages knowledge? That too is covered, along with strategies to mitigate and concrete examples of best practices of knowledge seeking organizations. The editor *models the way* in her book by conducting and collecting interviews across roles and responsibilities of individuals in healthcare to extract tacit knowledge. She then makes that knowledge explicit as part of this work.

A particularly engaging chapter in the book considers the role of improvisation – applying what is known while learning.

The editor has provided a timely contribution of the ins and outs of becoming active learners, both as individuals and as organizations. Our work is to embrace, apply, and practice what has been contributed. We owe it to those who need and depend on us for care; to the frontlines of the workforce who are at the heart of improving care; and to the greater community as we transform the healthcare system. While much is needed in policy, financing, and macro-system reform, the author and contributors are hopeful and confident that we can effectively achieve better care for individuals, improve the health of populations, and reduce the cost burden on our economy. Most of all, the book is about continuously learning how to learn.

Preface

The provision of clean clear knowledge requires 'the organised efforts of society' and may be regarded as being a health service no different from a health service such as cardiac surgery or the management of epilepsy (Gray 2011: 2).

My start in the field of patient safety in the mid-1990s coincided with my introduction to knowledge management. At that time, I was honored to interact with many experts in the field of patient safety, absorbing knowledge from them and applying it to the development of information services for a new organization: the National Patient Safety Foundation (NPSF). Years later I worked with hospital-based teams and others as a 2004–2005 Health Forum/NPSF Patient Safety Leadership Fellow. From that experience I became sensitive to the challenges associated with the "sharp end" of medical error reduction. During my career I have also been honored to interact with patients and families that have been harmed by medical error. Their knowledge and wisdom, frustration and pain contributed an essential element to my perspective. The richness of the stories I heard over time helped me fully appreciate the difficulty of achieving safety. It was my good fortune to engage with these experts: it brought passion and commitment to my work in the field. I would have never seen patient safety the same way by reading even the best book.

Knowledge ignites passion for goals. Knowledge bolsters the hard work of improvement. Knowledge provides context for effort. Knowledge feeds creativity and innovation. Enhancing the use of knowledge to render its reliable use, however, is a challenge yet to be recognized fully in healthcare. Yet through my exposure to quality improvement and patient safety work, it was evident to me that the following themes exist in enhancing both knowledge use and quality improvement that would make efforts synergistic:

- *Complexity*: Developing and staying aware is a complex business as is management of services and organizational entities that support staying aware (Kelly, 2010). Modes of organizing, accessing and sharing information, evidence and knowledge are becoming more diverse and ubiquitous, whether the mechanism is published literature, web sites, intranets, discussion lists, blogs, communities of practice, social media, or conversation over coffee or during rounds.

• *High Reliability*: The sensitivity of actors in risky environments to the ever present potential for failure and the engagement of all to do something about it in a robust dependable way. Knowledge feeds that sensitivity.

• *Multidisciplinary/Multi-industry involvement*: It is important to enrich how safety happens and ensure all the intellectual capital – residing from the sharp to the blunt end – is available to enhance improvement. Teams can help make that happen by sharing tacit knowledge. Looking outside one's own environment and mindset to gather tacit knowledge enables new perspectives to translate successes into innovation.

• *Sensemaking*: A concept associated with teamwork and mindfulness to enhance reliability of action in critical situations through tacit knowledge sharing and acceptance. In addition, knowledge management is conceptually connected with organizational sensemaking (Choo 1996).

• *Systems thinking*: Organizations learn through systems thinking, and the sharing of knowledge from all points in an organization enables an informed systems view. Sharing knowledge gleaned from failure is an element of a learning system. Learning from failure is heralded by experts as a driver of safety and quality improvement (Leape 1994; Kohn et al. 2000; Donaldson 2000). The creation of an environment where it is safe to learn from mistakes and share tacit knowledge to promote advancement is a leadership skill (Senge 1990).

These common themes provide a foundation for knowledge management and healthcare quality improvement. As leaders have noted, knowledge management is a vital mechanism for high quality care that contributes to improved care, reduced harm and waste, mitigated inequalities and inequities and improved health (Gray 2011). Clearly these concepts provide launching points to engage healthcare leaders and practitioners in seeking to improve tacit knowledge use in healthcare: this has not yet been addressed in a robust way by professional groups, organizations and educational programs to date. Why then, has knowledge management and tacit knowledge in particular not been emphasized as a strategy to address the challenges of quality and safety improvement in healthcare? If I could see the opportunities, why couldn't others?

This book seeks to address that gap. It won't answer all the questions or resolve all the challenges, but it hopes to raise awareness as to how to get there.

How to Use this Book

Knowledge Management in Healthcare aims to generate avenues for collaboration to provide evidence and direction for exploring tacit knowledge sharing competencies and strategies that have particular resonance for the acute care environment. However, to begin this work without understanding the themes noted above lends itself to a "quick fix" mentality, with no design to fuse learning from rapid improvement into tacit knowledge sharing processes to sustain them. One must lay a foundation for a structure to hold.

Despite the desire for specific "how to's" on implementing tacit knowledge sharing in healthcare, those stories and case studies have not yet been emphasized in the literature, conferences or social media. As is noted here, the research documenting the value of tacit knowledge is hardly evident in healthcare. Healthcare needs concrete examples that illustrate tangible strategies to enhance the process of sharing its tacit knowledge. This book hopes to initiate the dialogue needed to get there.

This book is divided into three sections that weave together foundational themes, frontline experience and practical direction for the reader:

> **Part 1 – Nature of Knowledge sharing Environments:** This section introduces the language of knowledge management and elements within the healthcare spectrum that influence both the quality of healthcare delivery and tacit knowledge sharing.

> **Part 2 – Knowledge Workers: Insights from the Frontline:** This section reports on perspectives from 20 active healthcare professionals and patients to outline barriers, strengths and values associated with tacit

knowledge sharing within the construct of highly reliable, high quality healthcare.

Part 3 – Knowledge Sharing Measurement, Practicalities and Future Directions: This section explores tools to track the impact of knowledge shared, methods of designing and launching initiatives to benefit from knowledge and closes with a broad vision for where it could take healthcare teams, units and organizations for the future.

The publication concludes with an in-depth reference list to illustrate the applied experience from business, the safety sciences, and healthcare, a glossary of select terms and an in-depth index to help readers explore these pages according to their experience in the work of knowledge management.

The book is intended for:

- Leaders who want to strengthen existing programs or enable a knowledge sharing culture in their institutions. It is envisioned that management will use this volume as a tool to visualize and implement knowledge management initiatives in their institutions.

- Administrators and managers who want to build teams to proactively structure knowledge sharing improvement efforts at their organizations and capitalize on the knowledge within their organizations – including the knowledge of patients – to improve quality of care.

- Quality improvement professionals who are exploring knowledge sharing strategies to improve care in their organizations.

- Medical librarians, clinical informationists, healthcare informaticists and technologists who want to apply knowledge management principles in their daily work or service design.

Quality improvement expert Donald Berwick, MD, predicts that the "transition of medicine from a 'contact producing' to a 'knowledge producing' enterprise is at the heart of medicine for the year 2020" (1999: n.p.). May this text guide the reader through transition.

List of Abbreviations

AHRQ	Agency for Healthcare Research and Quality
AHRQ PSNet	Agency for Healthcare Research and Quality Patient Safety Network
AHRQ OCKT	Agency for Healthcare Research and Quality Office of Communications and Knowledge Transfer
ABMS	American Board of Medical Specialties
ACGME	American College of Graduate Medical Education
CMS	Centers for Medicare and Medicaid Services (CMS)
CLABSI	Central Line-Associated Bloodstream Infection
CoP	Communities of Practice
CUSP	Comprehensive Unit-Based Safety Program (CUSP)
CE	Continuing Education
CRM	Crew Resource Management
DOJ	(United States) Department of Justice
EHR	Electronic Health Records
EBM	Evidence Based Medicine
FAQ	Frequently Asked Questions
HIPAA	Health Insurance Portability and Accountability Act
HRO	High Reliability Organization
HR	Human Resources
IT	Information Technology
IHI	Institute for Healthcare Improvement
ISMP	Institute for Safe Medication Practices
IOM	Institute of Medicine
ICU	Intensive Care Units
KM	Knowledge Management
MET	Medical Emergency Teams
MeSH	Medical Subject Heading
NCQA	National Committee for Quality Assurance
NHS	National Health Service
NPSF	National Patient Safety Foundation

OIG	Office of the Inspector General
PS	Patient Safety
PDSA	Plan-Do-Study-Act
QI	Quality Improvement
RRT	Rapid Response Teams
SBAR	Situation-Background-Assessment-Recommendations
SNA	Social Network Analysis
VA	(United States) Veterans Administration

Acknowledgements

If you have a candle, the light won't glow any dimmer if I light yours off of mine (Steven Tyler, see http://www.rockthisway.de/quotes.htm).

It's with humility that I recognize the immeasurable help of the colleagues and friends who collectively participated in the development of this book.

The 20 anonymous interviewees deserve special mention. Their candor in reflecting the state of knowledge sharing in healthcare today brought the reality of the frontlines to the work. They confirmed the value of conversation as a mechanism for knowledge sharing. The time spent with them reinforced not only the value of network and relationships in crystallizing the direction of the book but that they can and should be mobilized to drive improvement in healthcare. That confirmation and support for direction was invaluable.

I had the same experience with my chapter contributors. Each author developed content with "one foot in their box, one foot outside it." They rose to the challenge to apply what they know and work with regularly to an area that was potentially outside their thinking when they joined the project. The author teams were not always acquainted with one another before putting "pen to paper" yet their willingness to collaborate on their assignment is recognized. I value what I learned from all of them.

Beyond these two groups a rich network of colleagues bolstered the perspectives represented here. Pam Barnard – who first supported this idea for this text over a decade ago – came on board as a contributor without question. It would have felt wrong to proceed without her. Kelly Smith, Devin Carr, Katie Watson and Chris Wood provided insights and shared their time to explore one piece of this layered puzzle. Susan Carr, Barb Jones, Jan Sykes and Sarah Taylor provided helpful suggestions on the manuscript draft and clarified language for the stated audience. John Jackson helped technically to get the draft ready for submission. Michael Moore lent his proficiency in loop diagramming as a method of system analysis to again enhance a project of mine as he has done for years. Ross Vagnieres of Vagne Design kept the graphic elements for the book clean and simple. Margaret F. Tomaselli managed the interview transcription process in a timely and professional manner. Jeannine Gluck – who collaborated with me on a knowledge map article years before we met face to face – delivered capable indexing skill to connect the conceptual dots for readers. Jonathan Norman and his team at Gower supported the book concept early on and provided guidance as it matured. Collective thanks are also due to members of the Special Libraries Association. Their commitment to the role of information professionals as leaders in knowledge management helped me to see myself in this work and to translate it into a strategy to improve safety in healthcare.

A constellation of librarians enabled an array of multidisciplinary interactions that brought a dose of reality to my theory-based approach: Margaret Bandy, Cathy Burroughs, Barb Jones, Clair Hamasu, Beth Robb and Ruth Holst. Ruth and Beth years ago welcomed the chance to explore the role of librarians as true partners in knowledge management in hospitals. They initiated a series of workshops sponsored by regional offices of the National Networks of Libraries of Medicine that gave me the opportunity to work directly with librarians and ultimately frontline teams to explore how business knowledge management concepts might be applied and generate innovation in hospitals. The experience of facilitating multidisciplinary dialogue and thinking through these sessions helped confirm there was a value in the ideas presented here. A similar experience came through work with Dr. Paul Uhlig, Ellen Raboin, Cindy Dominquez and Jeff Brown (affectionately referred to as the "Way-Cool-X-Team") who supported my involvement in their observational research. There I was able to absorb how collaborative rounding teams share evidence, information and knowledge both in situ and during incident review discussions. This enabled me to infuse sharp end experience into my thought process. Cathy Tokarski served as the copy editor and contributed considerable expertise into the style and structure of the text. As book projects can spill into space normally occupied by family, I must acknowledge my husband Ross who was patient and supportive in every way possible during the process and my sisters, Mom and friends who heard more about knowledge management then they ever wanted to. In closing I must recognize Becky Steward whose commitment to this work helped to fortify my vision to apply tacit knowledge sharing to the important goal of improving patient safety. The book project wouldn't have begun without her support and belief in what it aims to accomplish.

PART 1

Nature of Knowledge Sharing Environments

Chapter 1 Synopsis – What is Knowledge?

This chapter introduces terms used to discuss knowledge management in a variety of constructs. The authors discuss the impact the lack of clarity around knowledge management and knowledge sharing may have on the widespread adoption of a culture of learning, and recognition of the importance of tacit knowledge in healthcare. The lack of consensus about what knowledge means and how it is managed influences efforts to define its impact on quality and safety.

Chapter 2 Synopsis – Healthcare Culture and Knowledge

The success of a knowledge management initiative hinges on whether or not the culture of an institution is ready and able to apply a knowledge sharing philosophy to its daily activities. This chapter will explore systems thinking, complexity, and other key characteristics of learning organizations as foundational concepts on which to build and sustain an effective knowledge sharing culture. The authors discuss the role of leadership in embedding knowledge, skills, attitudes, and beliefs across all levels of the organization (from front-line clinicians to board of directors) to gain traction for tacit knowledge sharing initiatives.

Chapter 3 Synopsis – The Healthcare Environment and Knowledge: Blunt End Experience

This chapter makes the case for an organizational commitment to shaping and nurturing a knowledge sharing culture. The authors explore the negative downstream effect of dysfunctional organizational knowledge sharing at the non-clinical level on the ability of front-line practitioners to benefit from their colleagues' experience.

Chapter 4 Synopsis – The Healthcare Environment and Knowledge: Sharp End Experience

The authors describe how effective tacit knowledge sharing can positively influence care delivery. Communication and teamwork mechanisms are opportunities to optimize knowledge sharing and can be leveraged to identify tacit knowledge sharing as a factor in quality improvement.

What is Knowledge?

Pamela Barnard, Judith Napier and Lorri Zipperer

> *Knowledge is experience. Everything else is just information.*
> Albert Einstein (quoted in McDermott 1999: 103)

Knowledge and its Management: Defining the Terms

What is knowledge? A wicked question?

Literature that describes how to define and describe knowledge management offers little support for these efforts (Hicks, Dattero and Galip 2006). In fact, it has been stated that this topic holds little interest outside of the information and library science fields (Wilson 2002). This lack of consensus has ramifications in healthcare where the clarity, immediacy and reliability of communication play a vital role in patient safety. In this context, the definition of knowledge management requires illumination.

Let's start by articulating basic definitions and introduce knowledge management concepts that support improvements in healthcare quality and safety.

THE CONCEPT OF KNOWLEDGE

While the modern concept of knowledge may have its origins with the ancient Greeks, the hierarchy of data, information, knowledge, understanding and wisdom was coined in the late 1980s with Ackoff's hierarchy (Hicks, Dattero and Galip 2006; Ackoff 1989). The term "knowledge management" traces its roots to the business improvement movement of the early 1990s, including

Figure 1.1   Knowledge Terms

initiatives such as total quality management, business process re-engineering and human resource management (Metaxiotis, Ergazakis and Psarras 2005). Myths about knowledge management persist, including the mistaken notion that it is an information technology function and can easily be outsourced to consultants or a new software system (Rogers 2007). Recent trends in the knowledge management literature emphasize the concept of individually "embedded" knowledge and discuss the need to share and exchange that knowledge to inform the actions of others (Beesley and Cooper 2008) and evaluate outcomes.

Healthcare demands extraordinary amounts of data collection and reporting to satisfy reimbursement and regulatory requirements. The intense focus on these activities may have resulted in a dearth of attention in the healthcare literature about knowledge management outside of data-sharing improvements (Wilson 2002). Attention has more traditionally focused on the introduction and maturation of evidence-based practice in healthcare, which includes the transfer of explicit knowledge, primarily in the form of research findings but with scant emphasis on the sharing of tacit knowledge (Kothari et al. 2011b).

However, an emergent body of literature may be indicating there is increased activity and growth in the actual study and implementation of knowledge management in healthcare (Nicolini et al. 2008). It is noteworthy that it was only in 2011, that the US National Library of Medicine introduced a new Medical Subject Heading (MeSH) for knowledge management for its PubMed®/MEDLINE® database. PubMed®/MEDLINE® is a premier database of indexed citations and abstracts to medical, nursing, dental, healthcare and preclinical sciences journal articles. The establishment of "knowledge management" as a subject worth indexing demonstrates its importance as a topic for research and reflection.

The use of electronic health records (EHRs) and incentives to adopt them through Federal payment incentives have created more opportunities to transform data into information that generates knowledge. Data "dashboards" capture important trends and care outcomes which provide clinicians and administrators with high-level summaries of their patients' care and well-being. This is an example of an innovation which permits administrators and clinicians to engage in the discussion of information while exchanging tacit knowledge unique to their relationship with patients.

ACKOFF'S HIERARCHY AND ITS APPLICATION IN HEALTHCARE

Applying the elements of the Ackoff's hierarchy to the context of healthcare will help provide a foundation for the discussions that this text will present. Let's look at the five levels of the hierarchy through a healthcare lens.

Data is gathered in the form of patient and family history, basic physiologic monitors (that is, height, weight, blood pressure), medication history, and so on. Each element represents a single value, but taken together, begins to frame the health status of the individual. Data may *"... an emergent body of literature may be indicating there is increased activity and growth in the actual study and implementation of knowledge management in healthcare" (Nicolini et al. 2008).* be provided in the context of normal lab values to provide *information* for comparison to the lab values in the patient's medical record. The structured data helps the clinician understand the patient's health status and inform decision-making.

Information is then integrated and put in context with the *knowledge* that the clinician possesses about disease process, clinical experience, knowledge of the patient and his or her preferences, familiarity with practice guidelines, and practice alerts that may be incorporated into the EHR. Applying knowledge to the unique consideration of individual patients allows the clinician to develop

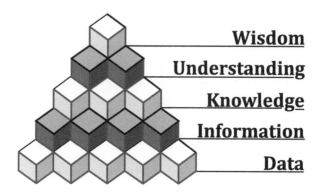

Figure 1.2   Ackoff's Hierarchy

Source: Ackoff, R.L. 1989. "From Data to Wisdom, Presidential Address to ISGSR, June 1988." *Journal of Applied Systems Analysis*, 16, 3–9.

a plan of care and demonstrates *understanding*, even if the care plan does not involve an intervention. Subsequent decisions about care that this patient may require, including discussions of preventive actions to ensure health, illustrate *wisdom.*

To illustrate further, examples within three specific contexts in healthcare can help describe the knowledge hierarchy (Ackoff 1989): medication administration, evidence review, and disclosure analysis. Understanding and wisdom, as elements that follow the base of data, information and knowledge are beyond the scope of this text.

Medication Administration

Data, represented by the medication name, dosage route of administration, and frequency is represented in the medical record through the physician order.

Information takes the form of a nurse's familiarity with the patient, the context of the care encounter, and documentation in the record; for example, speech therapy performed a swallow test and documented that a patient is unable to swallow solids, including pills.

Knowledge incorporates data, information and experience to develop the plan of care needed for this patient. Analysis of information, such as which food is preferred by the patient for the administration of oral medications, can lead to a strategy for future care. Nursing documentation and verbal reporting can provide important details for other staff members or for patient and family education. The nurse's experience with the administration of this patient's medication, and the nurse's experience with similar patients, will add knowledge to this process.

Evidence Review for Clinical Care

Data is used to define the care for a specific intervention, such as preventing blood clots following joint replacement, which is formalized into a guideline or care pathway. Hospitals have data on incidence of this complication on a local and national level. Patient risk factors are known. Studies may report success or failure rates associated with different interventions.

 If clinical variation is significant, such as using ambulation protocols, pain medication protocols, anticoagulant therapy or use of compression stockings (either knee-high or thigh-high) post-surgery, *information* may be gathered by an outside body, such as the American Academy of Orthopaedic Surgeons, to assemble and analyze the evidence. Reviewers (including clinicians, researchers, and informaticists) then develop a consensus statement or clinical guideline to inform clinical practice. Information about the recommended practice change is disseminated through meetings, seminars, professional societies and publications in major journals. Librarians can facilitate access to these guidelines through alerts and posts on internal web sites. The availability of data and information, however, does not itself mean that practice change will occur. Additional work will be needed to encourage adoption of the change.

 Certain organizations use a centralized entity, such as a clinical service line or an individual hospital department, to discuss whether and how to change clinical practice based on the information they have reviewed and their individual experience. These entities and the clinicians affiliated with them can anticipate and evaluate the impact on practice and outcomes of a system-wide change.

Changes may be made in an EHR that supports the practice change. In this way, information may be transformed into *knowledge* that will inform changes in the way care is provided.

Disclosure Analysis Following an Unanticipated Outcome

Data elements include facts of the event itself, details about the individual patient and family involved (age, relationships, siblings), and the objective specifics about the patient's condition that led to an unanticipated outcome.

Information includes the ability to disclose data that is relevant to the patient and family without supposition or opinion. It can also include data and written factual explanation about the type of incident that can be shared with the family to inform future care decisions.

Knowledge is the ability to identify and enhance what the patient and family can comprehend the situation at hand. Knowledge is required to help guide the patient and the family to understand the significance of the data and information as it affects the patient's outcome. It requires that clinicians draw from their experience to communicate both data and information as they apply to the patient, family and the care team. A root cause analysis is a process to identify what led to the adverse event, and can produce data, information and opportunities for knowledge sharing that can address an organizational failure or contribute to system-wide improvement.

KNOWLEDGE TYPES AND THEIR MEANING

Tacit knowledge is not black and white – it's more like the style and finesse; it is unique to a person (Interview 7/17–19).

In a broad context, knowledge falls into three categories: explicit, implicit, and tacit (Polanyi 1966; Nonaka and Takeuchi 1995). These types of knowledge exist on a continuum that flows back and forth and changes each over time

(Bohmer 2009). Table 1.1 defines these concepts and shows how they may exist in the healthcare environment.

Table 1.1   Tacit, Implicit, and Explicit Knowledge

Type	Definition	Application
Explicit _____ Knowing what	"Knowledge that is easily expressed, captured, stored and reused. It can be transmitted as data and is found in databases, books, manuals and messages" (Nonaka 1991, as captured in Zipperer 2011: 302).	• More easily shared through documentation and training (DeLong 2004). • Technical or data-oriented in nature. • Could serve as a synonym for "information or evidence" (Wilson 2002).
Implicit _____ Knowing how and being able to talk about it	Knowledge that influences action and is shared by others through common experience or culture (Wilson 2002).	• Has the potential to convert to explicit knowledge but has yet to be articulated (Bohmer 2009). • Transferred through interviews, mentoring, communities of practice (DeLong 2004).
Tacit _____ Knowing how but not being able to explain it	Practical knowledge, or "knowing how" to do something; is extended through "theory-based scientific investigations" and clinical experience to enhance practice (Benner 1984).	• Generated through discussion of explicit knowledge. • Transferred through observation, experiential learning, shadowing (DeLong 2004).

This book argues that opportunity lies in the optimization of managing the processes through which the sharing of the least tangible form of knowledge – tacit knowledge – takes place. Tacit knowledge is a resource that benefits from interactions with other people and from their experiences. It is a rich source of expertise that organizations can benefit from when employees are encouraged to cultivate it (Anderson and Willson 2009). Losing experienced workers and their accumulated, or tacit, knowledge is a significant drawback for many industries (DeLong 2004). Within healthcare, for example, this phenomenon has been noted to occur when experienced employees leave the workforce, taking their tacit knowledge with them (Hatcher et al. 2006). It should be assumed to be a concern for other exiting clinicians and non-clinical employees as well.

Healthcare delivery is a collaborative process, requiring the development and dissemination of explicit and tacit knowledge (Paul 2006). Multi-disciplinary interactions that occur in healthcare organizations have strong potential to be enhanced by a knowledge management approach from large scale collaboratives to bedside rounds. Healthcare organizations could benefit from a tacit knowledge management orientation to teamwork.

KNOWLEDGE MANAGEMENT: WHAT IT IS NOT

To enable discussion about knowledge management strategies and initiatives in any environment, it's helpful to understand distinctions between knowledge and knowledge-related terms (see Glossary).

The following all represent common terms that are often erroneously seen as synonymous with *knowledge* or used in its place:

Best Practice: This term infers that the activity is supported by evidence, thereby distinguishing it from tacit knowledge. Organizations also use "best practice" to brand their knowledge management efforts when these efforts do not succeed so they can gain acceptance for new efforts (Call 2005).

Communication: The term "communication" as a task can involve development of messages from an organizational perspective and considers large-scale distribution networks, messaging, and formats. This definition can create confusion with knowledge management efforts. Obviously individuals talking to one another serves as a knowledge conduit; yet they are not one and the same.

Evidence-based Medicine/Evidence-based Practice: Evidence-based medicine has been suggested as a potential deterrent to the application of knowledge management in healthcare (Kothari et al. 2011b). The emphasis on evidence can diminish the value of story and anecdote, which are building blocks of knowledge sharing.

Storytelling/Narrative: Sharing accounts of activities has been shown to be effective in business as a knowledge distribution tactic for strategic and engagement purposes (Denning 2004; Denning 2006). The value of stories has been diminished by an emphasis on measures, statistics, and quantifiable outcomes. Nonetheless, storytelling to chronicle personal experience has been a valuable tool in engaging residents in incident reporting and leadership engagement in patient safety (Cox and Logio 2011; NHS Wales 2010; Institute for Safe Medication Practices 2011).

Electronic Records Management/Data Warehousing: Focused on tangible data and information resources, records initiatives archive data and information assets rather than share knowledge in a hospital. Similar to explicit tools and cognitive aids, review of records may indirectly result in the surfacing and sharing of tacit knowledge, but in and of themselves do not represent knowledge.

Training/Education: Training and education programs are used by some organizations instead of tacit knowledge sharing mechanisms. Tacit knowledge sharing can result from training efforts, yet these didactic programs or online tutorial sessions are not designed for and do not foster robust and reliable tacit knowledge sharing.

> *We have become such a technologically oriented field in that the majority of our communication is now no longer face-to-face or verbal, it's through electronic documentation, it's through paging, it's through one way communication and that has created a barrier and an inability to share tacit knowledge (Interview 7/160–168).*

Tools/Technology Development: Tools and technologies are often mistakenly referred to as knowledge management. Technology may enable knowledge sharing but it can also present barriers, such as integrating across multiple sources. Technology can create challenges as organizations seek to develop knowledge sharing mechanisms while maintaining information and explicit knowledge sharing artifacts, such as policies, procedures, guidelines, and evidence. Resources are often applied to tools, such as the development of wikis, internal collaboration software, shared directories or drives, with an incomplete understanding of knowledge management as the strategy to which the tools contribute.

A Shared Mental Model

A variety of terms are used to define knowledge management, thus creating confusion in efforts to devote resources and commitment to knowledge management activities. Therefore, establishing a shared "mental model" of knowledge management is a necessary step to launch and sustain these programs and create the culture to support them.

Mental models help organizations, teams and individuals develop and nurture a shared understanding. They heavily influence what knowledge is developed and how it is shared (Davison and Blackman 2005).

In his classic text *The Fifth Discipline*, Peter Senge explains that mental models influence how people behave because models affect what people perceive as reality (Senge 1990:

"... a shared 'mental model' of knowledge management is a necessary step to launch and sustain these programs and create the culture to support them."

175). In healthcare, mental models may contribute to preconceived ideas about clinical hierarchies and support the stereotypes that exist within specialties (Furnham 1986). In addition, mental models can lead clinicians to incorrect diagnosis when the facts clearly support one diagnosis but the clinician fails to consider other less probable but possible diagnoses. For example, a 30-year-old woman who is brought to the emergency department with chest pain and difficulty breathing may likely be diagnosed with anxiety, given the low incidence of young females who experience myocardial infarction. A clinician who does not consider other diagnoses beyond anxiety may be constrained by his mental model.

Mental models can also affect understanding of initiatives and tools aimed at improving patient safety. For example, if a root cause analysis is seen as a reactive exercise to determine "who did what" rather than a proactive step in an effort to understand shortcomings in a process to minimize a repeat of the occurrence, staff are less likely to contribute and take the findings seriously.

A benefit of mental models can be seen in the connection of workers to values and beliefs that drive organizational culture and commitment to goals. They support communities of practice and provide a cognitive framework for enabling information and potentially knowledge sharing (Wilson 2002).

DIFFERENT VIEWS OF THE WORLD

Some experts contend that knowledge cannot be managed (Drucker 1969; Wilson 2002; Wilson 2005). A lack of a consistent mental model about knowledge management negatively affects healthcare organizations by:

- Diminishing the chance to share lessons without a common understanding for further dialogue and application.

- Failing to recognize the role of knowledge as a contributor to or detractor from "high reliability." This results from having no definition or standardization supporting the work (Resar 2006).

- Misusing the terms "knowledge" and "management," lead to their use as a marketing slogan with diminished effectiveness (Wilson 2002; Wilson 2005).

- Reducing multidisciplinary involvement, which can result in fewer successful programs for implementation in organizations and industries.

However, agreed-upon terminology can help minimize confusion. Collaborative efforts to develop terms to describe knowledge initiatives can enhance hospital uptake of these programs by:

- Allowing for alternative, innovative descriptions of knowledge management to be in use that are appropriate to the organization. This will reflect a local context to support success, much as checklists need to allow for a unique application to enable their success (Pronovost and Vohr 2010).

- Providing impetus for the organization to work across service lines and departments.

- Enabling team development and learning as consensus evolves.

- Serving as a provocative first step for program development by allowing a team to devise, develop and champion its own unique initiative.

- Allow the involvement of everyone within the organization in a successful effort.

Successful knowledge management initiatives require a basic agreement on the meaning of knowledge management (Call 2005). Arriving at collective clarity on terminology can help individuals seeking to develop and instill a knowledge sharing culture in their organization. The discussion of terminology currently is imprecise, dynamic and not easily categorized. As knowledge management becomes a more recognized process within healthcare, definitional rigor will evolve and guide more specific discussions.

KEY TAKE-AWAYS

- Knowledge is dynamic – a moving target.
- Knowledge, knowledge management, and other knowledge-related terms are often used interchangeably and are ill-defined in healthcare.
- Lack of definition can slow down knowledge management improvement processes.
- Initiating knowledge management programs without a clear understanding of terminology can contribute to frustration and program failure.
- Arriving at shared mental models of knowledge and knowledge management is an opportunity for hospitals.

Suggested Reading

Davenport, T.H. and Prusak, L. 1998. *Working Knowledge: How Organizations Manage What They Know*. Boston, MA: Harvard Business School Press.
Dixon, N. 2000. *Common Knowledge*. Boston, MA: Harvard Business School Press.
Nonaki, I. and Takeuich, H. 1995. *The Knowledge-Creating Company*. New York, NY: Oxford University Press.

2

Healthcare Culture and Knowledge

Barbara Balik, Margaret Moylan Bandy
and Michael Leonard

> *Organizations emphasize and pursue what leaders, by their*
> *example, believe is important (Kaplan 2013: v).*

Knowledge Sharing, Learning and Leadership

Knowledge management is essential for healthcare organizations to be successful at a time when widespread disruptive change is occurring. Healthcare economists talk of a "perfect storm," made up of a fast-growing population of baby-boomers seeking more complex care, a shrinking supply of skilled healthcare providers, and an unsustainable cost structure (Tucker and Spear 2006). As the complexity and pace of patient care has grown, the current care delivery model, based on the skill of the individual expert, produces high levels of variation in care processes, inconsistent clinical outcomes and an incidence rate of harm affecting approximately one in three patients (Classen et al. 2011).

With progressively increasing levels of scrutiny by regulatory agencies and publicly available data that measures quality of care, successful care delivery systems strive to continually improve organizational culture, reduce clinical variation and consistently apply knowledge through rapid sharing and practice adoption. Effective knowledge management is a vital component of this strategy. Organizations that are structured to create and develop an environment of continuous improvement – learning organizations – will have a distinct advantage in adapting and delivering the care they provide.

How Does an Organization Learn?

In 1993, David A. Garvin defined a learning organization in practical language: "A learning organization is an organization skilled at creating, acquiring, and transferring knowledge, and at modifying its behavior to reflect new knowledge and insights" (Garvin 1993: 80). Yet changes in behavior are also essential, "Without accompanying changes in the way that work gets done, only the potential for improvement exists" (Garvin 1993: 80).

He outlined the foundational activities of a learning organization:

- systematic problem solving;

- experimentation with new approaches;

- learning from their own experience and past history;

- learning from the experiences and best practices of others; and

- transferring knowledge quickly and efficiently throughout the organization.

Garvin also noted that each activity must be accompanied by a distinctive mind-set, tool kit, and pattern of behavior.

In discussing the stages of organizational learning, Garvin emphasized the importance of measuring employees' cognitive and behavioral changes, as well as any specific improvement that has taken place. Measuring all three is important, because some elements of change materialize over many years. Garvin and colleagues (2008) recently published tools for assessing the components of successful learning environments. They describe three building blocks of a learning organization: supportive learning environment, concrete learning processes and practices, and leadership that reinforces learning (Garvin, Edmondson and Gino 2008). Their survey tool can be used at the unit level and organizational level. The authors suggest that units within an organization partner with other units to improve weaknesses identified by the survey.

Developing a learning organization requires an understanding of complexity and systems thinking. Recognizing the healthcare organization as a complex adaptive system provides a foundation for creating and sustaining a learning culture and culture of safety. In 1998, Zimmerman, Lindberg, and Plsek (1998) applied the ideas from complexity science to healthcare. Complexity science examines the unpredictable, disorderly, non-linear, and uncontrollable ways in which living systems actually behave. In the context of a learning culture, complexity science reveals that outcomes emerge from the connections and relationships among the individual agents. In organizations, relationships among the individual agents in a complex adaptive system are often more critical than the individuals themselves. The authors identified nine organizational and leadership principles from the study of complex adaptive systems:

1.   View the system through the lens of complexity, in addition to the traditional metaphor of a machine or military organization. The delivery of healthcare is an extraordinarily complex process, with literally hundreds of steps in the process and often dozens of individuals having to coordinate care for a given patient. What makes healthcare unique is the inherent complexity of the human body and high degrees of uncertainty as how to disease processes manifest and respond to treatment.

2.   Build a "good enough" vision and provide minimum specifications, rather than trying to plan every detail. Having predictable and standardized care processes is essential to ensure the basic aspects of good care are being delivered, and there is a visible, measurable process that can be improved upon.

3.   Lead from the edge, using both "clockware" (mechanistic processes) and "swarmware" (processes that capitalize on chaos). Balance data and intuition, planning and acting, safety and risk, paying honor to each. Combining standard, clear processes and the "wisdom of the crowd," tapping the expertise of people who do the work every day is essential for learning and improvement.

4.   Foster the right degree of information flow, diversity and difference, connections inside and outside the organization, power differential and anxiety. Learning organizations have cultures that create the psychological safety that makes it safe to speak up and voice concerns that are weighed and acted upon. Systematic,

organizational learning will not occur in the absence of these conditions.

5.   Uncover and work with paradox and tension, rather than shying away from them as if they were unnatural. Smart people have strong opinions; the ability to openly air contrasting points of view and work toward a common goal is necessary for learning.

6.   Try multiple actions and let direction arise, rather than awaiting certainty before embarking on a change. Small tests of change and iterative learning engage people, and capture the wisdom of the people doing the work every day. Trying to plan for every contingency makes the plan of action so cumbersome and complex that it usually fails.

7.   Listen to the "shadow system." Realize that informal relationships, gossip, rumor, and hallway conversations contribute significantly to people's mental models and subsequent actions. Capturing the "real conversation" is quite valuable. It reflects how people really see the work, and is critical for effective implementation of change and learning.

8.   Grow complex systems by "chunking," or allowing them to emerge out of the links among simple systems that work well and are capable of operating independently. A common mistake is to try and fix complex problems all at once. This almost always fails, as there are too many variables. Breaking the challenge into "bite size chunks" allows people to manage complexity in an effective manner.

9.   Balance cooperation and competition, rather than relying exclusively on one or the other (Zimmerman, Lindberg, and Plsek 1998: 3–44). Collaborative work is essential, as is fostering an environment where the open, respectful exchange of ideas drives excellence and ongoing learning.

Organizational Readiness for Knowledge Sharing

DEVELOPING A CULTURE OF SAFETY

A culture of safety occurs in an environment where anyone is able to speak up and voice a concern without risk of ridicule or retribution. Of course, individuals must be capable, conscientious and provide safe care, but they also must know they will not be held personally responsible for system errors. In a culture of safety, transparency fosters the ability to learn from errors. Elements of a culture of safety include:

- *Psychological safety*: Psychological safety is necessary for learning at both an individual and organizational level (Edmondson 1999). Achieving psychological safety requires that everyone in a healthcare system, from housekeeping staff to senior medical staff, feel safe to voice a concern. In addition to an environment in which staff can ask questions and be treated with respect, psychological safety also includes a reliable process to act on these concerns and provide feedback. In the absence of psychological safety, or a system to share lessons learned, defects and harm persist because knowledge is not shared, thereby removing the opportunity to resolve the problem.

  Creating an atmosphere for psychological safety is a fundamental responsibility of leadership. Senior leaders must define and embody the behaviors that create value for patients, clinicians and the organization, and insist that behaviors that create risk will not be tolerated (Krause 2005). At the clinical unit or microsystem level, leaders must continually model the behaviors that promote psychological safety: sharing information, inviting team members into the conversations continually for their expertise and concerns, using people's names, and making it clear that staff can always speak up if they are concerned about a patient. Consistently acting on the concerns of their staffs, peers and clinicians and providing relevant, timely feedback is essential to maintaining psychological safety and supporting organizational learning.

- *Transparency*: Sharing and discussing tacit knowledge obtained from experiences are other key success factors in developing a culture of safety. Human performance is rarely error-free; thus, sharing how and why mistakes occurred and how they can be avoided is requisite for organizational learning. Because the prevailing culture in healthcare expects that clinicians never make mistakes, leaders must "give permission"

  "In the absence of culture that supports transparency, organizational learning and knowledge management to improve patient safety cannot thrive."

to others to talk about mistakes, near misses, and other issues. Leaders should continually reinforce the value of transparency as a mechanism to help the organization learn from its mistakes by modeling the behaviors as well.

- *Collaborative culture*: Healthcare's long-established hierarchies often inhibit the sharing of knowledge. Large authority gradients or power distances inhibit collaboration and decrease psychological safety. Effective leaders continually work to reduce hierarchies and enhance collaboration. Setting a positive, active tone and continually inviting team members to speak up minimizes the impact of hierarchy and enhances learning. Frontline care providers often have great insight into defects and opportunities, but not the status in the organization to generate momentum and work toward addressing potential safety risks. To maximize learning for everyone in an organization, a collaborative culture is necessary, and one that can be established and reinforced by leadership. In the absence of culture that supports transparency, organization learning and knowledge management to improve patient safety cannot thrive.

ENABLING PRACTICES TO ASSURE LEARNING AND KNOWLEDGE SHARING

Healthcare organizations can no longer manage rising complexity with outdated linear solutions (Weberg 2012: 268).

Given the importance of leadership commitment across an organization that is sensitive to needs and responsive to all, leaders at the senior, middle and frontline level have to be encouraged and committed to establishing a culture that supports effective knowledge sharing.

Senior Leaders

How do leaders build and sustain an effective knowledge sharing culture to assure safe care; to assure that systems embed knowledge, skills, attitudes, and beliefs for ongoing learning and innovation across the organization? Effective healthcare leaders recognize that they are crucial catalysts in shaping knowledge-generating and knowledge sharing environments that can transform their organization.

It's about establishing the entire culture ... to support and enhance the kind of environment that needs to be there so [leadership] has the ability to pay attention to the important stuff ... And challenge the status quo (Interview 13/169–173).

However, Kothari et al. (2011b) found that healthcare organizations lag in their knowledge management capabilities compared to organizations in the business sector. Key gaps in healthcare organizations include:

- Static information and communication technologies that were not purchased and implemented to fully support knowledge sharing; for example, a technology solution alone is often viewed as "the answer" rather than as part of a cultural process supported by a systemic approach which includes a technology.

- Groups formed with the goal for knowledge sharing across silos (that is, communities of practice discussed below) are not resourced for success. The lack of concrete support (that is, people and time) prevents the attention from being directed to the work realize success from the effort and obtain and sustain intended outcomes.

- Research is valued over tacit knowledge.

- A single-strategy approach is employed.

Learning Culture

A learning culture develops when leaders decide that new patterns of thinking and acting are essential for the organization. Fortunately, abundant leadership research exists that describes leadership behaviors, infrastructure, and enabling practices essential to transform healthcare.

Leaders should engage others to create organizations that Garvin (2008) describes as places where employees excel at creating, acquiring, and transferring knowledge. With colleague Amy Edmondson, Garvin (2003) identified three building blocks to achieve that outcome:

- A supportive learning environment includes psychological safety, appreciation of differences, openness to new ideas, and time for reflection.

- Learning process and practices that encompass experimentation (and associated tolerance of failure), information collection, analysis, transparency, education and training, and information transfer.

- Leadership that reinforces learning includes the visible support and infrastructure to ensure the vitality of the first two elements, along with a sense of curiosity, questioning, listening, and collaborating with the expectation that seeking and sharing tacit knowledge is essential. Kaiser Permanente (Schilling et al. 2011) employed these concepts when creating the systemic capacity for continuous improvement that characterizes a learning organization.

Challenging the Status Quo

After over two decades of experience with leaders in many sectors, Kouzes and Posner (2007) discuss the importance of challenging the status quo as one of five practices of exemplary leadership. Consistent with Garvin, these practices offer examples for healthcare leaders. This leadership practice step – called "Challenge the Process" – is exemplified by leaders who seek innovative ways to change, grow, and improve. These leaders also experiment and take risks by constantly generating small wins and learning from mistakes. Examples of this practice include constantly (continuously) learning from errors and failures, ensuring that there are processes for after action reviews, for example, short meetings to draw out lessons from a task or activity. These leaders also make it safe to experiment and learn from the results – intended or unintended. Examples of this behavior include open review of a project that failed – what worked, what did not, what would we do differently next time, and where did organizational hurdles impede success? These questions focus on *what* not *who*, create a curiosity instead of a blaming tone, and seek deeper levels of understanding rather than a quick, simplistic, answer.

Orientation Toward Complex Systems

Healthcare organizations exemplify complex systems that pose leadership challenges to assure safety and innovation. Through his studies of highly complex organizations, Steven Spear (2010) identified three capabilities for complex systems to succeed:

1. Seeing where knowledge is needed by identifying the gap between current and desired performance.

2.   Generating new knowledge by seeking solutions to the gaps.

3.   Sharing knowledge to build continued reliability and innovation.

Successful complex organizations show these capabilities in these ways:

- The expertise of one person is a function of their experience and tacit knowledge combined with that of many others.

- Success does not depend on a single event but on sharing the success and lessons learned so that others may build upon it.

- Outcomes are not viewed as successes or failures but are framed as successes or an opportunity to increase the chance of success the next time.

- Those who accomplish better outcomes do not share how they did that but show the problem in context with the discovery process; they tell the story of what happened and how.

- Training explains not just how but why, with a high reliance on visual learning and simulation.

- Leaders are accountable to develop knowledge sharing skill in others.

Embedding the Right Culture

Additional insight for leaders comes from Schein (2004), who identified primary means to embed culture to inform knowledge sharing. Leaders embed a knowledge sharing culture in many different ways; for example, how they react to critical incidents or crises, such as events causing harm to patients; how they allocate resources; what they recognize and reward; and who they recruit and promote. Leaders who pay attention to knowledge sharing in these instances will embed in their culture more quickly and thoroughly. Schein (1999) also notes that changes in essential components of an organization's culture require unlearning and relearning cultural behaviors. When professionals face changes, they can encounter learning anxiety that may highlight a fear of incompetence and personal or professional punishment for

"Leaders who pay attention to knowledge sharing ... will embed in their culture more quickly and thoroughly."

incompetence (real or imagined). An essential principle to guide leaders in transformative change is reducing learning anxiety while promoting the need for change.

Social learning theory provides effective means of advancing changes (Patterson et al. 2008). Their work points leaders to changing behavior as a means to changing thinking. Leaders often try to accomplish change solely by convincing others of the superiority of the new direction and by talking people into new behaviors. While people need to clearly understand why the changes are needed and be engaged in processes to achieve changes, the most effective first step is often small tests of change rather than large scale roll-out and expectation of new thinking immediately. Consistent with Dixon (2000), Patterson's work challenges the conventional wisdom that asks leaders to "fix the culture" by creating a learning culture, then get people to share. She sees this process occurring in the reverse, by getting people to share ideas about topics important to them, which creates its own learning culture. Leaders must also be clear on those specific and vital few behaviors that describe what individuals must do. Many of us confuse outcomes (such as weight loss) with behaviors (exercising 30 minutes a day) and create an extensive list of new behaviors. These lists often overburden people in complex systems, thus assuring failure.

Additionally, social learning theory points to the people who possess tacit knowledge – the positive deviants (Pascale, Sternin and Sternin 2010) – who are able to achieve the cultural outcomes sought. Leaders can stimulate curiosity and learning by asking the questions, "How did they do that?" and "How might we ...?" with expectations that people will uncover tacit knowledge that is already in use in the organization.

Transformation through Leadership

A study of transformational leaders exemplifies learning from positive deviants (Balik and Gilbert 2010). It identified leaders' behaviors that contribute to a culture of learning. Four personal characteristics underlie leaders' behaviors. These personal characteristics also express themselves in organizational action. The characteristics bring results that benefit those served and serving – safety and quality of care, patient and family experience, commitment of staff and providers, and financial vitality.

The four personal characteristics in transformational healthcare leaders are:

1.   A personally held passion for patient care.

2.   Consistency in words and actions, authentic, humble.

3.   Intelligence, eager to learn, reflective.

4.   A genuine concern and trust in others.

These personal characteristics help cultivate a learning culture at all levels within an organization.

Transformational healthcare leaders are able to instill these success factors within their organizations:

- A constant focus on patient care combined with disciplined action.

- An ability to challenge the status quo while maintaining a future orientation.

- An eagerness to engage everyone.

- An atmosphere of teamwork and problem solving.

- An ability to develop the talents of others.

These organizational success factors support learning and knowledge sharing. For example, by engaging everyone and maintaining a disciplined focus on patient care, healthcare staff are motivated to improve their performance and contribute to better outcomes. Leaders who possess the personal characteristics that inspire organizational success can create exceptional results.

Leaders committed to learning are able to foster a culture that values curiosity, improvement, and unrelenting attention to mission. Organizational learning encourages people to use their creativity and experience to generate changes in the system. This is supported and stimulated by leaders who enable individual and collective learning, who assure infrastructure that permits sharing new processes with others; and who help to institutionalize the learning in the organization (Fritz 2011). New approaches are taught, embedded in procedures, measured for results, and recognized in performance.

Finally, exceptional leaders have the ability to tap into the untapped wisdom and tacit knowledge held by patients and families. They have the unique experience of their healthcare journey, their fears and needs, and their preferences in health and healing. Leaders who are able to engage patients and families as full partners in care can leverage their tacit knowledge to improving the safety and experience of care (Balik et al. 2011).

"Building the Middle" – Connecting Senior Leadership with Front-line Clinicians

Organizations that effectively manage knowledge and continuously learn are able to build infrastructure in "the middle" to facilitate this knowledge sharing. This infrastructure requires leadership skills among physicians and middle managers, and a system to acquire, analyze, and act on knowledge. Technical expertise and clinical problem solving are the traditional hallmarks of physician education. However, physicians also need to know how to lead teams in an effective and inclusive manner. This type of behavior must be continually modeled through the sharing of tacit knowledge. Communication and teamwork are essential, so that reluctance to speak up is minimized or overcome if a risk to patient safety is perceived. Middle managers should also share tacit knowledge and develop effective communication and teamwork skills to ensure consistency and predictability.

> It all starts with the leader and the culture that they and their senior team build to allow [tacit knowledge sharing] to happen so as issues are identified … they enable the asking, probing, questioning; showing that they think it's important through their role modeling (Interview 13/241–247).

The other necessary component of "building the middle" is creating a system that insures the knowledge of the front-line clinicians and non-clinical staff is reliably captured and acted upon. Traditional models, like incident reporting systems, are inadequate for this purpose (Classen et al. 2011). For a variety of reasons, only a small number of incidents and learning opportunities are reported. First of all, if clinicians are unsure if they will be reprimanded for their role in an error, they are unlikely to provide vital insights as to how risk can be mitigated in future. Second, most organizations don't ensure consistent feedback after an incident is reported, thus reducing the confidence that an incident report will improve anything. Too often, front-line clinicians will say that certain problems have existed for years in an organization, even though the risk to patients' safety was apparent. Therefore, an organizational commitment to listen, analyze and provide feedback is essential.

In most healthcare organizations today, senior leaders and front-line clinicians still work in separate worlds. But these worlds need to be more closely aligned to create opportunities for knowledge and improvement to permeate the organization more consistently. A reliable structure for information and tacit knowledge flow and consistently reinforcing the behaviors that promote the open exchange of knowledge can help achieve these goals. Infobox 2.1 highlights one example that has effectively been implemented to span boundaries and provide structured opportunities for knowledge sharing: executive walk arounds.

INFOBOX 2.1: A TACTIC FOR EXECUTIVE ENGAGEMENT

The Executive WalkRounds™ at the Brigham and Women's Hospital. (Frankel et al. 2005) is a recognized example of a tacit knowledge sharing strategy that supports a learning organization. Senior leaders round with clinical staff on units and discuss clinicians' concerns about actual or potential threats to patient safety. All concerns, information, and tacit knowledge expressed during the course of the WalkRounds are recorded, analyzed and prioritized according to their potential severity of harm and frequency. The issues selected for intervention are placed in a database, assigned for correction, and followed up on. Every clinician who provided information received feedback in the form of a note, e-mail, phone call or conversation, continuing the invitation to share their tacit knowledge.

Unit Level – Role of Unit Level Leadership and Leadership Behaviors for Learning

Healthcare staff who work on an organizational unit are often known as "frontline" or "sharp end" employees. At this level, knowledge sharing frequently occurs informally. Waring and Bishop (2010: 325) describe it as "water cooler" learning or "backstage" communication. In a similar way, the "shadow system" contributes to individuals' mental models and actions

"[Unit level and informal leaders] are in the best position to nurture the community, and build the trust that enhances continual knowledge sharing."

(Zimmerman, Lindberg, and Plsek 1998: 37–8). While acknowledging that some back-stage knowledge sharing may be seen as a sign of a secretive or negative culture, Waring and Bishop (2010) hypothesize that it can also contribute to a positive problem solving environment. The authors observed situational informal knowledge sharing in a variety of surgery unit settings, including the staff lounge, the surgery store room, and the main corridors of the surgery unit. Discussions often related to patient care safety and quality. Authors identified six ways these types of interactions contribute to practice improvement and patient safety (Waring and Bishop 2010: 335–7). They are:

1.   Critical reflection with colleagues.

2.   Collective sense making of recent events.

3.   Functional contribution or problem solving.

4.   Communication and follow-up of identified concerns to the leadership.

5.   Supportive and emotional sharing that helps develop coping strategies.

6.   Reinforcement of cultural and professional norms.

Storytelling

Storytelling is another informal, yet powerful, practice for building knowledge at the unit level. The immediate impact of stories often makes them more powerful than events that are written down and read at a later point. For example, one nursing unit shared a story in which a family experienced confusion about the equipment being used with the patient. In addition to the factual details, the story included the emotional reactions of the family members and the positive effect of a different type of communication with the family. Following this experience in storytelling, nursing staff explained the workings of the equipment to other family members in a different way. Without a new policy or procedure, the story became part of the orientation of new nurses to the unit.

Communities of Practice

Storytelling and water cooler learning are examples of social learning that can build knowledge at the unit level. Another type of social learning has been described by Wenger as communities of practice (CoPs). They are "groups of people who share a passion for something that they know how to do, and who interact regularly in order to learn how to do it better" (Wenger 2004: 2). Richard McDermott (2001: 20) explains that they "form spontaneously as people seek help, try to solve problems, develop new ideas and approaches." McDermott suggests that these communities "are ideal vehicles for leveraging tacit knowledge because they enable person-to-person interaction and engage a whole group in advancing their field of practice. As a result, they can spread the insight from the collaborative thinking process across the whole organization" (McDermott 2001: 20). While these communities often form spontaneously, McDermott also thinks that organizations have "recently begun to understand their dynamics and tried to intentionally develop them" (McDermott 2001: 21).

Communities of practice often develop within a single discipline. In healthcare organizations, both single- and multi-disciplinary CoPs exist at the unit level (Li et al. 2009). Ideally, the unit or CoP leader should embody the same personal characteristics as the organizational leader to enable effective knowledge sharing. In the hospital environment, unit leaders can be the clinical manager, charge nurse, shift coordinator, or the unit educator. Informal leaders are also influential. These individuals know their associates on a personal and professional level. They are in the best position to nurture the community, and build the trust that enhances continual knowledge sharing. They can lobby the senior leadership to ensure that enough time is allowed for the community members to participate for knowledge sharing activities. This is especially challenging in environments that restrict non-productive time or if there is discomfort with conversations taking place that could challenge or question administrator or management actions.

The current CoP models include both single-discipline and multi-disciplinary structures. Single-discipline models are frequently unit-based nursing councils, and are usually focused on specific clinical issues. Discussions often begin with tacit knowledge sharing about the issue at hand, but expand to incorporate published evidence. Effective councils need to meet on a regular basis and often will have rotating leadership. They may also create subcommittees to address such topics as patient safety, family satisfaction, and introduction of new technologies.

Teams and Clinical Microsystems

In recent years, various methods for organizing multi-disciplinary unit teams have been adopted from other industries. Their language is increasingly becoming a part of the healthcare lexicon. For example, the aviation model of crew resource management (CRM) has been used in a number of healthcare settings, including the Veterans Health Administration.

The concept of clinical microsystems, another method for organizing multi-disciplinary unit teams, received a theoretical and practical foundation through the work of Dartmouth University's Nelson, Batalden, and others (*Acting Locally* 2005). They defined the clinical microsystem as:

> *a small group of people who work together on a regular basis to provide*
> *care to discrete subpopulations of patients. It has clinical and business*
> *aims, linked processes, and a shared information environment, and it*
> *produces performance outcomes. Microsystems evolve over time and*
> *are often embedded in larger organizations. They are complex adaptive*
> *systems, and as such they must do the primary work associated with*
> *core aims, meet the needs of internal staff, and maintain themselves*
> *over time as clinical units (Nelson et al. 2002: 474).*

Clinical microsystems are often developed to address patients cared for on specific units, such as mother/newborn or the emergency department, or to address patients who may be cared for on various units, such as those with heart failure. Each microsystem has a lead team, usually consisting of a physician, nurse, and administrator. The lead team brings together physicians, nurses (both managers and staff), pharmacists, dieticians, case managers, rehabilitation therapists, chaplains, and librarians/informationists. Often the microsystem lead team will invite a patient or patient's family member for a specific project or as a long-term member.

Lead teams collect and analyze data to select a focus for improving patient care. The data can consist of employee or patient satisfaction survey results, clinical performance data on selected measures, or experiences from patients or families. Once data has been analyzed and an improvement target selected, the team develops the specific aim for the improvement and determines how success will be measured. This collaboration requires time to develop as members exchange tacit knowledge that has evolved over months and years. The team typically includes members with varying degrees of experience, ensuring different points of view and levels of expertise. Leaders will allow sufficient time for the collaborative phase so that knowledge as well as information can shape the improvement activity. This is a useful illustration of the Ackoff hierarchy of data, information and knowledge, as the ideas and thoughts of the team emerge through the sharing of data to elicit what is known through their deliberation.

Briefings

Another multi-disciplinary structure for knowledge sharing at the unit level has developed through a process to address patient safety issues. Called a "safety briefing," this model was developed by the Institute for Healthcare Improvement (2004) as a non-punitive way to foster a safety culture. It is used to improve medication safety but can be adapted to other safety issues. The safety briefing should only last about five minutes and can be conducted by any member of the unit. It is important that the unit leaders act upon issues that are raised.

Safety debriefs can also be used to address a near miss (sometimes referred to as "close calls" or "good catches," near misses are events, activities or situations that could have resulted in a problem, but did not, due to preemptive action by others (Quality Interagency Coordination Task Force 2000)). The process brings together all involved parties on the unit before the end of a shift change to capture as many facts as possible while the incident is still fresh in everyone's mind. This type of informal knowledge sharing may lead to a formal process such as a root cause analysis. Like the safety briefing, the safety debrief is intended to be done in a non-punitive way, and the unit leader is responsible for setting this tone. Because of its immediacy, the safety debrief is a powerful way to spread lessons to the whole unit and ensure that everyone has the same information.

Unit-level Engagement

The Comprehensive Unit-Based Safety Program (CUSP) was developed at Johns Hopkins to provide a protocol to enhance improvement and safety culture on a unit. CUSP is a structured framework for safety improvement that integrates communication, teamwork, and leadership to create and support a culture of patient safety that can prevent harm. The program features: evidence-based safety practices, staff training tools, standards for consistently measuring infection rates, engagement of leadership and tools to improve teamwork among doctors, nurses, and other members of the healthcare team (Pronovost et al. 2006).

The following five steps from CUSP equip front-line providers with the tools, metrics, and framework to tackle the challenge of quality improvement:

Step 1:   Staff are educated on the science of safety.

Step 2:   Staff complete an assessment of patient safety culture.

Step 3:   A senior hospital executive partners with the unit to improve communications and educate leadership.

Step 4:   Staff learn from unit defects.

Step 5:   Staff use tools, including checklists, to improve teamwork, communication, and other systems of work.

CUSP was first applied on a large scale in the Keystone Project, which deployed this approach in more than 100 intensive care units (ICUs) in Michigan beginning in 2003. This project targeted clinicians' use of five evidence-based practices, recommended by the Centers for Disease Control and Prevention, to reduce rates of Central Line-Associated Bloodstream Infection (CLABSI):

1.   Practicing hand hygiene.

2.   Using full-barrier precautions during the insertion of central venous catheters.

3.   Cleaning the skin with chlorhexidine.

4.   Avoiding the femoral site when possible.

5.   Removing unnecessary catheters.

Using a checklist to ensure the procedures were followed, the Keystone Project:

- Reduced rates of CLABSI by two-thirds within three months.

- Saved more than 1,500 lives and nearly $200 million in the program's first 18 months.

- Decreased the rate of CLABSI to the point where these infections became rare events in the participating ICUs, which continued to sustain this reduction three years after first adopting CUSP.

A Calling to Commit to Knowledge Sharing

The success of knowledge management in healthcare organizations hinges on whether the leadership is ready, committed, and able to apply a knowledge sharing philosophy to its daily activities. Leaders who nurture learning and accelerated results through knowledge management demonstrate a combination of four essential elements: clarity of purpose, urgency, effective systems development, and courage.

Balik and Gilbert (2010) provide concrete examples of these four elements. *Clarity of purpose* is shown through an unwavering passion for patient care that engages others, "He defines the vision with great clarity but not the answers. He integrates the vision into everything he does" (2010: 5). *Urgency* is visible by constantly challenging the status quo and by aiming higher, "We can always be better. She is always asking 'What is the next best?'" (2010: 14). Learning enabled by knowledge management does not happen by accident or hopefulness, but through effective systems development. Several examples are noted in this chapter. *Effective knowledge sharing behaviors* that support effective knowledge management systems that stem from a combination of disciplined action and engaging all parties, "She has the ability to make people belong and matter and want to work hard for themselves and the institution" (2010: 16). And finally, leaders demonstrate *courage*. The courage to take meaningful actions every day to assure that their words and actions match, to make their clarity of purpose a reality, not a feel-good slogan, "I trust him with any decision because he will always do the right thing for patients, the business, employees – he will not accept otherwise" (2010: 3).

Leaders who demonstrate these four elements honor those who are close to the work, tap into the crucial tacit knowledge of those around them, and achieve results vital to serving those who entrust us with their care.

KEY TAKE-AWAYS

- Opportunities exist for leaders at the organizational, managerial and frontline level to be seen as knowledge sharing champions.
- System thinking, complexity, and the learning organization are foundational concepts to build and sustain an effective knowledge sharing culture.
- Behaviors and tactics to infuse knowledge must be embedded at all levels of the organization to recognize and adopt knowledge sharing skills, attitudes, and beliefs.

Suggested Reading

Balik, B. and Gilbert, J. 2010. *The Heart of Leadership: Inspiration and Practical Guidance for Transforming Your Healthcare Organization*. Chicago, IL: American Hospital Association Press.

Garvin, D.A. 1993. "Building a Learning Organization." *Harvard Business Review*, 71(4), 78–91.

Seaman, J.T. Jr and Smith, G.D. 2012. "Your Company's History as a Leadership Tool." *Harvard Business Review*, 90(12), December, 44–52, 133.

Smith, M., Saunders, R., Stuckhardt, L. and McGinnis J.M. (eds). 2012. *Best Care at Lower Cost: The Path to Continuously Learning Health Care in America*. Washington, DC: National Academies Press.

3

The Healthcare Environment and Knowledge: Blunt End Experience

Lorri Zipperer and Albert Wu

> *Tacit knowledge is the primary basis for effective management and the basis for its deterioration (Argyris 1999: 123).*

Knowledge Sharing as a Crucial Part of Improvement

A 1998 inquiry at Bristol Royal Infirmary in the United Kingdom examined the organizational and individual failures leading to a series of fatalities among infants undergoing pediatric heart surgery. The final report detailed some 200 recommendations for front-line clinicians, administrators, auditors, and the National Health Service (NHS) itself. Recommendations were put into effect quickly, launching improvements in how the NHS provides care, audits its organizations, and engages in quality initiatives and local improvement activities (Walshe and Offen 2001).

Despite this aggressive response, there were lapses in tacit knowledge between clinicians and administrators that also figured in these tragic events, but that received little attention. Fifteen years after the report, this gap in knowledge sharing may continue to hinder the success of other investigations that seek to identify ways of creating better, safer care processes.

This chapter argues for the importance of an organizational commitment to shaping and nurturing a tacit knowledge sharing culture. It illustrates the potential downstream effect of dysfunctional organizational knowledge sharing on the ability of front-line practitioners to benefit from tacit knowledge, sometimes described as "what the knowers know" (Davenport and Prusak 1998).

Organizational Personalities Shape Performance

Organizations have personalities. They are born, evolve, age, and die. They have their own cultures, failures, successes, and mechanisms for ebb and flow. They have structures that can simultaneously expose employees, customers and the organization to risk. All of these elements affect how work is performed, how information is developed, how explicit knowledge is disseminated, and how tacit knowledge is created, shared, and acted upon.

James Reason's oft-applied model, which illustrates systems failure across the structure of an organization, is useful for examining knowledge sharing within hospitals, and how it extends beyond the organization to affect the larger system of healthcare (Reason 1990).

The Blunt End and Knowledge Management

WHAT IS THE "BLUNT END"?

James Reason (1990) conceptualized the "blunt end" as the activities within an organization that craft and enforce the policies, programs, and rules that affect how clinicians on the frontline (those providing direct patient care), or "sharp end," carry out their work (see Infobox 3.1 and Chapter 4). In the context of knowledge management, the blunt end represents the forces that determine the resources, influence, access, rules, and incentives, including human resources and practice policies that affect how individuals share what they know.

INFOBOX 3.1: THE SHARP END

"The sharp end refers to the personnel or parts of the healthcare system in direct contact with patients. Personnel operating at the sharp end may literally be holding a scalpel (for example, an orthopedist who operates on the wrong leg) or figuratively be administering any kind of therapy (for example, a nurse programming an intravenous pump) or performing any aspect of care."

Source: Adapted with permission from AHRQ Patient Safety Network: Shojania, K.G., Wachter, R.M. and Hartman, E.E. *AHRQ Patient Safety Network Glossary*. Available at: http://psnet.ahrq.gov/glossary.aspx

---

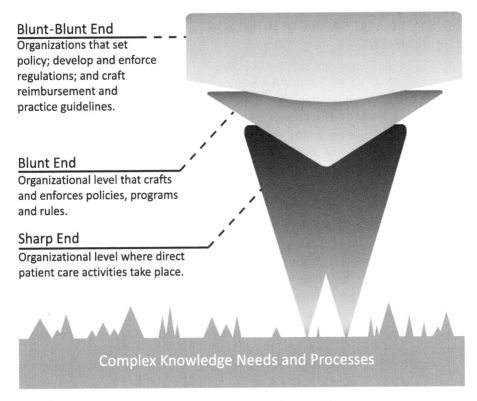

Blunt-Blunt End
Organizations that set
policy; develop and enforce
regulations; and craft
reimbursement and
practice guidelines.

Blunt End
Organizational level that crafts
and enforces policies, programs
and rules.

Sharp End
Organizational level where direct
patient care activities take place.

Complex Knowledge Needs and Processes

Figure 3.1   Sharp End, Blunt End, Blunt-Blunt End
Source: Adapted from Reason 1990.

Activities that occur at the blunt end enable an organization to convert tacit
knowledge and the "know how" of staff into explicit assets that can be used
to spur innovation and improvement in quality and patient safety (Choo
1996).

Expanding the definition of the blunt end from AHRQ's PSNet (AHRQ
Patient Safety Network Glossary) allows an insight into the meaning of
organizations located at the "blunt-blunt end." These are entities that are
external to the care delivery environment that play an important role in
influencing the decisions of those organizations and the actions of those at the
sharp end. For example, blunt-blunt end organizations set policy, develop and
enforce regulations, and craft reimbursement and practice guidelines. Their
actions often have a significant impact on the day-to-day activities of clinicians
and other practitioners.

BLUNT END STAFF AFFECT KNOWLEDGE SHARING IN THE HOSPITAL ENVIRONMENT

Boards of directors and executive-level administrators enable a knowledge sharing culture by engaging others, establishing a shared vision and building a supportive learning environment. In addition, a mix of clinicians and non-clinicians can help engender the trust needed among executive management for tacit knowledge sharing. Tacit knowledge provides value as it conveys know-how typically captured at the sharp end to influence decision-making at the blunt end. This transfer of tacit knowledge can benefit leaders by preventing the unintended, and potentially dangerous, consequences of uninformed decision-making.

Senior leaders must support and participate in a knowledge management initiative to ensure its success. With their 360-degree view at the blunt end, they help to allocate resources, set expectations, determine resource allocation, mentor psychological safety, and encourage improvement. In addition to senior leadership, other key departments at the blunt end who are well-situated to play a role in knowledge sharing include:

Risk Management: These individuals work collaboratively to provide their services across traditional organizational silos (Youngberg 2011). Collaboration allows risk managers to use the tacit knowledge of staff to assess strengths, weaknesses, opportunities and threats to the organization. Risk managers must be able to effectively access and utilize the experience, expertise, and knowledge of those at the sharp end, to specifically identify threats to the patient and to the organization. The risk manager can utilize this range of input to target threats across the organization and develop more effective means to ameliorate the potential or actual concerns. For example, in developing a crisis communication plan about a potential hazardous waste spill within the hospital, the risk manager would garner input from administration, public relations, environmental safety, clinical personnel, housekeeping, and others to organize a coherent communications response to the public, to employees, and to public safety officials.

Information Technology: Whether the data are clinical, financial, or legal, staff who design, build and implement information technology (IT) systems naturally accumulate tacit knowledge across the organization. This resource should be leveraged. Their experiences in working with a variety of personnel to understand workflow, process, and system integration issues situates IT staff to know who is doing what and how it is being done. This awareness can enable effective internal sharing across silos, while protecting privacy and confidential information. Whether engaged in systems development at the sharp end or the blunt end, IT departments are most effective when they include staff with an orientation and aptitude for knowledge sharing. This skill could enable IT departments to serve as "boundary spanners" to influence implementation of supportive technologies. For example, it has been suggested that such a failure contributed to the ineffective use of IT during the Bristol audit reviews (Walshe and Offen 2001).

Education and Training: Staff that design and implement resources (that is, continuing education (CE), general training and orientation) to educate non-clinical employees have an opportunity to improve knowledge sharing. Although training programs do not necessarily serve as tacit knowledge conduits (DeLong 2004), they can provide valuable opportunities for performance improvement and skill development (Hazlett, McAdam and Beggs 2008). Training is often erroneously equated with knowledge management; however, engaging staff to promote tacit knowledge sharing can be a beneficial strategy. Education staff need to recognize that knowledge sharing goes experts providing didactic presentations and short lists of steps to follow to build new skills. With this broader perspective in place, educational staff could facilitate the rich exchange of tacit knowledge in training sessions, mentoring and shadowing initiatives, thereby making knowledge sharing more accessible and impactful.

Libraries and Informationist Programs: Librarians in hospitals work with staff at the blunt end to help coordinate CE programs, develop policy, design web sites, and enhance performance improvement (Zipperer 2004; Gluck 2004; Garcia and Wells 2009; Robinson and Gehle 2005; Sollenberger and Holloway 2013). These information professionals belong to a category of librarianship referred to as special librarianship, and play a role in improved knowledge sharing in corporate healthcare settings (Wheaton 2009; Moore 2006). Their role and access to information can provide tacit, explicit and cultural knowledge. This occurs by helping clients understand and articulate needs; increasing value of resources through evaluation, summation and organization for specific purpose; and applying what is known to the acquisition of information and knowledge resources to address specific needs (Choo 2002).

Human Resources: DeLong (2004) discusses the importance of human resources (HR) in the design and implementation of an · infrastructure to embrace knowledge retention. Ideally, the experiences and insights from departing employees are captured through a defined process. In the quality and safety realm, confidentiality constraints may arise that make it difficult for exiting employees to share their experiences. However, HR personnel could share valuable lessons learned and maintain the employee's privacy. Because of HR's sensitivities into the gaps and strengths of employees and units, the organization could also benefit if that knowledge were accessible as part of hiring decisions.

Administrative services: Administrative staff serve as valuable disseminators of information and policy. Their role can be enriched by acknowledging the value of their tacit knowledge on how the organization, unit or team works. For example, administrative assistants can be adept at navigating hierarchies, personalities and organizational processes to get work done in a way that is tailored to a specific need. Exploration of this skill can shed light on the workings of activities that occur at the blunt end if incorporated into knowledge sharing and other types of process improvement.

> *Go ask the department secretaries … They know what to ask and who to ask and which rules can be bent and which rules can't be bent. And they're the only ones who really know how the [place] works (Interview 17/190–193).*

Staff whose expertise situates them at the blunt end exhibit knowledge sharing behaviors within their respective communities. These behaviors can be leveraged at the organizational level to enrich the sharing of knowledge (McDermott 1999). Leadership and management can facilitate this through supporting a culture of trust and transparency. They can recognize knowledge sharing as a viable employee skill, hire for it, and enable informal communities at organizations (McDermott 1999). Policies should be developed to leverage that knowledge more broadly as an organizational learning strategy, without deterring the sharing of tacit knowledge through discussion, or community involvement (online or face-to-face), or allowing disruptive management behavior toward staff that share their knowledge in good faith.

BOUNDARY SPANNERS: KEY ENABLERS

Certain individuals are well-positioned to facilitate knowledge transfer between the sharp and blunt end of an organization. A term that describes the quality these individuals possess is "boundary spanner." Whether officially appointed or simply recognized for this skill, boundary spanners serve as "go-betweens" and bridge information gaps between the sharp and blunt ends. They have ties both within the organization and outside of their work environment that others may not possess (Adler 2009). They are sometimes known as knowledge brokers, or gatekeepers (Davenport and Prusak 1998).

Boundary spanners should be active in the blunt-blunt end of an organization as well. Activities such as engaging in quality improvement work (see Infobox 3.2), providing CE, convening committees, and being members of professional associations provide staff with opportunities to translate tacit knowledge gleaned from their familiarity with the organization's sharp end.

INFOBOX 3.2: TACIT KNOWLEDGE SHARING THROUGH QUALITY IMPROVEMENT WORK

This story presents quality improvement education as a tacit knowledge transfer mechanism through the creation of boundary spanning opportunities.

Small multidisciplinary teams of clinicians first learned rapid cycle improvement processes and then implemented the learning by completing a process improvement project of their choosing within the organization. The rapid cycle improvement tool referred to as Plan-Do-Study Act (PDSA) facilitated a process of brainstorming and the collaborative, multidisciplinary team process enabled tacit knowledge to be transferred and then spread given the wide reach of the team on both the sharp and blunt end. The teams included nurses, residents, attendings, pharmacists, allied health professionals, librarians, pastoral care professionals and healthcare administrators.

Source: Christine Chastain-Warheit.

Although healthcare organizations are routinely separated into strict organizational silos, risk managers, librarians and human resources employees often provide their services at both the sharp and blunt levels of the healthcare system. For example:

- Risk managers advise on disclosures of error to patients and families.

- Coding specialists round with clinical teams to make sure insurance billing and paperwork issues are handled appropriately.

- Librarians participate in clinical rounds to provide a reference service for clinicians. The role of the clinical librarians and informationists in acute care environments has been established and studied, yet it is not an established practice in every healthcare environment (Davidoff and Florance 2000; Grefsheim et al. 2010; Committee on Quality of Health Care in America 2001).

- Human resources or employee assistance staff can support clinicians who are "second victims" of patient adverse events (Scott et al. 2010; Carr 2009).

COLLABORATIVES: WHERE BOUNDARY SPANNERS CAN SHINE

To be successful, boundary spanners should engage in knowledge sharing work and in the design, championing and peer assist efforts of knowledge management. Barriers exist to this concept, including organizational silos, protective views of roles, and negative mental models within an organization (Zipperer and Amori 2011; Currie, Waring and Finn 2008). The collaborative is one type of peer assist process where boundary spanning has been embraced (Peele, Goldberg and Trompeta 2011; Green and Plsek 2002; McCannon and Perla 2009; Leape et al. 2000). It can be used as a meaningful tacit knowledge sharing tactic.

For example, the Michigan Keystone Project has attracted international attention by reducing the incidence of catheter-related bloodstream infections in 100 intensive care units (ICUs) and sustaining that improvement over three years (Pronovost et al. 2006). Knowledge management successes in this endeavor, which is repeated now in hospitals across the US, include wide participation among staff and clinicians from the blunt end to the front-line ICU staff (Dixon-Woods et al. 2011).

The goals and means to get there were articulated by experts who condensed the explicit knowledge needed to follow the protocol into an easy-to-follow checklist. Adapting the knowledge of nurses and physicians to this protocol was instrumental in gaining and sustaining success for the project (Pronovost and Vohr 2010). Institutional leaders adopted both the goals and evaluation measures of the project. The existing culture toward learning from others across the program was foundational in the achievement.

Successful implementation at the unit level relied on tacit information about barriers to use. Hospital leaders used this knowledge to justify expenditures for infection control and implement policies to reduce costly and dangerous healthcare-acquired infections. Importantly, the project created a network of clinical managers and practitioners across hospitals that provided both normative pressures to improve as well as channels to convey practical improvement suggestions.

Despite the success of this and similar programs, the knowledge sharing that occurs in these improvement initiatives receives scant attention compared to discussions of other elements of the improvement process. Consequently, the generation of evidence has not formed around the construct of tacit knowledge management definitions, success mechanisms or metrics. It is possible that this failure results from a lack of rigor around exploring the workings of such networks within the blunt or blunt-blunt end environment (Braithwaite et al. 2009).

THE BLUNT-BLUNT END OF KNOWLEDGE SHARING

The multi-tiered US healthcare system includes several layers to its organizational blunt end, thus adding to the complexity of communicating information and evidence. As depicted in Figure 3.1, the blunt end operationalizes decisions made by external entities that shape regulations, policies, and procedures that impact the sharp end and the delivery of care. These policy-making entities, in addition to healthcare organizations, are considered to be "knowledge intensive" (Hurley and Green 2005). For the purposes of this discussion, they are the organizations considered to be on the blunt-blunt end of the healthcare system.

Blunt-Blunt End: Organizational Entities

Organizational structures, reporting requirements and financial arrangements can serve as barriers to streamlined operations between an organization's blunt end and its clinicians (Bohmer 2009). This creates a barrier to knowledge sharing. The following list illustrates some of the organizations that affect hospital operations through their rules, standards and policies:

- *Accreditors, Regulators*: The Joint Commission, Centers for Medicare and Medicaid Services (CMS), Office of the Inspector General (OIG), Department of Justice (DOJ).

- *Assessment Organizations*: Institute for Safe Medication Practices (ISMP), National Committee for Quality Assurance (NCQA).

- *Professional Boards*: American Board of Medical Specialties (ABMS), American College of Graduate Medical Education (ACGME).

- *Quality Improvement Organizations*: National Patient Safety Foundation (NPSF), Institute for Healthcare Improvement (IHI).

- *Funding and Research Agencies*: Commonwealth Fund, Centers for Disease Control & Prevention (CDC), Agency for Healthcare Research and Quality (AHRQ).

- *Government Payers and Providers*: CMS, Veterans' Administration (VA).

- *Private Payers*: United Healthcare, Humana, Aetna, Blue Cross Blue Shield, and others.

- *Purchasers*: Employers, retiree organizations, unions.

Blunt-blunt end organizations have mature monitoring and coordinating mechanisms to manage the data they collect and the knowledge they capture through interactions with their constituents (Lynn 2011). Policy-making bodies may approach knowledge management efforts using more of a marketing strategy approach, rather than one that seeks to enhance the value of their employees' knowledge and work process (De la Mothe and Foray 2001).

To be fair, some organizations on the blunt-blunt end face significant economic challenges due to decreases in membership revenue, reductions in public and private funding, non-profit status, and increased expectations from the marketplace and members. They can be slow to apply knowledge typically generated at the sharp end. However, enhancement of tacit knowledge sharing can drive innovation and facilitate quicker adoption of concepts and knowledge to generate the type of improvements these organizations are intended to foster. These organizations could benefit by empowering their own employees to effectively address knowledge gaps of peers, management and colleagues (DeLong 2004).

The Role of Knowledge Sharing in Blunt-Blunt End Quality and Safety Improvement Organizations

Many experts in quality improvement and patient safety believe that progress occurs far too slowly (Wachter 2010; Leape and Berwick 2005). Tacit knowledge can generate motivation and commitment to advance this work. Tacit knowledge can positively influence:

Timeliness: Gathering and organizing comprehensive evidence (guidelines, consensus statements, sentinel event alerts, etc.) is an essential function of many blunt-blunt end organizations. Knowledge that is separated by organizational siloes often leads to delays in developing such evidence.

Urgency: A collective recognition that delays reduce the value of the effort can enhance the willingness of staff to share what is known. A lack of knowledge sharing can delay or result in incomplete results that require re-work, which is frustrating and stressful for all involved.

Cultural norms: Unresolved problems due to cultural norms within an organization can lead to significant failure (Vaughan 1996, reporting on Turner 1976). Healthcare organizations that accept disruptive physician behavior, for example, reward that behavior through retention of the relationship, promotion, additional research funding or departmental improvements (Porto and Lauve 2006). Leadership and staff that exhibit poor knowledge sharing can retain their positions and influence due to an inability to recognize its downstream effects. This is detrimental to the organization's ability to address quality and patient safety issues and contributes to the healthcare industry's reputation for slow progress on these fronts. See Appendix 1 for illustrations of negative downstream impacts of poor tacit knowledge sharing.

The influence of responses generated by organizations whose activities occur at the blunt-blunt end can be formidable. One notable example is the 2010 Patient Protection and Affordable Care Act, including CMS' Innovation Center and the Partnership for Patients (see http://innovation.cms.gov/ and http://partnershipforpatients.cms.gov/). More efforts include Institute for Healthcare Improvement's 100,000 and 5 Million Lives Campaigns, National Quality Forum "Never Events" classifications, the World Health Organization Safe Surgery Checklist initiative, and NHS National Learning System evidence-sharing efforts (AHRQ, "Patient Safety Organization"; Wachter and Pronovost 2006; Haynes et al. 2009; NHS Scotland 2011; National Quality Forum 2010).

Organizations can commit themselves to benefiting from their own knowledge. For example, the NHS has been transparent in its efforts to translate its experiences externally through the distribution of information packaged in guidelines and policies (Donaldson 2000). Yet a lack of evidence exists about the internal use of tacit knowledge in the NHS and how that translates to affect improvements at the sharp end.

IMPORTANCE OF ENABLING INTERNAL KNOWLEDGE SHARING TO DRIVE EXTERNAL IMPROVEMENTS

The ability to manage knowledge internally by blunt-blunt end entities requires the same cultural and organizational attributes as those needed by hospitals and other healthcare organizations. However, because blunt-blunt end organizations exert a large influence on healthcare entities, their success in knowledge management can have more wide-ranging implications. For instance, the NHS has come under criticism recently for maintaining an ever-growing number of policies and guidelines from different sources, making compliance an increasingly impossible task (Carthey et al. 2011).

The inadequacy of information sharing is often accompanied by a broader problem: an over-reliance on unmanaged information. One manufacturing organization experienced quality and timeliness problems when staffs were unable to easily access an information-sharing system that reported how problems could be resolved. Timely information became even more problematic when the staff member responsible for this system transferred to another area, leaving workers ill-equipped to contribute information that could help quickly identify quality and delivery problems (Milton 2010).

These types of information failures can only suggest the types of knowledge shairing failures that occur. Authors were unable to identify discussions of specific blunt end or blunt-blunt end healthcare failures related to an ineffective internal knowledge sharing climate. However, Table 3.1 on the page opposite presents a selected list of potential problems due to poor knowledge sharing in blunt or blunt-blunt end organizations and the potential downstream impact.

A Paradox Between Internal/External Knowledge Flows: Robbing Peter to Pay Paul

Organizations tend to have a strong bias toward external information dissemination (that is, looking only at optimizing information distribution to be pushed outward) rather than internal knowledge sharing that can work against them. A typical scenario is a health system that devotes resources to developing an attractive public web site but does not develop a useful intranet or internal knowledge sharing strategy for its employees. To optimize a long term strategy to protect against this "fix that will fail" – seven steps can be conjoined with systems thinking techniques to illustrate the potential consequences:

Table 3.1 Poor Tacit Knowledge Sharing at the Blunt End: Potential Impacts on Quality Improvement and Patient Safety

Failure of tacit knowledge sharing	Impact on external organizations (blunt-blunt end) whose policies affect hospital decision-making	Impact on hospital administration (blunt end)	Impact where care is given (sharp end)
Lack of access to internal tacit knowledge from experts and staff with relevant experience.	• Reduced awareness of problem. • Delayed QI/PS policy statements/guidelines. • Reduced opportunity to influence hospital improvement efforts.	• Expert consensus not used to inform decision making. • Delayed internal policy development. • Misinformed or ineffective policy. • Delayed or ineffective resources for improvement due to lack of external leverage.	• Insufficient motivation by individuals for safety improvement. • Diminished engagement of front-line staff in cooperative efforts to reduce errors.
Lack of effective QI/PS program development due to unsuccessful application of organizational expertise.	• Wasted time, resources and dollars (Hurley and Green 2005). • Employee burnout. • Decreased efficiency resulting in increased product costs. • Reduced financial support for QI/PS efforts.	• Wasted in-house resources for QI/PS programs. • Increased employee cynicism. • Reduced management support due to intangible impact. • Reduced product uptake due to perceived lack of relevance. • Diminished trust in policy due to lack of timeliness.	• Reduced front-line access to material/explicit knowledge. • Reduced engagement of champions in QI/PS work. • Lag time in initiatives to explore QI/PS options.
Failure to share problems with a commitment to learning.	• Staff reduction due to failure of EHR implementation. • Lack of organizational learning from experience. • Diminished ability to prevent similar failures in the future.	• Lack of benefit from negative experiences of vendor. • Failed experience not translated into hospital program. • Failure is repeated.	• Delay in effective implementation of technology. • Lack of buy-in from practitioners. • Delayed access to EHR. • Delay in anticipated QI/PS intervention.

Step 1: Identify the Symptoms of the Original Problem.

Step 2: Map all "Quick Fixes."

Step 3: Identify Undesirable Impacts.

Step 4: Identify Fundamental Solutions.

Step 5: Map Side Effects of Quick Fixes.

Step 6: Find Interconnections to Fundamental Loops.

Step 7: Identify High-Leverage Actions.

The problem of disproportionate investing in external information distribution leads to a lack of investment in internal knowledge management, which makes the problems worse. This failure to address internal knowledge sharing difficulties even with commitments of time, effort, and expense is familiar to many organizations – yet not studied or discussed broadly in the literature. Eventually, the problem will recur and need to be addressed again.

Problems related to dissemination, human capital, employee stress and attrition can be exacerbated by an emphasis solely on external communications as a "KM strategy." Systems thinking and causal loop diagrams can serve as

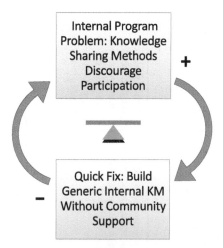

Figure 3.2   Balancing Loop Diagram of Quick Fixes
Source: Michael F. Moore, MLS, based on the work of Peter Senge.

tools to explore the long-term implications of a knowledge and information-sharing process and to envision its impact over time. Translated from the engineering field and popularized by Senge, causal loops can be used to explore a variety of changes and scenarios, including impacts of persistent information and knowledge sharing problems and proposed solutions to address them (Senge 1990; Senge et al. 1994; Tompson and Zipperer 2011). Appendix 1 illustrates the use of a causal loop diagram as a strategy for organizations to examine the steps outlined above to explore the impact of how knowledge sharing resources are distributed to support internal and external goals.

Commitment to Improvement

Successful organizations factor in the past, present and future in their knowledge sharing efforts. Past and current organizational cultures are influential and need to be considered in designing knowledge sharing initiatives (Wickramasinghe et al. 2009). Blunt end and blunt-blunt end organizations have more stable team structures than frontline care units, thus providing more staying power.

Mismanaged or unmanaged knowledge can affect an organization's ability to streamline costs and improve productivity (DeLong 2004). Given the national emphasis on increasing efficiency and quality in *"Successful organizations factor in the past, present and future in their knowledge sharing efforts."* healthcare, organizations can look "in-house" to improve knowledge retention and tacit knowledge sharing. The trend toward using less experienced staff may increase the risks of serious and costly mistakes, even at the blunt end of an organization due in part to the loss of important tacit knowledge. Diagnosing situations that put an organization at risk of failure requires knowledge of the situation, organization and activity (DeLong 2004).

Organizations can learn by looking internally. This requires the same level of commitment and resources as external information sharing programs. Leadership must persist in coordinating knowledge exchange across professional groups within complex adaptive organizations (Rangachari 2009). Robust strategies will provide opportunities to create connections, networks, and developmental models that include tacit knowledge sharing efforts and goals to connect them with the changing external environment.

Organizations that drive improvement, standards adoption, guideline uptake and care innovation should also share knowledge within their own walls. Increased efficiency and internal learning can improve efforts to be more effective, responsive, and reliable due to better member relations, improved employee retention and investment in proactive problem solving.

Non-profit organizations can "lack the critical processes and knowledge needed to help them develop, evaluate, document and share successful programs" (Hurley and Green 2005: 1). Failure by blunt-blunt end organizations to exploit their own work products, foster intellectual capital and encourage the formation of tacit knowledge perpetuate downstream failure. Because of their diverse and often competing stakeholders, these organizations can be handicapped by lack of access to the best practices, guidelines, information and evidence they create, let alone the tacit knowledge that resides within their organization.

Today's emphasis on learning from failures typically occurs first and foremost at the sharp end of care. A similar application of this insight to the blunt end and the blunt-blunt end is also warranted. At both the sharp and the blunt ends, openness to learning from failure helps organizations capitalize on the insights such failures generate (Edmondson 2011). To enable learning from failure in a complex organization, interdisciplinary teams need to be involved in the analysis. Enabling those improvements across an organization can spread effective practices that stimulate safety and quality improvement.

KEY TAKE-AWAYS

- Organizations should see tacit knowledge sharing as a primary responsibility and devote resources to its optimization.
- Ineffective knowledge sharing at the blunt-blunt end can affect overall knowledge use in the healthcare system which can affect safety and quality improvement work and contribute to large scale failure.
- Knowledge sharing ineffectiveness should be explored through complexity and systems-oriented diagnostic tools to elevate the conversation to run parallel with other systemic changes.

Suggested Reading

Committee on Quality of Health Care in America, Institute of Medicine. 2001. *Crossing the Quality Chasm: A New Health System for the 21st Century.* Washington, DC: National Academies Press.

Donaldson, L. 2000. *An Organisation with a Memory: Report of an Expert Group on Learning from Adverse Events in the NHS Chaired by the Chief Medical Officer.* London: The Stationery Office.

Gherardi, S. 2006. *Organizational Knowledge: The Texture of Workplace Learning.* Oxford. Blackwell Publishing.

Gray, M. 2011. *Report for the Mid Staffordshire Inquiry on the Benefits of Knowledge Management, 19 October.* Available at: http://www.midstaffspublicinquiry.com/sites/default/files/uploads/Sir_Muir_Gray_paper.pdf

Kohn, L., Corrigan, J. and Donaldson, M. (eds). 1999. *To Err Is Human: Building a Safer Health System.* Washington, DC: National Academies Press.

Meadows, D.H. 2008. *Thinking in Systems: A Primer.* White River Junction, VT: Chelsea Green Publishing.

Senge, P.M. 1990. *The Fifth Discipline.* New York, NY: Random House.

Weick, K.E. and Sutcliffe, K.M. 2003. "Hospitals as Cultures of Entrapment: A Re-analysis of the Bristol Royal Infirmary." *California Management Review,* 45(2), 73–84.

4

The Healthcare Environment and Knowledge: Sharp End Experience

Christine Chastain-Warheit and Lorri Zipperer

Healthcare professionals value and pursue local and tacit knowledge (Nicolini 2008: 249).

Knowledge Sharing in a Complex Space

Tacit knowledge helps clinicians make decisions that are efficient, effective, and patient-centered with greater confidence (Clarke and Wilcockson 2002; Nicolini 2008). The interaction among jazz musicians as they make music together provides a useful metaphor: "They take in information, make sense of it, generate new musical ideas, and apply their insights to the ongoing musical conversation ... Jamming is a kind of musical thinking" (McDermott 1999: 106). With the ongoing, highly complex nature of activity at the sharp end of clinical care, this metaphor may help visualize how tacit knowledge is shared during direct care delivery.

A consistent theme in the knowledge management literature for healthcare notes "the preference for local knowledge in the making of clinical decisions" (Nicolini 2008: 247). Seeking this readily available source of knowledge is understandable. With the overwhelming amount of new information that clinicians need to access, interpret and apply, they may turn to colleagues when they need additional expertise. Although relying on colleagues can be an imperfect method for gathering evidence about a preferred course of action (Schaafsma et al. 2005), tacit knowledge may best be shared through this conduit. Low quality, unsafe, effective and model behaviors can also be normalized through tacit knowledge sharing (see Chapters 3, 6, and 9). Thus great care must be taken to derive from tacit knowledge the effective lessons as they are applied at the sharp end to generate improvement of healthcare delivery.

This chapter will explore tacit knowledge sharing at the place where clinicians provide care to patients: the sharp end. It is at this point in the process where effective, accurate, and accessible knowledge has the greatest potential of good – or harm. The local area of focus, where tacit knowledge is typically shared, is the clinical microsystem and its related subcultures. Actions and relationships at the local level influence how care is delivered from clinicians to patients (Nelson et al. 2003).

Front-line Learning, Decision-Making and Tacit Knowledge: Exploring their Relationships to Care Provision

Whether acknowledged or not, tacit knowledge is a part of every clinician's repertoire. It contributes to clinical confidence, expertise and maturation of critical thinking skills. Concepts that relate to mindfulness, expertise and judgment and decision-making can help illustrate how tacit knowledge can be applied by clinical teams.

MINDFULNESS

Use of tacit knowledge helps people become more aware and "weave the stitch" in new or different ways. For clinicians, this could mean examining how care could be delivered in a mindful way. Mindfulness involves self-critiquing even the ordinary active and obvious tasks while in process and is based on the interweaving of action, thought, memory, and feeling. Mindfulness is the contradiction of multitasking (Epstein 1999; Sibinga and Wu 2010). Developing mindfulness may reduce errors by helping clinicians appreciate the value of "reflective practice." For example, a resident may weigh the consequences of asking for help from others in a dubious situation. The mindful resident reflects on the impact on the patient of an incorrect or delayed diagnosis, the effect on his or her self-esteem and the desire to learn. The "unmindful

"Whether acknowledged or not, tacit knowledge is a part of every clinician's repertoire."

practitioner" may avoid these questions, become more preoccupied with expediency or blame on others, even the patient or patient's family. This behavior thusly leaves the resident unprepared for a similar situation the next time it might arise (Epstein 1999).

Mindfulness can affect how, why, with whom and when knowledge should be shared to prevent or intercept problems that could contribute to failure, such as sharing a near-miss experience shortly after it occurs. The reluctance among clinicians to share knowledge of a potential failure precludes the opportunity for other clinicians to learn from that negative experience and incorporate it into their own knowledge base, thereby enhancing safe care delivery.

EXPERTISE

Nursing educator Patricia Benner (1984) points out that educators may believe "expert decisions" are made by "explicit evaluation of alternatives," while in reality "expert decisions are more holistic" (Benner 1984: 31). In essence a focus on data and evidence is not all that is needed to be expert. Though she does not use the term tacit knowledge, she describes the use and acquisition of tacit knowledge at the bedside. Benner compares the expert nurse to a chess master in her ability to access and make decisions quickly in the same manner that Goldman describes the ability of an experienced pediatrician to quickly and accurately assess the state of an infant's health just by looking (Goldman 1990). Benner (1984) also notes that the performance of an expert can actually degenerate as the granular process and details of a particular task are explicitly described or contemplated in the act of doing. This is a similar phenomenon as described by Goldman (1990) involving a master pianist who freezes during a live performance if he focuses on the movement of his fingers, not the music. Using this analogy, Goldman refers to the surgeon's precise knowledge of how much tension to put on a scalpel or a suture as the "tacit dimension" or knowledge, which cannot be articulated in explicit terms (Goldman 1990: 51).

JUDGMENT, DECISION MAKING, AND CONTEXT

Two contrasting positions describe knowledge to support clinical judgment and decision-making. One emphasizes that important clinical judgment is supported by explicit knowledge through the use of defined process, practice, and evidence (Goldman 1990). The second argues that the tacit aspect of clinical judgment is often overlooked, yet can play a significant part in the development of a clinician's mental model and influence activities such as confirming or refuting diagnostic hypotheses (Goldman 1990).

Practicing evidence-based medicine is considered the coin of the realm by policymakers and clinical groups. However, this poses the risk that the "conscious application of formal, defined rules and explicit knowledge in medicine" overlooks the "neglected tacit dimension of clinical judgment" (Goldman 1990: 48). This analysis of the nature and development of the explicit and tacit sides of clinical judgment is aligned with Benner's discussion of a nurse's knowledge rooted in competency, where know-how and expertise is acquired through active performance of a task. Effective interpretation of clinical events requires this capability to meld the evidence with the tacit knowledge of practice.

An appreciation and understanding of the context of decision making and the resulting action contributes to mindfulness and to mindful practice. Errors often occur due to an ineffective reaction to context and its ability to cloud the decision-making process (Croskerry 2009). The ability of expert clinicians to perceive and recognize subtle physiologic changes and discriminate disaster from the beginning of a care process is often context dependent (Benner 1984; Goldman 1990).

Knowledge transforms as it moves through an organization, department, unit, or during interactions between individuals (Wickramasinghe et al. 2011; Bohmer 2009). The following section explores how mindfulness and expertise may be applied to understand tacit knowledge sharing at the several locations within the sharp end care delivery environment: subculture, embedded, and location specific.

Subculture Tacit Knowledge Sharing

Subcultures refer to groups of individuals who share a set of customs and principles (Boisnier and Chatman 2002). In knowledge management, subcultures can be referred to as silos or individuals that share similar mental models. Subcultures can be both a conduit and barrier to successful tacit knowledge sharing. Their customs, ideas and principles can influence organizations at all levels; from the frontline through the administrative ranks to the executive suite. Subcultures need to be identified so they can be dismantled or capitalized upon, depending on their potential to improve knowledge sharing and patient care (see Chapters 3 and 8). Once organizations understand subcultures and their potential, they can utilize them to enhance culture

"Subcultures can be both a conduit and barrier to successful tacit knowledge sharing."

programs and other team-based initiatives. Samples of subcultures that can influence knowledge sharing include the following.

Profession-centric

Subcultures and silos can make knowledge sharing "difficult to realize in practice because of professional boundaries" (Nicolini 1998: 248; Powell and Davies 2012). These boundaries also affect knowledge sharing in healthcare. However, the growing use by organizations of multidisciplinary teams who perform cross-functional activities is helping to diminish and overcome these boundaries. Tacit and explicit knowledge sharing increases when individuals belonging to different professional groups work side by side in an organization or when individuals in different professional groups share organizational values, such as patient safety improvement work. Knowledge transfer across professional groups can alter the behavior of organizations, prompting them to develop and sustain consistent routines, actions and values, and to incorporate new layers of knowledge sharing (Tagliaventi and Mattarelli 2006).

Communities of practice (CoP) is a strategy that can help build common understanding. They can enhance tacit knowledge sharing within subcultures (Tagliaventi and Mattarelli 2006; Wenger 2000) and be facilitated by electronic or social means (Russell et al. 2004; Kothari et al. 2011a, 2011b). Social networking technologies such as a wiki, can increase dialogue among colleagues who do not work in the same space but share a similar mission and set of goals. Technology can stimulate the sharing of tacit knowledge, but that outcome is by no means assured (Call 2005; McDerrmott 1999). But even organizations with established information sharing and team development efforts find that the technologies are most often embraced by innovators and early adopters (Schilling 2011); therefore, it's unclear how well social technologies will enhance the knowledge transfer capabilities in the complex day-to-day activities of a healthcare organization. Building COPs with boundary spanners, exhibiting interests and skills that enable information and knowledge sharing connections to prosper, are useful to engage in this work.

Patient-centric

> There is a good chance that the patient knows more about the practicalities
> of that [chronic] illness than you do (Interview 4/422–423).

Shared common values, such as the "centrality of the patient," enhance the opportunities for ongoing, productive knowledge exchange (Tagliaventi and

Mattarelli 2006: 303). This observation supports the potential value that tacit knowledge exchange could have on patient-centered care. The single-mindedness of the care team to ensure that a patient receives appropriate care illustrates a shared mental model precipitated through tacit knowledge sharing during a specific activity. However, this same single-mindedness can create in clinicians a type of tunnel vision; an unwillingness to participate in improvement and safety work or to participate in activities that could enhance their clinical expertise.

Patient-centric subcultures have a direct resource for tacit knowledge: patients themselves. Patients and family members possess tacit knowledge gained through previous hospitalizations, surgeries, or emergency room visits. These experiences allow patients and families to gain an awareness of their reaction to the care environment and interventions. Clinicians should respect the patient and family as a tacit knowledge conduit and be willing to listen to and ask for the insights based on patient experiences. For example, sharing of and learning from a patient's previous negative (and positive) experiences with hospital processes – a patient's tacit knowledge – may help avoid adverse events and errors. Patients can educate themselves about a procedure or illness. Engaged patients exhibit interest in the care they are provided and how it is delivered. They can help hospitals reduce harm, prevent errors and work as partners to improve the hospital experience (Edgman-Levitan 2004).

Strategies associated with patient-centric subcultures and their tacit sharing opportunities include:

Collaborative patient rounds: Multidisciplinary collaborative patient rounding has demonstrated positive improvements in cardiac surgery mortality, patient satisfaction and quality of clinicians' work life (Uhlig et al. 2002). Collaborative rounds can also assist in bridging professional and departmental boundaries and result in improved shared mental models about the patient care plan. This strategy can reduce profession-centric divisions within the care team. In traditional rounds, the staff would ordinarily have very different ways of interacting with each other within their specialized boundaries (for example through the use of jargon, leveling of hierarchy or use of humor others won't understand). During a collaborative rounding process, ideally with the family present, the flow of information and recognition of team knowledge is enhanced as people work together over time. While the focus of the exchange is primarily information-based, the trust developed can facilitate tacit knowledge exchange through increased awareness of other roles and competencies and flattening of hierarchy (Dominguez et al. 2005).

Patient navigators: Patient navigator initiatives recognize that hospitals are complex organizations that are difficult for patients and families to understand. These initiatives, often staffed by nurses or patient educators, help patients navigate these complexities in a variety of ways. These initiatives also provide tacit knowledge sharing opportunity at the sharp end. For example, a nurse navigator, using tacit knowledge of the patient's home environment can assist a patient and his/her family during care transitions and hand-offs with specialized providers. This knowledge is invaluable in avoidance of potential harm during care transitions. Finding appropriate ways to encourage and collect this knowledge can enhance patient safety within the organization. For example:

- Patient escort staff can share impressions with other clinicians and family members of how a patient responded to transport en route to tests and procedures.

- Dieticians and certified nursing assistants who prepare and serve patient meals and menus, can note food consumption changes. That "know-how" could be shared with the clinicians and homecare-givers.

- Nurse navigators coordinate care, answer questions and explain diagnoses and medical information for the patient and family about process. They can help patients make informed medical decisions, schedule appointments and tests, run interference on insurance issues, assist with getting translators, even negotiate social services in the community. Their intimate (and abundant) tacit knowledge of the healthcare system procedures and policies and the specific hospital environment helps to enable quality care.

As well as reducing potential problems for individual patients, the insights of patient and family, their tacit knowledge, can be applied more broadly, and thereby may help improve safety and quality throughout the organization.

Structured care communications: Multidisciplinary structured care communication points, such as handoffs, sign outs, huddles, and transfers enable the clinical team to prepare for patient transitions from one team, unit or level of care to another. This exchange should facilitate the application of team member expertise to use the information and data from one place or state of care to another to assign future tasks between similar clinical teams or patients with similar care needs (Seager et al. 2012). Handoffs, for example, have been identified as key communication activities that are often ineffective and prone to missing information (Ong and Coiera 2011). While it is primarily considered an information exchange, the handoff could be enriched by recognizing it as an opportunity for tacit knowledge exchange (Cohen, Hillgross and Kajdacsy-Balla Amaral 2012). How to take this structured exchange beyond information transfer, design it to be mindful and use existing tacit team knowledge to raise concerns and discuss potential problems and errors is just beginning to be examined (Matney et al. 2013).

Embedded Expert Tacit Knowledge Sharing

Embedded experts practice at the unit level within an organization. These professionals apply their expertise at the sharp end of care delivery. In the process, they absorb and share tacit knowledge through both observation of and active participation in sharp end activities, such as the provision of care to individual patients, patient rounds, unit meetings and informal consultations. Through these interactions, they glean knowledge. In essence, they learn.

These experts also become potential conduits of tacit knowledge. Through sharing the tacit knowledge obtained while performing their primary duties, these individuals could provide important feedback during their interaction with the unit. Tacit knowledge gathered while working in an environment may enable an embedded team member to intuitively distinguish between important and trivial issues, or to provide nuanced and proactive service without being explicitly asked. Embedded experts can gain and apply tacit knowledge in the following ways:

Embedded pharmacists: Research studies have shown that pharmacists who participate in rounds and other activities associated with clinical care can help reduce medication error, address overuse and under use of medications and positively affect the medication reconciliation process (Kaboli et al. 2006; Leape et al. 1999; Cohen 2006). Catching a near miss is a clear-cut application of how tacit knowledge is applied at the frontline. Pharmacists' expertise in managing the complexity of medication therapy *in situ* can be shared explicitly through reports, as well as through tacit knowledge exchange as a unit-level team participant. This knowledge informs productive discussions of symptoms, dispensing, reporting of the misuse of drugs (Waterfield 2010).

Embedded clinical librarians: The embedded clinical librarian or informationist can enhance effective use of evidence at the bedside and at the unit level (Davidoff and Florance 2000; Davidoff and Miglus 2011; Banks et al. 2007;

Mulvaney et al. 2008). Their expertise and tacit knowledge in collaboration with clinical faculty can help teach residents about health literacy (see Infobox 4.1). The routine presence of the clinical librarian at education rounds and evidence-based medicine (EBM) training allows the librarian to both acquire and share tacit knowledge. By interacting at the information seeking interface to share what they know about identifying and using the literature, they gain richer understanding as to how that activity is embedded in care processes while sharing knowledge acquired by experience and informal discussion (Aitken et al. 2011). By interacting with and observing unit staff, residents and others the clinical librarian becomes more mindful of how care is delivered. This tacit knowledge can then be used to design and implement programs and services that make sense in daily care delivery.

INFOBOX 4.1: SHARING KNOWLEDGE TO ENHANCE EVIDENCE SEEKING

A clinical informationist for a family medicine department with 22 family medicine residents, six attending physicians, up to six medical students is part of a national program to revise residency education entitled, *Preparing the Personal Physician for Practice* (Leach and Batalden 2007). For four hours each week in a block, the librarian works with small groups of residents in 30-minute increments to help them identify and learn to use evidence-based resources for patient-care decision making using small group case discussions to stimulate the use of evidence-based resources at the point-of-care. Through the development of safe and trusting relationships over time in weekly meetings, values, worldviews, problems and much tacit knowledge is shared. The librarian's health literacy skills and knowledge were also shared. This knowledge transfer improved the residents' abilities to craft clinical questions and locate evidence to support their patient-care decision-making.

Intensivists: Intensivists are physicians with advanced clinical training in both a primary clinical specialty (that is, anesthesiology or surgery) and critical care medicine. These specialists are embedded in intensive care units (ICUs) in a closed staff model (Popovich, Esfandiari and Boutros 2011). In this model these clinicians are dedicated solely to ICU practice. Studies indicate that units staffed with intensivists have lower turnover rates, improved working relationships with nursing staff, and reduced mortality rates (Popovich, Esfandiari and Boutros 2011; Leapfrog Group 2011). Their direct engagement in critical care gives them responsibilities that involve sharp end concerns which they must then, at times, translate to blunt end decision makers. However, given the immediacy of the decision making that often needs to take place in the ICU, tacit knowledge of the unit, the human resources and the practice of critical care is paramount to the success of this role. In this complex setting, use of information technology for decision support may not be as useful as it is in other areas. Instead, the experience and knowledge of a physician who is embedded in the ICU serves the care process more effectively (Lundgrén-Laine et al. 2011). The intensivist must make decisions quickly and effectively, using knowledge, clinical judgment, and mindfulness. The ability to do this is enhanced due to the proximity of the intensivist with the team in the closed staff ICU. They are a part of a team that works together and builds trust which enables tacit knowledge to be capitalized on due to shared values, mental models, and goals.

Clinical Event-Related Tacit Knowledge Sharing

Events at the point of care require that clinical experts identify subtle indications of problems when formal "clinical triggers" may not have been activated. Such a proactive response draws from tacit knowledge. Opportunities to capitalize on this phenomenon and measure its impact can be designed into programs already active in the organization such as rapid response initiatives, debriefings, simulations or event analyses.

Rapid response initiatives: The use of Medical Emergency Teams (METs), Rapid Response Teams (RRT), and other clinical expertise teams, correspond to the shared mental model concept (Chan et al. 2010). Teams with members who have cultural values in common as well as a shared mental model of how to best interact when faced with critical or unpredictable clinical events are likely to be more effective. Practice sessions, drills and simulation training among these specifically coordinated teams as well as among professional colleagues who are not part of defined teams (nurses on units, residents and medical students in training) can provide a collective understanding of a team's specific environment. Results of recent studies reveal that a team benefits when members have shared mental models of the team's task (Lim and Klein 2006, McComb and Simpson 2013).

Similar to an airline's cockpit crew, RRTs are examples of the successful application of tacit knowledge for mindfulness and mindful practice. These multidisciplinary teams rely on practice and trust in each other's expertise as well as on individual mindfulness that relies on context and analytical thinking (Croskerry 2009). Mindfulness includes several characteristics, identified by Epstein (1999: 835) as active observation, peripheral vision, preattentive or meta-processing, "critical curiosity," humility, and more. These are the skills and the mental processes needed for successful situational awareness for solving problems and for making decisions. How the team interacts, even the point at which an RRT team is called (by family members or by other clinicians) is influenced by tacit knowledge gained through prior rapid response calls and activity.

Debriefing: Debriefing, or the constructive discussion of a team's activities following an episode, can enhance learning beyond catastrophic or traumatic events. Instead, debriefing can be used routinely for problem solving, team training and organizational learning. It is a means of soliciting and sharing ideas from a range of clinical experts on the unit (Leonard, Frankel and Simmonds 2004). A common type of debriefing occurs following a traumatic event, when those involved can reflect on it and process its impact. The value in debriefing is to enable psychological coping but can also facilitate insight and demonstrate tacit knowledge by encouraging shared cultural values and an increased understanding of expectations. Debriefing improves situational awareness through the development and application of a shared mental model of what took place. Situational awareness is a "shared understanding of the situation at hand, what is likely to happen next, and what to do if the expected does not happen" (Leonard, Frankel and Simmonds 2004: 49). Another debriefing strategy is highlighted in Infobox 4.2.

INFOBOX 4.2: DO NO HARM LUNCHES

Patient Safety Rounds in the form of "Do No Harm" lunches (about every other month) with internal speakers, open to all, are a tactic for surfacing and sharing tacit knowledge. Specific instances of failures or near misses are showcased by the clinicians involved in order to encourage everyone to share knowledge gleaned from the experience that could prevent future harm to patients and sustain a culture of "no blame" with a systems approach to improvement. The "Do No Harm" debriefs enable learning "by communicating a motivating rationale for change and minimizing concerns about power and status differences to promote speaking up in the service of learning" to encourage the sharing of safe practice (Edmonson 2003: 1491).

Holding such a debrief or a dialogue in response to an actual incident at a hospital can bring awareness of care processes and team weaknesses to other clinicians and staff – though context may be absent, lessons can be learned. The sessions are not limited to only those involved in the original event. Instead all clinicians as well as all department directors and managers are invited.

Simulation: These technologically sophisticated events – often situated in simulation laboratories – can enable tacit knowledge sharing to become explicit for personal and team learning at the microsystem level. Simulation labs spread tacit knowledge (know-how) as residents, medical students, nurses and others (novices and experts) have opportunities to respond to unexpected or complex clinical events to make explicit team and individual behavior. Simulation training makes tacit knowledge more explicit and can help others understand context through learning modules that train users for both the positive and negative events. Mindfulness could be enhanced by simulation training. Tacit knowledge is heightened by prior experience so RRTs improve their team and personal mindfulness through practice and repeated opportunities to perform.

Event analysis: Knowledge sharing through incident reporting and proactive risk and failure assessment can reduce risk and change an organization's culture. Learning opportunities occur when medical errors and near misses are discussed with the clinicians, such as at weekly morbidity and mortality rounds. Lessons learned are shared by individuals involved in the event, with the intent to "make sense" of what happened from a root cause analysis perspective. The structured investigation should be designed so the organization can benefit from what is shared and so that other staff not directly involved in the event can learn what happened to enable learning and behavior change (Waring and Bishop 2010; Mengis and Nicolini 2011).

How clinicians make sense of risk is complex and closely related to professional identity (Waring and Bishop 2010). Open forums for discussion can share what is learned from a near miss or medical error without departmental or professional boundaries. These mechanisms create opportunities to share tacit knowledge about similar experiences thus drawing from and enhancing the broader tacit knowledge base of the organization.

Informal Opportunities: A Point to Consider

Informal discussions that take place away from the daily clinical tasks can significantly facilitate the exchange of tacit knowledge and enable collaborative bonds between individuals (Waring and Bishop 2010). Informal knowledge sharing and its contributions to patient safety are taken for granted. They are a part of daily work that makes a marked impact on organizational learning (Waring and Bishop 2010).

Individuals engaged in this type of knowledge sharing can belong to a single profession, such as nurses, librarians, or medical residents, who meet in a shared environment, such as a hospital cafeteria. Environments that provide opportunities for individuals to informally interact, such as on-call rooms, storerooms, staff lounges, and other gathering places can serve as hubs of tacit knowledge sharing if leadership and management recognize this potential with an eye toward learning and juggling the importance of maintaining patient and professional confidentiality. Individuals continually modify their tacit knowledge by infusing it with everyday interactions with colleagues. It is "context-specific, non-individual knowledge" (Tagliventi and Mattarelli 2006: 293) that is part of all social interactions (Chang et al. 2012).

In a similar way, important knowledge can be imparted through social interactions. Casual conversation among individuals can reinforce how one goes about a task or practice. Changes in these cultural norms can model a change in culture (Waring and Bishop 2010). Hospitals can still harbor a culture of blame regarding medical errors and ineffective practice which may reveal itself informally at first. Although organizations are moving toward a culture of no blame and mitigating harm by openly discussing near misses, the fear of risk to one's professional reputation continues to thwart both informal and more structured communication regarding error. Sensing where the culture is on how error is discussed informally can reveal knowledge about the state of the current environment's true acceptance of learning from failure.

The Case for Collaboration to Enable Sharp-End Tacit Knowledge Sharing

Tacit knowledge sharing accelerates when individuals and organizations have a common understanding and commitment to safe care delivery. This goal serves as a motivation to enable knowledge sharing to occur through robust and reliable means. Technological tools to enable this have yet to be fully adopted at the sharp end. Technology – with emphasis on decision support software/analysis – might ignore activity-based knowledge, the context of the care environment and the value that tacit knowledge can provide (Goldman 1999; Lundgren-Laine et al. 2011). The notion of spread of knowledge within the unit, within teams in the unit and out to other frontline units has yet to be embraced proactively as a factor in quality care. Embedded professionals can model the role of boundary spanners as a knowledge sharing mechanism by translating tacit knowledge from the frontline to other areas of the organization that might benefit from those lessons.

In an inspirational speech from 2000, healthcare quality and patient safety leader Donald Berwick, MD, described the frustrating results of silos in healthcare (Berwick 2002: 31) that occurred during his wife's multiple hospitalizations for a complex, difficult diagnosis. Berwick attributes the failures in communication to a loss of "sensemaking" among her clinical teams and a greater need for "improvisation" as the care did not yield the hoped-for results (Berwick 2002). Could his experience confirm a failure among clinicians to share tacit knowledge at the bedside? The capacity of a healthcare organization to "preserve sensemaking" requires "preconditions" or a set of shared assumptions (core values, for example) and "designs" or new ways of thinking about what is done according to Berwick (2002: 35). This may require increased attention and accountability for tacit knowledge sharing among clinicians, patients and families at the sharp end.

KEY TAKE-AWAYS

- Tacit knowledge sharing contributes to effective frontline care as it affects individual decision making and team-based activities.
- Both structured and informal multidisciplinary mechanisms which exist at the sharp end can be optimized to improve the reliability of tacit knowledge sharing.
- Culture plays an important role in dismantling negative influences on knowledge sharing and enabling the establishment of relational behaviors that can support it.

Suggested Reading

Benner, P. 1984. *From Novice to Expert: Excellence and Power in Clinical Nursing Practice.* Menlo Park, CA: Addison-Wesley.

Goldman, G.M. 1990. "The Tacit Dimension of Clinical Judgment." *Yale Journal of Biology and Medicine,* 63(1), 47–61.

Polanyi, M. and Sen, A. 2009. *The Tacit Dimension.* Chicago, IL: University of Chicago Press; Reissue edition.

Rowley, E. and Waring, J. 2011. *A Socio-cultural Perspective on Patient Safety.* Farnham: Ashgate Publishing Limited.

PART 2

Knowledge Workers: Insights from the Frontline

Chapter 5 Synopsis – What Healthcare Knowledge Workers Can Teach Us About Knowledge Sharing

This chapter will describe how the knowledge workers were identified and interviewed. Their roles, skills, and behaviors are outlined, as well as their potential contribution to knowledge sharing activities in an effective learning culture.

Chapter 6 Synopsis – Tacit Knowledge: Insights from the Frontline

This chapter reflects interviewees' observations about tacit knowledge as a potential contributor to high-quality care. Their insights illustrate how ineffective tacit knowledge sharing can contribute to system failure. Interviewees discuss the potential of tacit knowledge management to quality improvement initiatives.

What Healthcare Knowledge Workers Can Teach Us About Knowledge Sharing

Lorri Zipperer and Becky Steward

> *Knowledge workers have high degrees of expertise, education, or experience and the primary purpose of their jobs involves the creating, distribution or application of knowledge (Davenport 2005: 10).*

Learning from the Field

Knowledge management and healthcare delivery are complex, interdependent processes. A deeper awareness of the relationship between tacit knowledge and healthcare can foster opportunities to develop and implement strategies to improve safety and quality. Gathering these perspectives through conversation can serve as a useful first step to understand how – or whether – tacit knowledge sharing is understood in the hospital environment. The process and results of the interviews undertaken on this topic serve as a proof of concept, with the hope that the findings will spur further development of knowledge management study methodologies in healthcare.

The Interview Process

Interviews were conducted with 20 healthcare professionals to capture real-world perspectives and experiences. Half of the interviewees were known to the interviewer; the rest were suggested by colleagues of the interviewer who were familiar with the project. Individuals were selected based on their roles and interest in how knowledge management may serve as an opportunity to contribute to quality and safety improvement.

Interviewing knowledge workers with differing professional backgrounds can illustrate the varied ways in which these individuals and their established roles can support knowledge sharing initiatives. Discussions sought to identify knowledge sharing roles, attitudes and behaviors to support and to clarify assumptions held by the authors. Insights will inform future explorations of how a knowledge sharing culture can be embedded into an organization.

INTERVIEW METHODS

Semi-structured, hour-long interviews sought to engage healthcare knowledge workers on:

- How they define key terms, such as tacit knowledge and knowledge sharing.

- The power and value of sharing tacit knowledge based on their personal experience.

- Behaviors that support sharing and response to tacit knowledge.

- How tacit knowledge sharing enhances and supports safe, high-quality care.

- Individuals' perspective on tacit knowledge sharing within the hospital environment.

Questions were shared with interviewees before the interviews to allow them to become more familiar with key concepts.

KNOWLEDGE WORKER ROLES

Interviewees were selected based on their capacity as knowledge workers in three distinct healthcare settings:

- Individuals currently providing care within the hospital environment on a regular basis (that is, the sharp end).

- Individuals with in-depth knowledge of hospital-based care but working in an administrative capacity (blunt end).

- Individuals who observe and interact with hospital-based staff to design improvement efforts (blunt-blunt end).

Appendix 2 lists the roles of each interviewee. They represent a range of expertise and experience that could be used to engage productive knowledge management initiatives within a hospital (see Chapter 8 for more details). Individuals were selected in part on their ability to:

- Illustrate the hierarchy and siloes that are typical of many healthcare organizations.

- Represent different ways to receive, apply, use and share tacit knowledge.

- Illustrate how individuals who work across professional settings, often referred to as boundary spanners, can enable support for learning organization concepts that are critical to safety and quality improvement.

- Participate in both sharp and blunt end activities (clinical and administrative) in the hospital setting.

- Validate the connection between knowledge sharing and improvement in quality and safety.

- Articulate knowledge management synergies across different roles.

Knowledge Sharing Roles and Attributes: Hospital-Based Participants

CASE MANAGER

Perceived knowledge sharing role: Case managers identify and address patients' needs and interact with a variety of medical, social, financial, and insurance entities to address them. They perform their work inside and outside of the hospital setting.

Unique attributes that enable or have the potential to enable knowledge sharing to support quality and safety: Case managers build personal relationships with the patient and the family. They put multiple aspects of the patient's care process into action and provide feedback that can influence quality and safety improvement. Their ability to determine the optimal course of action for varying patient and family circumstances draws from a wide range of experiences and tacit knowledge.

FAMILY ADVISOR

Perceived knowledge sharing role: Family advisors reflect the priorities and concerns of patients and of an organization's quality improvement efforts. In this capacity, family advisors can generate tacit knowledge that can improve both blunt end and sharp end activities. This knowledge, in turn can inform and educate decision makers, clinicians, hospital staffs and the community.

Unique attributes that enable or have the potential to enable knowledge sharing to support quality and safety: Family advisors engage others through storytelling. Their familiarity with real-life circumstances brings a sense of urgency to the abstract concepts of patient safety and tangible power to identify and address poor-quality care.

HEALTHCARE PROFESSIONAL AS EDUCATOR

Perceived knowledge sharing role: The healthcare professional as educator plays a key mentor role. It is, inherently, a knowledge sharing role as mentoring and coaching are tacit knowledge sharing activities.

Unique attributes that enable or have the potential to enable knowledge sharing to support quality and safety: Their skill as mentors through the sharing of experience and stories can influence and develop a commitment to quality and safety among trainees. Educators share and learn through tacit knowledge exchange to enhance safe practice.

HOSPITAL ADMINISTRATOR

Perceived knowledge sharing role: Hospital administrators can champion knowledge sharing culture and behaviors in their organization. Their visibility and authority allow them to elevate the role of knowledge sharing among administrative and clinical colleagues and staff, as well as governing bodies of the organization (such as the board of directors and hospital trustees).

Unique attributes that enable or have the potential to enable knowledge sharing to support quality and safety: Administrators can share knowledge through strategic planning, priority-setting and key hiring decisions. They have valuable opportunities to serve as models of knowledge management through resource allocation and recognition of tacit knowledge. They routinely interact with individuals and groups that can embed knowledge sharing as an organizational value, ensuring integration to all initiatives and sustainability.

HOSPITALIST

Perceived knowledge sharing role: Hospitalists are responsible for the integration of an episode of care in the hospital setting. In this capacity, they engage with other physicians, interpret and incorporate clinical information, and oversee and evaluate the care plan.

Unique attributes that enable or have the potential to enable knowledge sharing to support quality and safety: Because a good deal of knowledge sharing occurs when patients are discharged from the hospital, hospitalists ideally can apply tacit knowledge derived during the course of the hospital stay to inform patient care decisions at discharge. Hospitalists engage in shared problem solving and are familiar working in interdisciplinary teams with a broad set of clinicians. This enables them to work effectively across organizational silos while recognizing trends in care quality and delivery (Wachter 2009).

INFORMATION SYSTEMS SPECIALIST

Perceived knowledge sharing role: Information systems specialists engage with their customers to provide access to explicit knowledge, information and data. In this role, individuals take the tacit knowledge of end-users and translate it into tools, processes and systems that can address those needs within the limitations of the environment, the user base and the available resources.

Unique attributes that enable or have the potential to enable knowledge sharing to support quality and safety: Health system information specialists are well-positioned to understand the limits and the potential of a solely technological approach to knowledge management. They should be able to articulate the unintended consequences of an ineffective or abbreviated approach that could affect administrative (blunt end) or clinical care (sharp end) activities.

INTERNAL KNOWLEDGE MANAGEMENT LEADER

Perceived knowledge sharing role: Internal knowledge management professionals such as chief knowledge officers and knowledge managers can identify others who demonstrate knowledge sharing behaviors and assess to what extent their experiences can enable mentoring and systems to support organizational and knowledge sharing goals.

Unique attributes that enable or have the potential to enable knowledge sharing to support quality and safety: Individuals in this role can influence how a hospital builds learning into its regular processes and to what extent technology, personal observation, staff interaction and structured communication can orient a hospital toward becoming a learning organization. The individual can leverage and align explicit and tacit resources to enhance organizational intellectual capital.

LIBRARIAN/CLINICAL INFORMATIONIST

Perceived knowledge sharing role: Hospital-based librarians oriented to knowledge management have the capacity to work outside the conventional boundaries of managing materials and artifacts (Keeling and Lambert 2000; Donaldson and Gray 1998). This expanded skill set can build upon established knowledge management activities in corporate, law and other special libraries (Zipperer and Sykes 2009).

Unique attributes that enable or have the potential to enable knowledge sharing to support quality and safety: Clinical librarians who draw from their expertise to identify and provide relevant information and evidence demonstrate their enhanced role as knowledge management champions and team members (Banks et al. 2007; Aitken et al. 2011; Grefsheim et al. 2010; Sollenberger and Holloway 2013).

NURSE

Perceived knowledge sharing role: With their continual interaction with patients, physicians, other clinicians and administrative leadership, nurses are ideally suited as knowledge and information conduits (Aiken et al. 2011).

Unique attributes that enable or have the potential to enable knowledge sharing to support quality and safety: Through their knowledge of patient safety, nurses are instrumental in achieving success in communication improvement initiatives focused on care delivery teams, patients, and families. The perception of trust and shared vision by nurses has been shown to positively influence knowledge sharing (Chang et al. 2012).

PATIENT

Perceived knowledge sharing role: Patients, more than anyone else in the healthcare continuum, understand their care experience and its effect on their well-being.

Unique attributes that enable or have the potential to enable knowledge sharing to support quality and safety: Patients and their families are uniquely positioned to articulate, question, and seek additional information on their care experience. The saying, "Nothing about me without me," has become an increasingly popular expression by patients that reflects their expectation of a high-quality, safety-oriented healthcare experience (Delbanco et al. 2001: 144).

PATIENT SAFETY OFFICER

Perceived knowledge sharing role: Patient safety officers utilize process improvement and assessment activity to create information and understanding of factors contributing to process ineffectiveness or medical errors. They typically are clinicians who coordinate the activities of the patient safety bodies within the institution, advocate for organizational learning opportunities on the systemic medical failure error, and apply evidence with hospital management and staff to communicate patient safety improvement strategies throughout the organization ("Patient Safety Officer Job Description" 2009).

Unique attributes that enable or have the potential to enable knowledge sharing to support quality and safety: Patient safety officers represent a boundary spanning role in their capacity to work outside of organizational silos, improve teamwork, and encourage multidisciplinary efforts on both the blunt and sharp ends. These efforts can facilitate learning from failure among individuals, teams, and organizations (Kohn et al., 2000).

PHARMACIST

Perceived knowledge sharing role: Pharmacists, like librarians, increasingly interact with staff and teams outside of their traditional role. They have shown a demonstrated value by their presence in multidisciplinary care teams, in hospital units, and in blunt end patient safety and quality improvement project teams (Glassman 2013).

Unique attributes that enable or have the potential to enable knowledge sharing to support quality and safety: Pharmacists apply their knowledge not only to understanding the scientific formulations of modern medicine but also to the design of systems and processes that improve the safety and quality of care for both patients and providers of care. They also develop and interact with protocols to ensure cost-savings, quality, and confidentiality.

PHYSICIAN

Perceived knowledge sharing role: Physicians occupy positions of continuous learning and teaching. In this capacity, they can validate the value of tacit knowledge demonstrated by individuals in other roles and professions. Physicians' ability to serve effectively as boundary spanner and their professional authority provide additional knowledge sharing opportunities.

Unique attributes that enable or have the potential to enable knowledge sharing to support quality and safety: Physicians continue to hold enormous influence over the successful execution of quality and safety improvement efforts (Wachter 2011). Their engagement can determine the success or lack of adoption of these efforts. A similar dynamic applies to physician involvement and support of knowledge sharing initiatives.

RISK MANAGER

Perceived knowledge sharing role: Risk managers communicate with a wide variety of stakeholders in healthcare organizations, from hospital administration to clinicians to patients. In this capacity, they also build relationships and share knowledge both inside and outside of the organization.

Unique attributes that enable or have the potential to enable knowledge sharing to support quality and safety: Risk managers contribute to high-quality healthcare by ensuring a steady flow of information between departments while protecting their organization from undue liability exposure and financial loss (Youngberg 2011; Zipperer and Amori 2011). This role allows them to share tacit knowledge to enable information exchange in support of safe and effective practices and care processes. Their perspective can enhance the design of systems that minimize future risk at the system level (Zipperer and Amori 2011). The application of this blunt endrole to knowledge initiatives in hospitals is also explored in Chapter 3.

UNIT ADMINISTRATIVE STAFF

Perceived knowledge sharing role: Unit administrative staff play ongoing and visible roles in the front-line care team. They are aware of interpersonal characteristics of team members and can be highly skilled at navigating the unit culture in the course of their daily activities (Reddy and Spence 2006).

Unique attributes that enable or have the potential to enable knowledge sharing to support quality and safety: The specific knowledge gained by unit administrative staff can contribute to patient safety in unexpected ways. For example, unit secretaries have been shown to identify exceptions to prescribing process due to their close proximity and presence in the unit (Swinglehurst et al. 2011; Adler and Kwon 2009).

Another Point of View: External Experts

To broaden the perspectives of the 20 individuals questioned, a cohort of interviewees with expertise outside of the hospital environment was also selected. Their insights were sought to bring greater generalizabilty to the results. By working and interacting outside of the hospital culture, these individuals could more readily identify and recognize tacit knowledge sharing behavior and its contribution to patient safety and quality improvement.

Gathering Insights to Formulate Strategy

> *The biggest information repository in healthcare lies in the people working in it, and the biggest information system is the web of conversations that link the actions of these individuals (Coiera 2000: 278).*

The insights from both the hospital-based and external interviewees shed additional light on how tacit knowledge might be shared and valued in a healthcare setting. This qualitative informal approach illustrates a process to gather perceptions from a representative range of healthcare knowledge workers who collaborate on patient safety and quality improvement efforts. Information gained as a result of the interview process can help reveal the complexities of the tacit knowledge sharing environment that typically exists in hospitals. Findings can identify barriers associated with knowledge sharing, and help gain support for a sustained effort to creating a reliable, metric-driven knowledge sharing process. The exploration and analysis in Chapter 6 illustrate this point in greater detail. Future work is needed to extend this concept further.

KEY TAKE-AWAYS

- A variety of staff can share insights to understand tacit knowledge sharing and how it works in an organization.
- Qualitative methods of collecting these insights are apt to be richer than straight data capture to ascertain knowledge strengths and weaknesses.

Suggested Reading

Davenport, T.H. 2005. *Thinking for a Living.* Boston, MA: Harvard Business School Press.

Tacit Knowledge: Insights from the Frontline

Lorri Zipperer and Cathy Tokarski

> *In medicine, we ever hardly think about how to implement what we've learned. We learn what we want to when we want to (Gawande 2012: 60).*

A Basis for Learning and Innovation

From hospital operating rooms to housekeeping departments, individuals who work in healthcare settings seek, use, and share tacit knowledge. Too often, though, the insights gleaned from this knowledge aren't widely or routinely distributed. Consequently, colleagues frequently miss the chance to acquire the knowledge of others, recognize its benefits or apply it in their practice. However, organizations that learn to routinely capture and use tacit knowledge could enhance the high reliability characteristics associated with top-performing teams and health systems (Waring and Bishop 2010).

Suggested readings and references included in this book discuss various knowledge sharing mechanisms, applications and processes observed in organizations outside of the healthcare sector. A wide range of research methods, disciplines and theoretical constructs can enhance the understanding of how explicit and tacit knowledge in healthcare can contribute to performance and reliability (Orzano et al. 2008; Kothari et al. 2011b). A valuable perspective on the feasibility of applying these mechanisms in healthcare organizations could come from active knowledge workers, who can demonstrate how these theories could be put into daily practice.

Knowledge sharing enhancement presents an opportunity for improvement. As with any improvement endeavor, insights from the individuals engaged in the daily activities of an organization, such as a hospital, are essential to identifying problems, exploring innovations, developing consensus and sustaining change. Organizations must seek to apply experience from these frontline workers to understand how to enhance their tacit knowledge sharing culture for the desired changes and innovations to occur effectively and reliably.

As described in Chapter 5, clinicians, executives, and healthcare professionals were interviewed to explore how tacit knowledge sharing could be optimized in the care environment. Interviews sought to identify potential synergies between quality and patient safety improvement activities and activities that aligned with effective tacit knowledge sharing. This chapter reflects interviewees' observations about tacit knowledge as a potential contributor to high-quality care. Their insights also shed light on how ineffective tacit knowledge sharing could contribute to failure. Interviewee comments support experiences drawn from the literature and identify new perspectives on the topic.

Assumptions: Individuals and Tacit Knowledge Sharing Practice

Assumptions – whether right or wrong – are powerful forces that can shape behavior. Related to the concept of mental models, assumptions are often unrecognized despite their profound influence on patterns of thought and behavior. In the in-depth discussions conducted for this book, interviewees shared responses that addressed assumptions about tacit knowledge in healthcare held by one of the chapter's authors (LZ) which served as a drive for the research effort.

Assumption – Tacit knowledge is not a collectively understood or used term in healthcare: Most interviewees weren't acquainted with the term "tacit knowledge." However, they were serious about considering its meaning and invested time in considering responses to the questions developed by the author. Despite their initial unfamiliarity, the concept of tacit knowledge appeared to resonate with individuals. The interviewees more familiar with the term drew from business, managerial or blunt end experience. As interviewees explored the concept of tacit knowledge, they became more comfortable with the concept as a factor in the workplace and were able to articulate a value in its application to healthcare improvement.

> *… Somehow [tacit knowledge] is very different, and with my background in learning, I thought … 'Wow! This is a very different concept to wrap your arms around' (Interview 18/298–301).*

Assumption – Tacit knowledge is more likely to be shared by team-oriented individuals: Interviewees could identify a relationship between tacit knowledge and individual and team learning. They could see the distinction between team members capable of garnering a commitment to improve knowledge sharing within and outside of the team, and those who are insular about sharing what they know.

> *Exchanging tacit knowledge is an underpinning of the cultural imperative necessary for a learning environment that is a baseline, validation component of a safety culture (Interview 16/420–421).*

Assumption – Tacit knowledge sharing is enabled through leadership: Interviewees in leadership positions understood their responsibility to serve as a conduit of tacit knowledge. Some described experiences from earlier points in their careers that illustrated how they benefited from leaders who shared their tacit knowledge. Interviewees who had this experience adopted that philosophy and were prepared to do the same.

> *Managing, to me, seemed more technical and more black-and-white in some things … Although there is a lot of literature out there about behaviors and activities of good leaders, there was a lot more tacit knowledge that was shared with me to transition more [successfully] into a true leader role (Interview 7/90–93).*

Assumption – Tacit knowledge is more effectively shared face to face: Storytelling and verbal exchange of tacit knowledge can have lasting impact in ways that are different than information conveyed through communications and information technologies. The visual engagement and connection generated by direct interaction enhances the nuance and sensitivity of the exchange. Interviewees valued the dynamic of conversing face to face and shared examples of how this promoted knowledge exchange.

> *A memo … can't deliver the message with the caring attitude that was intended and the directness to help you see it. There is a relationship that goes a long way, the communication of this knowledge and how the message plays out and how all that happens is so much a part of the meaning of the information that's shared. You can't do that through a memo (Interview 1/332–339).*

> **INFOBOX 6.1: POWER OF TACIT KNOWLEDGE EXCHANGE – WHY MEETINGS MATTER**
>
> *I have a real "a-ha!" moment that actually relates to my boss ... it was one of those moments where the light bulb went off.*
>
> *[He] was showing the differences between two different patient care units around management of pain for patients, which is a particular favorite of many nurses because we worry a lot about our patients having pain. I observed that the one unit's root causes for why the interventions didn't work were quite different than the other patient care unit's root causes.*
>
> *The reasons why the solutions don't work equally well in different settings is that the root causes are different for the problem. And the solution, of course, has to speak to the root cause of the problem. If you have a solution that is not related to the problem, it won't be as effective.*
>
> *So it truly was a moment of tacit learning for me. I was in his conference room with a couple of my peers and I remember the moment the light bulb went off. I said, "I just realized I've something that's haunted me for years and I've never been able to piece it together quite the way that I can now." So that was my tacit knowledge learning (Interview 15/73–108).*

Assumption – Teams enable tacit knowledge sharing: Team-based work builds experiences that enhance tacit knowledge sharing. The collective interaction builds trust and provides communication behavior patterning through mentoring, modeling and repeated exposure to distinct ways of doing things. The ability to gather this knowledge can be enhanced by being in the same place, performing specific activities, and observing others with direct knowledge of the results.

> *I'm the new guy, I show up and within no time at all [the nurses in the ICU] knew exactly the things that I liked ... Fast forward 10 years later. Same intensive care unit ... the population of nurses in that unit had tremendously changed. And each of these nurses was wonderful ... But in the process of that sort of outflow of the experienced nurses and the inflow of the well trained, but not of that environment, nurses, a huge amount of tacit knowledge was lost (Interview 5/49–79).*

Assumption – Time and workload issues impact personal knowledge sharing behaviors: Time constraints affect the robustness and reliability of tacit knowledge sharing. Interviewees identified the hectic work environment of all healthcare organizations as a barrier to seeking, distributing and receiving tacit knowledge.

Tacit knowledge sharing takes time ... The busy-ness of getting all the tasks done gets in the way of people having a chance to talk to one another and share experience, information and knowledge (Interview 1/450–453).

What Was Uncovered: Individual Actions and Responsibilities

Beyond their confirmation of assumptions about tacit knowledge and its influence on how individuals function in the workplace, interviewees provided broader insights about the applicability of knowledge management improvement strategies. The interview process also confirmed the value of this method for organizations that wish to examine the role of tacit knowledge sharing in the hospital environment as a mechanism to generate learning and change in knowledge sharing.

INSIGHTS AND RESPONSES

Mechanisms to share tacit knowledge are in place in the hospital environment: Despite an inconsistency in understanding the term, "tacit knowledge," the interviewees revealed established knowledge sharing activities as helpful to accessing tacit knowledge. Strategies include: rounding, storytelling, mentoring, regular meetings, formal and informal observations/interactions, and social activities. Many of these were seen as organizational facilitators of knowledge sharing.

> *... There's nothing better than storytelling. When we're doing seminars, we open with a story because the greatest fear for a healthcare provider [is to cause] injury to a patient. Storytelling is exactly 'spot on' if you will, to get people engaged (Interview 14/104–109).*

> *Executive rounding could work, Great Catch could work, just proactive reporting into a hotline, a patient safety hotline or something like that, but you have dedication to the program to make it work and you can't be judgmental of the individuals who are reporting into it. It may start as a trickle, but it will develop into a waterfall (Interview 14/487–491).*

What does this suggest? Opportunities to leverage tacit knowledge sharing as a factor in quality improvement initiatives could help trends emerge that would recognize knowledge sharing as a strategy worth resourcing. Hospitals could then benefit from enabling the elements of such programs in a robust way by building tacit knowledge sharing functions into them. For example: If unit meetings encouraged storytelling around near misses, the expense for the coffee served at this meeting could be supported due to the enhanced learning from the conversations and the incentive to linger and talk informally. Tracking that element of unit meetings as a defined knowledge sharing strategy would enhance the connection of storytelling, near misses and tacit knowledge as that would have a distinct impact on quality.

Sharing of tacit knowledge has a significant and easily recalled impact on people: Interviewees recalled key tacit knowledge exchanges (good and bad) that affected their subsequent behavior, practice, and management style. These exchanges were recalled in vivid detail (see Infobox 6.1 and 6.4).

What does this suggest? Understanding the personal impact of tacit knowledge sharing should be leveraged to enhance its viability for quality improvement. Measuring the impact of tacit knowledge exchange and designing mechanisms to track it presents opportunities for further improvements. For example, measures that track workplace culture could provide a platform for metrics that measure tacit knowledge exchange.

Technology was rarely mentioned as an enabler of tacit knowledge sharing: In general, healthcare is considered a latecomer to industries that use social networking tools to facilitate information and knowledge sharing (Schilling et al. 2011). Omitting technology as a tool to enhance tacit knowledge sharing may be a factor in the lack of connection between knowledge management and terminology associated with clinical decision making, practitioner order entry systems and the like.

What does this suggest? An overt emphasis on technology as the "answer" to improved personal knowledge sharing may not align with the knowledge sharing goals of frontline or blunt end hospital staff. It also implies that an emphasis of knowledge management as a person-centered rather than a technology-centric process may be accepted in the healthcare environment given the person-centered focus of most safety, quality and safe culture improvement efforts.

Tacit knowledge sharing roles identified with distinct professions did not emerge: Outside of leadership, distinct professions, such as nursing, were not identified as key enablers of knowledge sharing. Interviewees did not identify distinct tacit knowledge sharing roles among clinical or administrative professionals that could be further enhanced for implementation or innovation.

What does this suggest? Tacit knowledge sharing is inherent in individual behavior and skills, not categorized into explicit roles and responsibilities.

However, social networking analysis or a visualization technique such as the Wagon Wheel concept (see Klinger and Hahn 2003) can help identify individuals best positioned to serve as conduits of tacit knowledge for distinct units or departments. Individuals should be strategically placed in the organization. In addition, skills should be nurtured and hired for, rather than being left to chance to allow a knowledge sharing role to develop to its full potential.

There is a relationship between tacit knowledge and confidence: Connections exist between tacit knowledge and confidence across the continuum of sharp end, blunt end, and blunt-blunt end. Interviewees recognized that confidence in their ability enables action, and that tacit knowledge sharing supports team engagement, problem identification, and resolution. Tacit knowledge also helps individuals take on new challenges.

INFOBOX 6.2: WAGON WHEEL DIAGRAM

Nurses interviewed in a collaborative rounding project revealed the highest number of nodes they interacted with on the patient care "Wagon Wheel" (Figure 6.1). Both patient and nurse are situated in the middle of these nodes, or relationships. The use of only using data and information found in the medical records were shown to be imperfect in helping assemble the "big picture" (Dominguez et al. 2005).

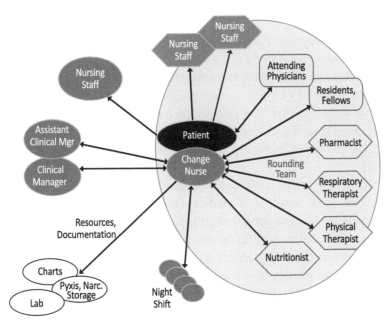

Figure 6.1   Wagon Wheel Diagram
Source: With permission, Cynthia O. Dominguez et al. 2005b.

> *When I'm pressed against the wall to perform, I've learned to really*
> *rely on my tacit knowledge to get me through. It's also getting to know*
> *myself and trusting that I do have a knowledge base that will get me*
> *through or can be validated on past experiences (Interview 13/71–74).*

What does this suggest? Tacit knowledge coincides with a level of maturity gained through experience. Individuals new to their role, who exhibit confidence should be able to leverage their experience in one area and apply it as they obtain knowledge in another. Actions taken with confidence affect how teams came together to quickly address problems to tackle challenges or avert failure.

Tacit knowledge is respected, regardless of where it resides: While not unique to healthcare, interviewees recognized the value of gathering knowledge wherever it exists. At the same time, they understood the reticence of junior staff, students and clinicians to ask questions, raise awareness of problems, or share ideas for improvement. Their hesitance created gaps in knowledge that could affect care, improvement activities and recording of near misses. Interviewees valued tacit knowledge, although they noted that organizational silos, hierarchy, and professional pride created barriers to seeking and sharing. Respondents said leadership should have the responsibility to enable the effective use of tacit knowledge. Leadership should also create a culture that energizes tacit knowledge to drive care improvement and quality.

> *… The whole premise of tacit knowledge exchange … is centered around*
> *appreciating the entirety of a person's experience and knowledge base*
> *and those people to share that with others. There's a role for everyone*
> *here, and there's a value in every single job, and it drives the results*
> *that we have. That is a cultural contract and that is a leadership*
> *responsibility. It goes back to requiring a very particular type of [vision]*
> *when you hire people (Interview 16/480–498).*

What does this suggest? As healthcare strengthens its commitment to safety culture and organizational learning, a dedicated consideration of tacit knowledge could contribute to sustaining that culture. Tacit knowledge processes should be designed into daily work to facilitate that knowledge is shared, no matter where it resides, through conversation, interaction and collaborative work. This emphasis should apply to novices, who need encouragement to share and gather tacit knowledge. Newcomers to positions at the sharp end and blunt end have less task-specific tacit knowledge to draw from. They should be encouraged to request help, seek assistance and clarify their results.

Tacit knowledge sharing enables a proactive mindset: Tacit knowledge was recognized as giving organizations the opportunity to address problems before they became institutionalized or directly affected patient care. Identifying and addressing near misses at both the sharp and blunt end provide dramatic evidence.

> *When I went to the IHI Patient Safety Executive training course, my project was [executive walkarounds]. Weekly we would have a patient safety person … and at least one senior leadership team member and then usually one or two other folks along with unit director. Every week we would go to a different place. Typically for 20 minutes or so, have a very non-threatening conversation with staff. These have been very successful. Some of the little nuggets that we've picked up over the last three years … we would not have picked up until something bad happened (Interview 2/242–254).*

What does this suggest? The link between organizational culture, patient safety, and knowledge sharing is genuine. Opportunities exist to share tacit knowledge that aligns with other initiatives. In addition, informal opportunities to tap into this rich knowledge base could contribute to a knowledge management strategy not yet fully operationalized in healthcare organizations (Waring and Bishop 2010).

Teamwork and trust lay the groundwork for tacit knowledge sharing: Team-building is of increasing interest and importance in healthcare organizations (Edmondson 2012). Teams can help address complexity and can more fully respond to spreading innovation, handling critical incidents, and improving safety and the overall patient experience (Wachter 2012). Interviewees articulated team-related experiences that enhanced their ability to share what they knew. Conversely, the absence of a team orientation minimized their ability to share and act on tacit knowledge.

> *Being able to create an environment [that enables staff] to share explicit and tacit knowledge builds trust and ultimately can impact our outcomes tremendously because people are more apt to do things for people if they trust that person (Interview 7/582–584).*

What does this suggest? Opportunities exist to build tacit knowledge components into established teamwork and communication improvement initiatives. They could enable mental models that support tacit knowledge sharing as part of daily work activities.

Patients' tacit knowledge has not been fully leveraged: Room for improvement also exists for putting a value on the tacit knowledge of patients. Interviewees were aware that this knowledge was a resource that is not often recognized.

> *The fear of what patients may come up with prevents a lot of people from engaging patients differently. Once you engage patients, they are actually quite realistic about what they expect and what they want. Being a patient sometimes helps us to better understand and get rid of some of the waste in our system that we think is good stuff. The patients say, 'It's not helping me, why are you doing this?'" (Interview 10/358–365).*

What does this suggest? The gap in capturing and sharing patients' tacit knowledge may correlate with ineffective patient experience and improvement efforts. Efforts must extend beyond communication mechanisms (such as change of shift and transitions improvement) tools and processes. To develop trust and familiarity, as well as incorporating patients' knowledge into improvement activities, organizations should design patient advisory councils and other formal mechanisms with knowledge sharing in mind. Tacit knowledge could provide rich context to data from survey mechanisms to better understand the patient experience.

Assumptions: Organizational Roles, Respect, and Resources

Assumptions held by the chapter author (LZ) on the organizational role individuals play in effective tacit knowledge sharing were confirmed by interviewees. In addition, they acknowledged the value in connecting tacit knowledge sharing improvement efforts to the quality aims identified by hospitals.

The interviewees also identified the presence of barriers that can scuttle implementation of tacit knowledge management programs. Indeed, responses to questions about barriers generated the most robust examples.

Organizations and their leadership enable a knowledge sharing culture: Interviewees echoed expert opinion, confirmed in the literature, that organizational culture is a precursor to successful tacit knowledge sharing. Leadership has a defining role in shaping that culture through decisions about how to manage and lead the organization. Some might say that one cannot be disconnected from the other. For better or worse, an organization's culture is a fundamental determinant in whether tacit knowledge will be valued and shared. Culture strongly influences, and often defines, the ways in which individuals and organizations respond to new ideas or initiatives. Therefore, efforts to recognize tacit knowledge and encourage its potential to enhance patient safety and quality must recognize the pervasive nature of organizational culture.

> *[You need to have] a culture where individuals are going to be able to tell you about those near misses, because there's nothing more anxiety-provoking to a risk manager than to go into an event that occurs and speaking to someone who says, 'I knew that was going to occur.' Until you really get down into the culture, nothing's going to be sustainable (Interview 14/287–294).*

Tacit knowledge is intangible; impact is difficult to measure: It may be difficult to comprehend today, but in the early days of the patient safety movement, leaders would bristle at the notion of having to measure safety. Their rationale: Making care safer was the right thing to do, and their organizations did the right thing, so why measure it (Weeks and Bagian 2003)? Nonetheless, measures more clearly illustrate the need for improvement, progress, impact, and results. They also drive widespread improvement, as evidenced by the adaption of safety measures in hospital intensive care units to lower infection rates (Pronovost and Vohr 2010).

Many holes exist in existing processes to share tacit knowledge. Interviewees readily identified obstacles to inhibit or block tacit knowledge sharing in hospital settings (see Infobox 6.3 for a selected set). These barriers create weakness in the knowledge sharing processes that can be likened to latent conditions that can lead to failures in care delivery. Similar to the Swiss Cheese Model (see Figure 6.2 on the next page) of accident causation, in which imperfections in safeguards can contribute to significant patient safety lapses, existing knowledge sharing processes have numerous holes that can thwart effective knowledge exchange and safety improvement efforts.

> *Through our knowledge sharing and our experiences … we've informed [the in-house product recall response] process so that it's much more rigorous and structured than it would have been otherwise without us sharing that knowledge … Now where it fell apart, is the silos we all live in. With every product alert we get, [there's] another example of somebody who wasn't aware that we had this process, that somehow we didn't reach them even though we tried all sorts of communication vehicles to get the word out (Interview 1/418–431).*

INFOBOX 6.3: TACIT KNOWLEDGE SHARING BARRIERS

- Time.
- Information overload.
- Hierarchy, status and silos.
- Fear of looking stupid.
- Blame.
- Disconnect between process and workflow.
- Sharp end/blunt end disconnect.
- Unstable teams.
- Lack of awareness of personal knowledge to share.
- Lack of willingness to listen.
- Lack of organizational resources committed to knowledge sharing improvement.
- Pressure to manage rather than lead.
- Reliance on information rather than knowledge.
- Lack of understanding of "tacit knowledge."

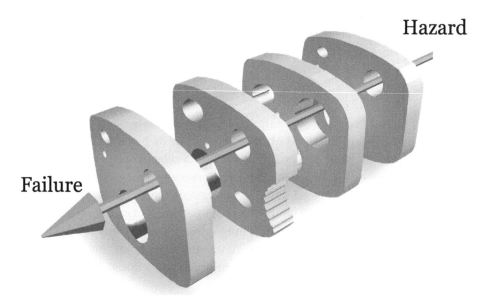

Figure 6.2   Reason's Swiss Cheese Model
Source: Adapted from Reason 1997.

Time is a barrier to individual tacit knowledge sharing: Time pressures are a concern for organizations and individuals. For organizations this can be seen in an environment of production pressure and the falsehood of urgency that keeps people from communicating and gathering knowledge. Time constraints demand that information, but not necessarily knowledge, be shared. This extends to relationships among peers, between administration and clinicians, and between patient and clinicians.

> *If tacit knowledge is valued, time will be allowed for people to discuss the topic, whether it's called tacit knowledge or experience, life experience or whatever. There would be time to talk about that, time to talk about the value of that and what it could bring to better decision making (Interview 13/290–293).*

Workflow doesn't enable knowledge sharing: The daily process of providing care inhibits the opportunities for tacit knowledge sharing in an ongoing way. Care teams can be temporary due to turnover, and silos develop easily.

> *It's very difficult to get the nurses and doctors together [to share tacit knowledge] because they each have different workflows (Interview 4/401–402).*

> *The OR team can definitely be a silo because they're behind doors, always covered up except for their face, so you don't really exactly know what they look like outside the OR (Interview 20/400–402).*

> *The hospitals of yesterday are not designed to encourage effective flow of people or anything, information or anything ... It's almost more like a 'Stop what you're doing and now do this,' as opposed to it being part of the natural constant flow of everyday life inside an organization. And so the sharing of knowledge has a lot of times been structured around having to attend something that causes you to stop your workflow and interrupt your process ... Those things have a tendency to become viewed as not only interruptive but as burdensome (Interview 16/265–280).*

Sharp end/blunt end communication is fragmented: Knowledge is not sought because administration may not be aware of a problem or not know how to approach a solution. Decisions are made outside of a system-oriented fashion.

> *Well-intended ideas to try and make things more efficient and more explicit ended up making a nightmare for the unit and everyone that worked in it (Interview 5/115–117).*

> *The reason this new policy isn't going to work is that you don't realize that to get this stuff done, get it done well, you have to do this and this and this and you can't even spell it all out. That's why it's tacit knowledge (Interview 4/463–465).*

What Was Uncovered: Organizational Roles, Respect, and Resources

Harnessing tacit knowledge and the value it can bring to safe, high-quality care requires organizational attention and support. Interviewees agreed that:

Recruiting for tacit knowledge sharing skills is crucial: Interviewees identified the need to hire for tacit knowledge sharing skills, such as willingness to mentor, effective communication, partnering, and non-technical skills that support team-based effort.

> *I'm very particular who will be sitting on the committee, because they need to be people that are open-minded and want to participate. Quite frankly there are some individuals that are just not suited to that type of environment. So to encourage better knowledge sharing, I think you have to have committed individuals that want to be in a group, want to participate (Interview 12/247–255).*

What does this suggest? Knowledge sharing is an essential component of healthcare. Therefore, hiring, teaching and mentoring decisions have significant consequences for how and to what extent knowledge will be shared. Knowledge distribution opportunities are embedded in established care and administrative team activities. Their impact could be enhanced by purposefully engaging individuals with a knowledge sharing orientation. For example, mentoring/shadowing programs are likely to support exchange of tacit knowledge but only if both participants are open and willing to engage in it. The right people with the right capabilities can enhance the spread of tacit knowledge most effectively.

Organizations can (and do) reward poor tacit knowledge sharing: Individuals who exhibit poor or obstructive knowledge sharing behaviors do not necessarily suffer any negative professional consequences. When this occurs repeatedly, organizations in effect reward poor tacit knowledge sharing. The impact on colleagues can be profound.

> *Mentoring is an important piece of ongoing communications and learning in healthcare ... [It's] important that the people identifying those mentors make sure [they] have [identified] good mentors because bad mentors can teach bad habits (Interview 11/477–480).*

What does this suggest? Organizations should not ignore the potentially disruptive, high-risk and dangerous consequences of individuals who are unwilling to share knowledge. Such behaviors are often due to turf, hierarchy, lack of skill development or professional respect. Rewarding such behavior through promotion or increased responsibility serves to perpetuate such behavior, even if that is an unintended consequence. In addition, tacit knowledge sharing considerations should be articulated within the "unwritten curriculum" in medical and nursing schools. Teaching these concepts to students could positively influence their behavior early in their profession (Lucian Leape Institute 2010).

Technology is not universally seen as a tacit knowledge sharing enabler: Many interviewees noted the value of face-to-face interactions that serve as an effective tacit knowledge sharing conduit while recognizing its demand on resources. Relying on technology was also seen to minimize opportunities for face-to-face interactions, thus reducing opportunities for tacit knowledge sharing. If not managed appropriately, the expanded reliance on technology can merely reinforce existing siloes and hierarchy (Stoller 2013).

> *What we have traditionally done and what we need to do in the future is different. In the same way that we've traditionally focused our technology to support the explicit and sort of missed the point that it really needs to be focusing on supporting the tacit (Interview 5/495-498).*

What does this suggest? Emphasizing technology as the sole facilitator of knowledge sharing in the healthcare environment could be counter-productive. This stems in part from a lack of a collective recognition of knowledge as something other than data. This mental model inhibits a broader understanding of technology's potential as a knowledge sharing tool. Given the acceptance of social media in other domains as a knowledge sharing facilitator, further innovation and research are needed to help create opportunities to infuse the use of these mechanisms in healthcare to enhance knowledge sharing (Coiera 2000).

Standardized communications is not knowledge sharing: Standardized communication through tools, such as the use of checklists and Situation-Background-

Assessment-Recommendations (SBAR), protocols can indirectly enable tacit knowledge sharing, but they are not designed to do so. Instead, these tools are designed to facilitate information gathering and sharing rather than direct knowledge exchange.

What does this suggest? An over-emphasis on standardized communications between team members could reduce opportunities for tacit knowledge sharing. Notwithstanding their value for effective and safe care delivery (Pronovost et al. 2006; Gawande 2009), it appears that mechanisms to share tacit knoweldge should also be designed and studied to document their impact on care quality. In addition, measures could be devised to understand how tacit knowledge could make standardization efforts useful and beneficial in care delivery and improvement. It remains unclear to what extent the shortcomings in standardized communications efforts affect the value and limit the collective impact (Ko, Turner and Finnigan 2011).

INFOBOX 6.4: A STORY OF POOR KNOWLEDGE SHARING

I had somebody in the hospital for six weeks one time and the patient's sister was the power of attorney.

... After six weeks in the hospital, the patient was home for 13 minutes before they dialed 911 to get an ambulance to bring her back because the patient's daughter was the one that was actually taking care of her and had a special needs child of her own. She took one look at her mom and said, "I can't take care [of her]. She can't even walk."

We were told we've got to send her home, but we didn't ask the question, 'You're making the decisions, are you the one who is going to be taking care of her?'

So we dropped the ball big time on that one.

... And [in this] case, we didn't ask the right questions.

... The problem with using the checklist is that we're not flying planes, we're not running nuclear submarines. We're dealing with patients, and there are a lot of nuances that we haven't figured out all the right questions to ask sometimes (Interview 9/288–331).

Information overload and excessive organizational communications can negatively affect knowledge sharing: The constant need and desire to update information can contribute to inattention, fatigue, and awareness gaps. Information overload can result in the false sense of being informed and therefore knowledgeable. Organizations and their staff believe they are communicating if content is distributed, regardless of whether that information is received, understood or acted on.

> We are bombarded with so much knowledge every day. All of it seems important. There's improvement knowledge and then there's the science of the work that we do every day ... Some of our improvement work is getting to that point that people are getting so bombarded with things they should be doing that it becomes yet another piece of paper ... How do we do it in a way that is truly helpful to those who actually need it? (Interview 10/660–674).

What does this suggest? Strategies are needed to manage information flow with an eye toward its unintended consequences on fatigue, lack of concentration and willingness to engage in knowledge sharing. Extraneous information can reduce opportunities to engage in tacit knowledge sharing. This situation should be seen as a system failure; however, remedies should be identified and implemented. The responsibility of managing this process should be assigned to a variety of boundary spanners, such as organizational change experts and practitioners with information dissemination skills, such as librarians (Macintosh-Murray and Choo 2005).

Metrics cannot identify whether knowledge sharing improves quality: Leadership and management assume metrics from existing information tools can effectively translate the value of knowledge sharing. For example, an internal community of practice (COP) may improve the sharing of lessons learned to develop a new in-house patient safety curriculum for nurses across a large hospital system. If the metrics to judge its value focus only on how many people join that community, access the site or download shared documents (which can be automated and easily generated for review), the actual impact of the discussions facilitated by the COP will not be factored into the return on the investment.

> Someone runs a report, how many after-visit summaries could we have printed and how many did we print? Oh, we printed 98 percent; we're doing great. So, if X amount of doctors are just throwing them away or if X amount of parents aren't even reading them, what does that really say? They're getting knowledge or they think they have this

impression about how we're doing, [but] that's really not accurate or true (Interview 6:510/515).

What does this suggest? Collecting and analyzing data to understand the value of a knowledge sharing tactic is only one method to track impact of an initiative. Perceptions on how the knowledge shared brought value to the task or activity, while potentially more expensive or time consuming to collect, may yield more impactful insights (for more on metrics, see Chapters 7 and 8).

Orienting staff to a systems orientation could help engage them in knowledge sharing: Enabling staff to see the "big picture" and create opportunities for them to see how their knowledge could be useful to others could facilitate knowledge sharing buy-in.

> *[Sharing of tacit knowledge] ... is very much creating the will, the atmosphere, the good will of sharing information. Since we've been trying to go for Magnet status, we have this thing called shared governance. Every single unit has a team of people, a leader on each unit where suggestions are given of any kinds of problems we're having ... The committee works on trying to improve the outcomes or deal with problems. Shared governance is one of the aspects of the Magnet status besides evidence-based practice and promoting and supporting nurses to look at evidence-based information to use at the bedside. So shared governance is a really good example of how tacit knowledge is being shared (Interview 3/551–562).*

What does this suggest? A strategy to engage staff in collective accountability for knowledge sharing would parallel safety and quality improvement initiatives in place at the hospital level. Recognizing that there is value in each individual's contribution to a tacit knowledge sharing process could build on synergies with other quality improvement efforts that are weakened by individuals who do not participate. Involving frontline employees in a way that would leverage their knowledge and allow them to engage in their roles more fully due to that feedback represents a communication challenge that would require skillful leadership.

Tacit Knowledge Supports Care Quality and High Reliability: How Well Do the Concepts Align?

A secondary expectation of the interviews was that they would reveal how tacit knowledge sharing could address the concept of high reliability organizations, which are reflected in the quality aims articulated by the Institute of Medicine (IOM) (see Table 6.1 and Infobox 6.5).

Table 6.1   High Reliability Organizations (HRO): Defining Characteristics

HRO Element Concepts (drawn from Weick and Sutcliffe 2007: 10–16)	Brief Description of Element
Tracks small failures.	HROs are "preoccupied with their failures" while realizing that small problems could combine to result in failure (Weick and Sutcliff 2007: 10).
Resists oversimplification.	HROs see the complex nature of their work and resist efforts to oversimplify. They shun "power-pointing" their efforts and encourage boundary spanners to share what they know to foster deeper understanding.
Remains sensitive to operations.	HROs are able to anticipate unexpected factors that can occur in the workplace with a keen interest in latent failures.
Maintains capabilities for resilience.	HROs capitalize on the knowledge of workers within their organizations by being prepared to address errors while they are small. They improvise to address manageable problems before they develop into complex issues. They create knowledge to address their problems through tactics such as simulation to practice and prepare to address failures.
Takes advantage of shifting locations of expertise.	HROs defer to knowledge and expertise at hand despite established hierarchies and chains of command when rapid access to knowledge in a unique situation is required. This recognition of decision-making autonomy shifts from standard mechanisms in times of crisis to enable safety to emerge.

INFOBOX 6.5: QUALITY AIMS

Safe: Avoid injuries to patients from the care that is intended to help them.

Effective: Services based on evidence to those who could benefit; refrain from services without benefit to patient.

Patient-centered: Care that is respectful and addresses patient needs, preferences and values.

Timely: Care that reduces waits and delays for patients, families, and clinicians.

Efficient: Care that avoids waste of both tangible (supplies and materials) and intangible resources (staff energy and effort).

Equitable: Care that is not influenced by a person's race, gender, and economic status.

Source: Committee on Quality of Health Care in America, Institute of Medicine 2001: 5–6.

Interviewees were asked about the role of knowledge sharing in supporting high reliability. While they showed varying levels of understanding about HROs, they confirmed assumptions that a relationship could be drawn between knowledge sharing behaviors and high reliability. This relationship should be defined as a potential opportunity for tacit knowledge sharing resources to be enriched due to its role in bolstering high reliability behavior in hospitals (see Table 6.1).

ROBUST AND RELIABLE TACIT KNOWLEDGE SHARING SUPPORTS IOM QUALITY AIMS

In the initial review and categorization of the interview transcripts safety, effectiveness, and patient-centeredness were more often identified as being influenced by tacit knowledge sharing than timely, efficient, and equitable (see Appendix 3). The importance of connecting improvement initiatives to strategic goals and organizational vision is a recognized approach to generating sustainable change (Kotter 1995).

Interviewees confirmed the chapter author's assumption that they could articulate how tacit knowledge sharing supports the IOM Quality Aims. This analysis sheds light on questions about the intangible nature of tacit knowledge and lends credibility to its ability to contribute to quality improvement processes. Consequently, the concept of tacit knowledge as a "soft" contributor to patient safety and improvement can be refined to one that has significant potential to move these goals toward completion (for a selection of interview quotes supporting this conclusion see Appendix 3).

Questions Could Highlight the Role of Tacit Knowledge and High Reliability

Interview discussions revealed topics that could benefit from an in-depth discussion to examine to what extent tacit knowledge sharing could contribute to the reliability of the care environment.

Questions that deserve further examination include:

- How do elements of knowledge sharing explicitly support high reliability?

- How can tacit knowledge be shared reliably?

- How can tacit knowledge impact be measured?

- What is the negative impact of poor knowledge sharing behaviors on direct patient care?

- How does blunt end knowledge sharing affect frontline processes?

- What is the relationship between production pressure, time demands, and lack of knowledge sharing?

- Which types of tacit knowledge have the most potential for greatest impact?

- What is the impact – both positive and negative – of technology on tacit knowledge sharing?

- Which elements of high reliability would best enhance knowledge sharing processes?

- Which of the IOM Quality Aims are more likely to see a direct benefit from enhanced tacit knowledge sharing?

- Can distinct roles in the clinical environment be established as knowledge conduits?

- Which distinct skills should be explicitly engaged in knowledge sharing work?

- Which failure modes would be revealed should a knowledge failure be examined through system safety assessment methods?

- What is the role of tacit knowledge in supporting the learning organization?

Tacit Knowledge Sharing: a Key Component of Quality Healthcare

At the individual and organizational level, tacit knowledge sharing can support high-quality care. Hospitals seeking to routinely capture and use tacit knowledge could enhance the high reliability characteristics associated with top-performing teams and health systems (Waring and Bishop 2010). To date, this capacity has not been identified and cultivated as a mechanism to improve quality, enhance patient centeredness, reduce patient harm and second victim stress.

For this awareness to develop, healthcare organizations will need to first develop consensus on the value of tacit knowledge sharing. This is no small task: little clarity exists on terminology, as interviews for this chapter confirmed. Yet once tacit knowledge was defined and its relationship to high-quality care articulated, interviewees recognized the potential value and understood how robust tacit knowledge sharing initiatives could enhance quality improvement. Further, interviewees also acknowledged the connection between tacit-knowledge sharing and the principles of high reliability organizations, which serve as a catalyst to many successful organizational improvement efforts.

Beyond developing consensus on the value of tacit knowledge sharing, organizations must also seek and welcome different points of view on how to best encourage its exchange. Despite the best intentions by leaders to reduce silos and hierarchies, it's naïve to assume they don't exist or pose barriers to widespread improvement efforts. No single approach has been identified to seek and welcome varying viewpoints on tacit knowledge exchange; however, identifying champions within clinical and administrative departments is a good first step. Champions must have the visible and ongoing support of executive leadership for tacit knowledge initiatives to develop and thrive.

As the patient safety improvement field continues to mature, the impact of system behaviors – both positive and negative – on patient safety and outcomes becomes increasingly clear. Tacit knowledge sharing can rightly be viewed as one of many behavioral components in a complex system situated within a unique organizational culture. Organizations that recognize the powerful potential of tacit knowledge sharing and harness it to further enhance quality improvement efforts can reap the benefits of a more engaged and committed healthcare team.

KEY TAKE AWAYS

- Tacit knowledge is used throughout the sharp end – blunt end continuum in healthcare to support quality healthcare delivery.
- Tacit knowledge was more easily defined as a factor in enhancing safety, effectiveness and patient-centeredness of care processes than efficiency, timeliness and equitableness.

- Tacit knowledge was recognized as a contribution to high reliability.
- Given the ability of staff to share stories of tacit knowledge as an element of high quality, reliable care, it would benefit healthcare to embrace tacit knowledge as a factor worth studying, resourcing, and enhancing.

Suggested Reading

Batalden, P. and Davidoff, F. (eds). 2011. "Knowledge for Improvement." *BMJ Quality & Safety,* 20(suppl 1), 1–105.

Bohmer, R.M.J. 2009. *Designing Care.* Boston, MA: Harvard Business Press.

Committee on Quality of Health Care in America, Institute of Medicine. 2001. *Crossing the Quality Chasm: A New Health System for the 21st Century.* Washington, DC: National Academies Press.

Griffith, J.R., Fear, K.M., Lammers, E., Banaszak-Holl, J., Lemak, C.H. and Zheng, K. 2013. "A Positive Deviance Perspective on Hospital Knowledge Management: Analysis of Baldrige Award Recipients 2002–2008." *British Journal of Healthcare Management,* 58(3), 187–203; discussion, 203–4.

Weick, K.E. and Sutcliffe, K.M. 2007. *Managing the Unexpected: Assuring High Performance in an Age of Complexity,* 2nd edition. San Francisco, CA: Jossey Bass.

PART 3

Knowledge Sharing Metrics, Practicalities and Future Directions

Chapter 7 Synopsis – Can We Measure Knowledge Sharing Effectiveness?

This chapter discusses the elusive and organic nature of tacit knowledge as a social construct that is integral to quality healthcare, but remains challenging to measure and assess. The authors discuss opportunities for measurement in the context of teams, networks, and organizations.

Chapter 8 Synopsis – To Boldly Go … Initiating Knowledge Management

This chapter introduces elements supporting the implementation of a knowledge management program with sensitivity to the complexity of the process and the environment the initiative will change. Recommendations on how to prepare, design, and launch these culture-changing initiatives are discussed.

Chapter 9 Synopsis – Strategies for Knowledge Sharing: Lessons from Improvisation

This final chapter will close the publication by looking ahead; to envision where knowledge management and effective tacit knowledge sharing can and should affect healthcare delivery. The authors aim to advocate, motivate, and inspire healthcare workers, leadership and organizations to embrace knowledge management to improve the quality and safety of healthcare for the future.

PART 3

Knowledge Sharing Metrics, Practicalities and Future Directions

7

Can We Measure Knowledge Sharing Effectiveness?

Margaret H. Burnette, Michael G. Dieter and Annette L. Valenta

The trouble with measurement is its seeming simplicity (Anonymous, see http://www.quotecosmos.com/quotes/36 355/view).

Tracking a Valuable Intangible

Knowledge management in healthcare is a complex, multi-faceted undertaking. Solutions require consideration of organizational culture and work to engage large numbers of staff. The efforts must incorporate systems, processes, data and documents and how people use them to achive an understanding of what needs to be accomplished and how it needs to be done. As healthcare organizations build effective and efficient delivery systems, they must recognize where knowledge resides and understand how it is stored, accessed, shared, and used.

Explicit knowledge, such as the type of information contained in clinical protocols, guidelines, and the professional literature is accessible via databases, the Web, and hospital system intranets. The accessibility of data and information available in patients' health records, for example, can allow for retrieval and analysis to enhance reporting and planning requirements. Certain types of resources, such as patient data, require adequate privacy protection.

Tacit knowledge, which represents the social and adaptable knowledge vital to collaboration and patient-centered care, is harder to quantify and capture. It is intangible. The healthcare knowledge management literature offers few tools or strategies to successfully track the exchange of tacit knowledge (Hoss and Schlussel 2009; Leonard and Insch 2011). Attempts to specifically measure tacit knowledge sharing, if it is to be measured at all, call for indirect, qualitative, and innovative approaches (Liebowitz and Suen 2000). Tacit knowledge transfer can be explored by focusing on the impact of the interactions of individuals, teams, or entire organizations. Attempts to measure this have limits. Previous efforts to identify tacit knowledge transfer have relied on questionnaires, surveys, group discussion, interviews, as well as direct observation and audio or video recordings. Analysis of social and knowledge networks using text mining and text analysis may provide additional insight into designing measures of knowledge sharing effectiveness within distinct communities; however, technologies to accomplish this goal for large-scale enterprise discovery are lacking. This chapter discusses the elusive and organic nature of tacit knowledge as an integral social construct that is challenging to measure and assess. Opportunities for measurement will be discussed as they present themselves in the context of teams, networks, and organizations.

The Elusive Nature of Tacit Knowledge

Whether tacit knowledge can be measured depends on how the term is interpreted. Building on Polanyi's view of tacit knowledge as "knowing how," Greenhalgh et al. (2008) focuses on the personal, experiential, and contextual nature of tacit knowledge, suggesting that these characteristics render it too changeable to be made explicit. Some argue that tacit knowledge is expressed through actions that can be observed, not articulated. Delen and Al-Hawamdeh (2009) distinguish between tacit knowledge as experientially driven behavior and tacit knowledge as the expression of thought through language.

"Attempts to specifically measure tacit knowledge sharing, if it is to be measured it all, call for indirect, qualitative, and innovative approaches" (Liebowitz and Suen 2000).

Within healthcare, tacit knowledge represents individual intuition and competencies that reside with a practitioner (Abidi 2007). Tacit knowledge is typically regarded as a component of broader knowledge management models and frameworks that include both tacit and explicit knowledge creation and exchange. The tension between tacit and explicit knowledge in the healthcare knowledge management literature is illuminated in the following four themes:

1. The lack of developed, practical knowledge management strategies and infrastructures beyond conceptual models (Kothari et al. 2011a).

2. Ambiguity and lack of consensus on knowledge management concepts and goals for knowledge transfer and exchange to inform knowledge management planning (Mitton et al. 2007).

3. The complexity of tacit health knowledge and the extent of its role in healthcare delivery, as well as the tendency to overlook its importance in evidence-based practice (Kothari et al. 2011a).

4. The lack of specific strategies to evaluate tacit healthcare knowledge sharing (Sullivan et al. 2010).

Acknowledging that tacit knowledge is a function of knowledge, behaviour, and context leaves little room for direct measurement. While it may be difficult for a health provider to articulate what he or she knows in a given situation, there are means by which this knowledge can be transformed through written, verbal or observed processes so that it becomes explicit, tangible, transferable, and measurable.

> *I think the challenges with measurements should never be a reason to not pursue a direction that is very logically appropriate (Interview 16/353–354).*

Tacit Knowledge as Intellectual Capital

Attempts to measure tacit knowledge sharing are associated more readily with the construct known as intellectual capital. Literature outside of the healthcare profession provides models, methods, and potential measures to assess tacit knowledge as intellectual capital using tools such as questionnaires, rating scales, interviews, observation, and storytelling. As with tacit knowledge, the discussion of intellectual capital begins with interpretation.

Intellectual capital represents organizational knowledge, information, and experience that can be used to create wealth. As a pioneer of intellectual capital research, Bontis (1998) recognized three subcategories of intellectual capital: human capital or pure intelligence; structural capital, which includes the functional organization and relationships; and customer capital, or what customers and suppliers know. Tacit knowledge is included under the human capital subcategory and is represented by "nodes," – individuals who perform the work (Bontis 1998). An organization's intellectual capital contributes significantly to its overall worth and success, but its value can be difficult to quantify. While the intent of intellectual capital measurement is to assign value to the organization's intellectual assets, this undertaking can also help in the capture and assessment of tacit knowledge (Kannan and Albur 2004; Poyhonen and Smedlund 2004; Van Deventer 2002).

Leibowitz and Suen (2000) developed a comprehensive inventory of metrics to measure intellectual capital. To apply this to tacit knowledge, one might identify a subset of employee demographics, such as "average years of service" and "average age of employees" as benchmarks of individual expertise. Other proxy measures, such as "hours spent in training," "hours spent in debriefing," "employee suggestions," "contribution of performance," "peer skill recognition," and "idea generation" serve as indicators of experience and, by extrapolation, may contribute to a model of tacit knowledge sharing effectiveness (Leibowitz and Suen 2000: 56–7).

The Knowledge Audit

> If only HP knew what HP KNOWS, we could be three times more productive ... (Lew Pratt, former chief executive, Hewlett Packard, as quoted in Garfield 2007: n.p.).

To assess the impact of tacit knowledge sharing, it's essential to capture and codify that knowledge. A good starting point is the knowledge audit, which can provide a clear picture of knowledge creation, utilization, and movement. The knowledge audit reveals what knowledge exists where, whether it is accessible or hidden, if it is used, how it is used, and how it is shared. The knowledge audit reveals organizational experts and whether those individuals share their wisdom and expertise. Further, the knowledge audit illuminates significant knowledge gaps and bottlenecks for internal and external processes. Finally, the knowledge audit can provide a framework for subsequent measurement and evaluation (Wu and Li 2008; Liebowitz and Suen 2000; Bartholomew 2005; Hylton 2002). Multiple models of the knowledge audit process are found in the literature.

INFOBOX 7.1: ELEMENTS OF A KNOWLEDGE AUDIT

PLANNING

- Identify what is missing.
- What needs to be known.
- Who needs to know it.

WHO

A designated KA team of experts representing distinct areas such as HR, finance, knowledge experts, and IT can provide input that addresses multiple aspects of knowledge management.

WHAT

Define the problem, goal or issue. Bartholomew (2005) supports a framework built on a single knowledge problem or issue; however, more ambitious projects assess the overall knowledge health of the entire organization. Determine budget/financial demands and establish a timeline. Decide on specific methods for data collection; establish benchmark determinations, if appropriate.

METHODS

Multiple options exist that can capture various types of knowledge systems, resources and movement, including but not limited to questionnaires, focus groups, group/individual interviews, surveys, scoring, statistical data, and mapping.

DATA ANALYSIS

Qualitative and/or quantitative methods can be used to capture knowledge assets and flows. Qualitative measures are more likely to apply to tacit knowledge assessment and the sharing of tacit knowledge.

REPORT

A knowledge map is a useful visual representation of knowledge flows.

Models of organization-wide knowledge audits can help distinguish between explicit and tacit knowledge assets. One approach uses the construct of systems and assets as the two major knowledge areas. The systems audit identifies information repositories, tools for accessing information, organizational structure, and cultural characteristics. The assets audit reveals both critical knowledge that is explicitly recorded and tacit knowledge, represented by knowledge experts and their capacity for sharing what they know. This type of audit captures tacit knowledge so it is identifiable, sharable, and measurable (Bartholomew 2005).

In the business community, the knowledge audit contributes to the valuation of tacit knowledge through metrics such as education and training participation and skills development as measures of experience and expertise. Data collected from surveys and interviews provide measures for skill level, corporate knowledge culture, access to knowledge, and staff relationships (Hylton 2002). The focus of the knowledge audit within healthcare organizations can be an assessment of how well tacit knowledge is shared to improve outcomes through tracking elements such as the adoption of new guidelines and how they might affect improvements in patient health status or outcome.

Knowledge audit outcome products may include written reports, data sets, and maps that depict relationships or patterns of knowledge dissemination. Collectively, these provide a snapshot of the entire network of knowledge assets and how these assets move throughout an organization based on system, user, and location. While the knowledge audit can address a single unit, a specific process, or an entire organization, the optimal approach is to start with one specific issue, barrier, or gap. Participants in this type of audit are typically a collaborative group representing multiple units of the organization.

In healthcare organizations, the team might include management, physicians, nurses, technicians, IT personnel, and librarians. Librarians are uniquely positioned to contribute to knowledge management efforts and the knowledge audit specifically by conducting research and providing support for data collection, organization, storage, and retrieval. Librarians who serve as boundary spanners are able to recognize weaknesses in knowledge sharing mechanisms, networks, and behaviors that can help to improve the reliability and effectiveness of the processes.

Social Nature of Tacit Knowledge

As human-centered constructs, tacit knowledge sharing processes are largely socially oriented. Because tacit knowledge sharing occurs through interpersonal communication and behavioral observation, settings where these interactions occur are most likely to capture and measure impact. The patient care team acts as a collaborative unit, representing an interdisciplinary approach to caring for the individual patient in the context of that patient's unique health status, beliefs

"Because the [patient care] team relies on collective evidence and wisdom for decision making, the team environment is an opportunity for examining tacit knowledge sharing."

and preferences. Because the team relies on collective evidence and wisdom for decision making, the team environment is an opportunity for examining tacit knowledge sharing. Using a variety of constructs that allows tacit knowledge to be identified and transformed, teams communicate, exchange ideas, and continually build new knowledge. Several identification tactics such as social network analysis, foresight and hindsight tracking, after action reviews, knowledge harvesting and communities of practice are discussed below.

SOCIAL NETWORK ANALYSIS

The social network analysis (SNA) is a commonly used tool in the knowledge audit process. This analysis looks at people or "actors" and interactions or "relations" (Liebowitz 2005). As a formalized process that seeks to capture tacit knowledge specifically, the social network analysis illuminates both knowledge experts and the flow of knowledge between individuals, groups or units. Questionnaires, surveys and interviews are designed to reveal patterns of interaction in a visual manner, making it immediately apparent who communicates with whom, who the major communicators are, and where communication is bottlenecked or non-existent. Feedback to the group of interest highlights specific areas for improvement and identifies people who may need to be more engaged (Liebowitz 2005; Bartholomew 2005).

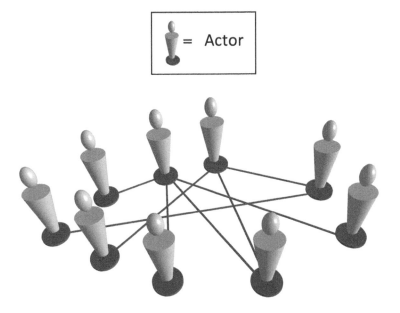

Figure 7.1   Sample SNA Diagram

Recent studies have demonstrated the potential benefits of using social networks to improve patient care quality and safety. Using interviews, surveys, and ethnography, multiple studies have demonstrated the importance of experts, vigorous network participation, engagement, and the quality of relationships as factors for successful collaboration. No concrete connection has been made between healthy networks and high quality care as of yet (Cunningham et al. 2012), the structural elements of a social network may serve as proxy benchmarks for analysis of network effectiveness and its impact on patient care. Rangachari (2008), for example, found that hospital coding and quality reporting performance are associated with rich knowledge sharing in a robust network structure. Sharp end communication sharing has been tracked by social network analysis in a variety of constructs, such as during rounds and patient handoffs to illuminate patterns that could inform improvement in health information technology design and enhance the learning opportunities inherent in rounds (Walton and Steinert 2010; Benham-Hutchins and Effken 2010). Both these vehicles are thought to have implications to improve communication and thus patient safety and quality.

FORESIGHT AND HINDSIGHT TRACKING

Bartholomew (2005) suggests "foresight" and "hindsight" as viable processes for codifying tacit knowledge, thereby illuminating knowledge creation and sharing. Foresight joins lessons learned with new thinking to stimulate innovative problem solving that targets a specific issue. Hindsight examines retrospectively what went wrong and what might be improved to address a specific problem. Both processes rely on group communication, sometimes in conjunction with questionnaires, to promote knowledge sharing in an open and non-threatening environment, with the goal of teasing out explicit knowledge from tacit knowledge.

AFTER ACTION REVIEW

After action reviews draw on hindsight, encouraging the open sharing of tacit knowledge for capture and documentation after an incident or activity (Milton 2010). This structured technique, originally developed for the military has been used by the UK's National Health Service and others as a process to gain rapid feedback on what happened during an incident. The dialogue exploring the groups' actions can help identify opportunities for improvement and how to best share that knowledge with others in the organization (Collison and Parcell

2004; Cronin and Andrews 2009; Milton 2010). Large projects benefit from routine after action reviews to help recirculate knowledge into the teams doing the work, leading to enhanced learning and performance. The process enables the emerging knowledge to be vetted and analyzed in both real time and through the subsequent reports generated to support organizational learning (DeLong 2004; Savoia, Agboola and Biddinger 2012).

KNOWLEDGE HARVESTING

Knowledge harvesting also makes tacit knowledge explicit through interview questions that are designed to elicit the when, where, why and how of behavior and decision-making of key individuals. Knowledge harvesting reveals important undocumented aspects of the employee's work and relationships. It can be crucial to capture information before the departure of a valued or long-term employee (De Brun 2005; Bartholomew 2005).

All of these processes are designed to codify tacit knowledge and are appropriate for organizational worth and knowledge management. The extraction of tacit knowledge activity resulting from these efforts provides opportunity for additional analysis to assess impact on established healthcare outcomes. The feasibility of assessment increases when a project focuses on high-value knowledge issues for specifically targeted teams, units, or processes (Bartholomew 2005).

COMMUNITIES OF PRACTICE

The association of tacit knowledge with social process extends to the model of communities of practice (CoP), which provide insights into tacit knowledge sharing. CoPs can be formal or informal, large or small, and represent a wide range of purpose and participation. CoPs are relatively new in the healthcare environment; however, their value as a means to create and share collective knowledge that may improve patient care is widely acknowledged (Ranmuthugala et al. 2011; Li et al. 2009). CoPs are often highlighted as an effective way to promote tacit knowledge exchange in a manner that creates a newly explicit knowledge base (Ranmuthugala et al. 2011). The CoP literature focuses on the creation of and participation in communities as social entities or knowledge sharing repositories. Efforts to measure the impact of these communities on care delivery may provide meaningful evidence for the importance of tacit knowledge. The social value of CoPs as knowledge repositories is recognized as important, even when evidence of the positive impact on healthcare delivery is largely anecdotal (Valatis et al. 2011).

As a tactic to support knowledge sharing, CoPs facilitate the symbiosis that should occur between researchers and users of research. CoPs provide opportunity and means for researchers to disseminate findings quickly to interested individuals who in turn apply the research in the real world. Results from implementation then inform further research. Elements of open communication, mutual interest, negotiation, and trust contribute to the success or failure of the process. This method accelerates the research to practice and practice-informed research paradigms, while providing valuable data for research, funding, real-world application, and outcomes measurement (McDonald and Viehbeck 2007).

The knowledge audit, social network analysis and CoPs offer methods and tools for capturing and mapping the diffusion of information and knowledge among members of a professional community, workgroup or team; however, they do not offer a method of tracking the diffusion of knowledge via these tools or a way to facilitate its storage and retrieval for subsequent application.

Knowledge Discovery through Technology

Tacit knowledge sharing can be examined from the perspective of research or discovery. Research implies that specific outcome measures or endpoints should be established at the beginning of the project. Discovery implies unexpected or even serendipitous revelations of specific needs or gaps resulting from analysis of existing knowledge or data collections.

INFOBOX 7.2: THREE TOOLS FOR KNOWLEDGE DISCOVERY

CONTENT ANALYSIS

A research technique that analyzes word use, it offers opportunities to explore narrative for examples to draw experience from incident reports that are richer than numbers alone (Ruben 1999).

TEXT MINING

A process that converts terms into numbers to draw conclusions as to value of word order and occurrence. Given the increased use of electronic health records, text mining shows great promise for capturing context and experience in healthcare (Raja et al. 2008).

ONTOLOGY APPLICATION

Ontologies are terms that connect related concepts that enable text to be classified to reflect those relationships (Wickramasinghe et al. 2009). Applying these concepts in a specific way can help knowledge inferred in the written word become collectively accessible and applicable. They are used in healthcare to do things like map medication use in medication administration records or identify and organize factors noted in malpractice claims.

In research, benchmarks or outcome measures are established at the outset. In healthcare, standards of care provide concrete benchmarks for success, such as treatment effectiveness, reduced hospitalizations, and others. The consideration in this context is how to equalize standard outcomes in such a way that allows for the measurement of the influence of tacit knowledge (Cunningham et al. 2012; Braithwaite, Runciman and Merry 2009; Reinders 2010).

Because of their highly collaborative nature, the exchanges and documentation found in CoPs can provide meaningful input about effective knowledge sharing. CoPs often rely on wikis or other online social or collaborative tools to facilitate communication and collaboration. When shared tacit knowledge becomes codified in these environments, it can be exploited in order to measure or analyze impact.

At a basic level, keyword searching may reveal patterns of activity or users; however, keywords don't account for context or interpretation. Nevertheless, this approach can illuminate areas of need. Documentation of activity in a community of practice over time may reveal not only experts, but individuals who are most willing to share knowledge. Usage or page access statistics reflect strong areas of interest or highlight areas of need that can inform future planning or research. Similar results are possible by mining organizational "yellow pages" or frequently asked questions (FAQ) lists. A tag cloud (Figure 7.2) based on a select block of text or document is an easy way to extract key terms for further exploration (Bartholomew 2005; Delen and Al-Hawamdeh 2009).

In knowledge discovery, new advances may provide solutions for analyzing information and evidence objects, entities, and repositories. Text mining and content analysis are two such tools. Both tools can return not only useful, but often surprising, results that would not be otherwise accessible.

Figure 7.2   Tag Cloud of Chapter 7

Understanding the Content of Shared Knowledge

Communities of practice offer hospitals opportunities to enable collective tacit knowledge to be explicitly transformed into text. As components of COPs, social networking tools such as discussion boards, blogs, and wikis provide a shared context for interactions within these organizational knowledge sharing groups.

"Advances in knowledge discovery methods may hold the key to progress in knowledge classification in order to track and measure knowledge sharing."

Knowledge translated into evidence and information can be stored in databases via explicit, structured representation of that knowledge (that is, a PubMed® abstract). However, text is typically unstructured in social media. Making this knowledge accessible requires application of terms and descriptors (that is, keywords or subject headings) to ensure context is translated for and findable by a broader audience. Three such methods are described on the following page: content analysis, text mining, and ontology application.

CONTENT ANALYSIS

Content analysis allows for analyzing language in multiple formats. It offers a potential method of categorizing writing shared via social media. Content analysis, while time and labor intensive, is a well-established method of text analysis used in qualitative research. Content analysis also represents a practical method for CoPs to ascertain what knowledge their members may hold (Titscher et al. 2000). Although computer tools can facilitate the content analysis process, social media discussion postings may result in thousands of messages conveying clues about the tacit knowledge of the participants. Limitations of content analysis include the inconsistent use of terms considered primary to the text (that is, keywords) for indexing, which provides descriptors for topics covered by the content, but lacks robust structure and organization. Additionally, existing sets of related terms (that is, vocabularies) may be inadequate to describe knowledge content semantically, necessitating new classification frameworks using knowledge discovery tools automated by technology. Advances in knowledge discovery methods may hold the key to progress in knowledge classification in order to track and measure knowledge sharing.

TEXT MINING

Text mining allows users to discover information by automatic computer extraction from written resources (Gupta and Lehal 2009). While text mining offers a number of potential applications, its use represents a step towards automatic classification of the representation of connections to knowledge in social media texts using pre-defined classifications (Gupta and Lehal 2009). While less accurate than human coding, text classification by automated processes that become more robust as the technologies gather word use patterns (that is, machine learning) represents a potential solution for large bodies of text (Scharkow 2011). The development of technology that can uncover potential meaning through how terms are used may represent an improvement over text mining, which is limited by its reliance on pre-existing classification schema. The ability to index around meaning and exploration of semantics could improve retrieval capability to differentiate meanings for the same word and named entities to denote persons, roles, and organizations (Davies et al. 2011).

ONTOLOGY APPLICATION

The emergence of ontologies to characterize social media texts represents a potential breakthrough in organizational knowledge sharing and provides a framework to characterize the nature of shared knowledge. Ontologies provide structure for indexing unstructured texts to facilitate their organization for retrieval by classifying relational meaning of text. There are a number of ontology modeling tools and software currently available for use in a staged methodological approach that defines the scope, users, uses, and prioritized requirements for ontologies prior to extraction of terms for structuring (Casellas 2011).

Within organizational COPs where the meanings intrinsic to knowledge are negotiated and validated, the large-scale use of discovery tools in social media, along with social network analysis, can provide a more definitive understanding of who is sharing and tracking knowledge. These tools can also provide evidence of what is being shared to uncover where knowledge may reside within the organization.

An Important yet Intangible Piece of Knowledge Sharing Work

> *An intangible is something that cannot be touched. Intangibles are nonetheless valuable, and in today's world, possibly more valuable than tangible assets (Wickramasinghe et al. 2009: 28).*

The tenets of evidence-based medicine and knowledge transfer rely on tacit knowledge in the form of professional experience and expertise and patient preferences to apply evidence from research. Both processes speak to the social, complex, and changeable nature of healthcare delivery. Greenhalgh et al. (2008) focus on the sociology of knowledge creation in the clinical practice setting, whereby new explicit knowledge is borne out of personal interactions in which tacit knowledge is continually exchanged and transformed. These elements are intangible, drawing from the interplay of individuals and their creative and rapid application of their clinical knowledge to the patient's needs.

The collaborative nature of patient care teams, the experience of the patient, and knowledge and wisdom of the clinician as expert and mentor, represent the contextual environments from which tacit knowledge appears. These moments in time provide instances where tacit knowledge may be extracted, recorded, and rendered explicit and measurable. Beyond verbatim audio or video recordings, mechanisms exist to capture the knowledge sharing they represent and the potential to improve healthcare delivery.

Research into the effectiveness of social networks to share knowledge is still new in healthcare. More research is needed to establish benchmarks and indicators for longitudinal study. Data collection strategies include questionnaires, surveys, self-report, audio or video recordings, ethnographic observation, content analysis of emails, and discussion forums (Ranmuthugala et al. 2011; Li et al. 2009).

Social networking and the use of social media, like blogs, is an established cultural phenomenon. Efforts to better understand how social media communications can facilitate the transformation of tacit, experiential knowledge into explicit formats for knowledge as the information content of blog posts offers the opportunity for exploring ways to measure the information transfer process. The use of discourse analysis in its most elementary form, content analysis, provides a means to create structure to facilitate access and retrieval of tacit experiential knowledge rendered explicit in text.

Emerging knowledge discovery technologies may provide the structure and organization of recorded social media and other digital knowledge platforms in a measurable form needed for knowledge sharing. As this transformation occurs, healthcare organizations will learn to identify and evaluate the feasibility of applying these tools to knowledge management to track its potential impact on high-quality healthcare. Given the increasing infusion of health information and social networking technology into healthcare to track safe, effective care, the opportunity to excise information to connect healthcare workers to knowledge to improve quality should be accelerated. It is the task of leadership to optimize these tools to understand and track impact to ensure transformation (Gowen, Henagan and McFadden 2009).

KEY TAKE-AWAYS

- There are challenges in creating processes and metrics to track the impact of knowledge sharing.
- Established social constructs in healthcare provide opportunities to explore effective knowledge transfer measures.
- A variety of technological strategies and tools exist that can track knowledge within an organization.

Suggested Reading

Cross, R., Singer, J., Colella, S., Thomas, R.J. and Silverstone, Y. 2010. *The Organizational Network Fieldbook: Best Practices, Techniques and Exercises to Drive Organizational Innovation and Performance*. San Francisco, CA. Jossey-Bass.

Gowen, C.R., Henagan, S.C. and McFadden, K.L. 2009. "Knowledge Management as a Mediator for the Efficacy of Transformational Leadership and Quality Management Initiatives in U.S. Health Care." *Health Care Management Review*, 34(2), 129–40.

Rangachari, P. 2008. "Knowledge Sharing Networks Related to Hospital Quality Measurement and Reporting. *Healthcare Manage Review*, 33(3), 253–63.

Zack, M., McKeen, J. and Singh, S. 2009. "Knowledge Management and Organizational Performance: An Exploratory Analysis. *Journal of Knowledge Management*, 13(6), 392–409.

8

To Boldly Go ... Initiating Knowledge Management[1]

Lorri Zipperer, Kathryn Eblen Townsend and Heidi Heilemann

> *Pockets of excellence exist in our healthcare systems, but knowledge of these better ideas and practices often remains isolated and unknown to others (Massoud et al. 2006).*

Knowing Where Knowledge Exists as a Quality Improvement Strategy

It is unacceptable to be complacent about failing to draw from the lessons that exist within an organization that operates in a high risk environment. Without them, an organization will waste valuable resources, both human and financial. In a hospital, the potential delay in improvement, or possible worsening of care due to a lack of optimizing "what the knowers know," could adversely impact those who have entrusted their lives or the lives of their loved ones to the organization.

Yet in hospitals it is not known that the proactive and strategic use of tacit knowledge is established practice. Interest in improving knowledge sharing processes peaks when organizations realize they can't locate and draw from

---

[1] This section is adapted from: Zipperer, L. 2011. "Knowledge Services." In The Medical Library Association *Guide to Managing Healthcare Libraries, 2nd edition*, edited by M.M. Bandy and R.F. Dudden. New York, NY: Neal-Schuman, 301–19 [page 313 MLA Guide].

"It is unacceptable to be complacent about not drawing from what lessons exist within an organization that operates in a high risk environment."

their own knowledge (Call 2005). This past knowledge is often buried deep within an organization and difficult to retrieve. Knowledge management initiatives can surface internal tacit knowledge. For a hospital or healthcare system this work needs to be approached as a complex implementation challenge such as other quality and safety initiatives. With strategies, commitment and motivations similar to those, progress can be made.

This chapter provides a series of suggestions to support the launch of knowledge management initiatives within the complex environment of a hospital. It recommends steps to help healthcare organizations understand what knowledge it may have and where that knowledge exists within their walls. It highlights the value of tacit knowledge – the sum of the experience and expertise of its clinicians, leaders, managers, and patients – as a key quality improvement resource.

A CHALLENGE WORTH ACCEPTING

For over a decade the Institute of Medicine has been challenging healthcare via its publishing output to think differently about what it does and how to learn from it (Kohn, Corrigan and Donaldson 2000; Committee on Quality of Health Care in America, Institute of Medicine 2001; Smith et al. 2012; Institute of Medicine 2004). With the attention by regulators, insurers, and consumers to improving healthcare quality generated by these reports and others, organizations have become increasingly motivated to identify and replicate the quality and patient safety improvement lessons they have already absorbed. Learning what those lessons are and adopting those changes can be a difficult task. The challenge often begins with discovering what is known, learning how to effectively synthesize and disseminate that knowledge, and understanding the lessons of it. The discovery and sharing of this knowledge then becomes a critical ingredient in creating and sustaining meaningful care improvement solutions.

Integral to this pursuit is a commitment from leadership to discovering not only *what* was done in connection with a distinct outcome and *how* it was

"The challenge often begins with discovering what is known, learning how to effectively use and disseminate that knowledge, and understanding the lessons of it."

done, but *why* it was done. The "why" may initially seem somewhat straightforward – perhaps a patient safety issue was encountered and a decision was made to resolve it; however, the nuances that enable a contextual understanding are much broader in scope. Capturing this knowledge to enable its use organization-wide is complex and therefore challenging to accomplish. The rationale for why a process is being changed (to harness knowledge) and effectively articulating how the change affects the individuals engaged in that process is critical to its successful implementation. Individuals charged with transforming their work and changing their behavior to carry out the objectives of the initiative must be convinced that the revisions are of value and will be supported by their leadership (Chuang, Jason and Morgan 2011). Learning what constituted successful motivation for behavior change then becomes an important aspect in identifying and transmitting existing knowledge. This awareness enhances an organization's ability to learn, which is essential for hospitals to become learning organizations through more effective application of knowledge management principles (Institute of Medicine 2004).

IMPLEMENTATION THROUGH THE COMPLEXITY LENS

Knowledge evolves. Teams shift constantly. Workforce turnover is at its height. Resources – both financial and personnel – are stretched. Impacts are formidable. Time is of the essence. All of these elements place the work of developing knowledge sharing processes in hospitals in the construct of complexity.

Given time demands, keeping interest in the work of change – across the blunt end/sharp end continuum – is also difficult. Employees of healthcare organizations are all too familiar with the adoption cycle of new improvement initiatives. The latest improvement scheme is launched, participants are informed why they should want it and are instructed that changes will be made to their work, and hoped for improvements are described. Over time, the improvements may not be realized, or communicated, and the participants' support for, and adherence to, process changes may begin to wane. Change fatigue sets in. Enthusiasm dims, trust ebbs, and skepticism materializes, thereby making the next initiative more difficult to implement (Gollop et al. 2004).

To avoid this scenario, participants must understand the context of the requested change. New initiatives need to be distinguished from past programs in order to demonstrate why the new initiative will be successful in contrast to former failed attempts. The suggested strategy of placing knowledge management and sharing initiatives within the construct of quality and safety improvement has been illustrated through the insights of healthcare workers as discussed in Chapter 6. If the former is seen as an element of the latter, the mission and professional motivation to contribute to high quality, safe care can keep interest and energy focused on the work at hand. Orienting the effort as a standalone program with no identified sharp end improvement outcome may cause interest to wane and accountability toward its success to soften.

General Implementation Elements for a Knowledge Management Initiative

Sometimes it takes a large and complex idea to capture a large and complex phenomenon (Weick and Sutcliff 2001: 42).

Knowledge management is a cultural initiative. It needs to be approached this way to ensure it is enveloped, embraced, and engaged in by all to be successful. It cannot be left to chance to achieve success. Organizations must approach knowledge management work as a designed innovation. Common considerations launching the work are to articulate the value of tacit knowledge, understanding why knowledge initiatives fail, seeing the process as a complex one and recognizing how these initiatives can help institutions become more accountable for safer care.

To do that, the process needs some structure.

The following elements provide that. Each organization may begin their work to address knowledge sharing improvements from a different state or in a slightly different order given their culture, leadership commitment and available resources. Knowledge management is not a "cut and paste" project and it should not be approached that way.

IDENTIFY THE CURRENT KNOWLEDGE SHARING STATE

Determining and articulating the need for a knowledge initiative is essential. The need for knowledge service improvement is best placed in the context of quality and patient safety strategic concerns. The concerns to be addressed and the limitations of the initiative should be articulated at the outset to manage management and leadership expectations (Riege 2005). During this exploration step, input from others in the organization can better shape and prioritize the most important needs that an initiative will address. Steps to identify and provide important context for work and identify existing knowledge sharing needs include:

Determining what exists and where the gaps are: In determining what knowledge sharing practices exist, and identifying the barriers that may be impeding staff from sharing knowledge. Knowledge gaps can be inadvertently created when processes block individuals from sharing what they know with others and then capitalizing on existing tacit knowledge.

Considering and collecting real-life examples: Identifying examples of failures that illustrate the importance of an endeavor will help generate commitment, engagement and a sense of purpose to that work (Gollop et al. 2004). Generate language and advocate for involvement using real terms and situations; if the "ask" is too theoretical, skepticism will inevitably arise. However, the underlying theory is important. It should be presented so that individuals are introduced to the systemic issues involved. The discussion, must be translated to illustrate the practical impact for workers at the sharp and blunt end so they can contribute in a meaningful way.

Defining and recognizing context: The context of how knowledge is created is crucial in determining how it can be applied, distributed, valued, and retained over time. Suggested tactics for assessing the current state of knowledge sharing and its relationship to the daily work of providing healthcare service are:

- *Conducting group interviews and/or focus groups*: Focus groups can be invaluable in assessing the context and eliciting tactics for addressing the knowledge gaps and culture barriers which are known to exist. This information can provide invaluable insights into the current social infrastructure and the ways in which groups share or don't share knowledge. Questions about what has worked and has not worked in the past can ascertain guidance in developing tactics.

- *Conducting a team-focused assessment*: Assessments of knowledge sharing gaps and strengths can help gain insights into what processes and behaviors are in place that support improvement. The dialogue required to complete the assessment will review different perceptions of what the current state is, garner cross-disciplinary insight and generate the needed buy-in for improvement.

- *Employing Social Network Analysis tools*: Social Network Analysis can be used to examine knowledge flow and knowledge conduits within teams, units or organizations. Often associated with software applications, social network analysis can provide visual representations of interconnectivity of individuals to highlight patterns of information seeking and collaboration that help to identify trust in individuals, while labor intensive, social network analysis provides unique opportunities given the appropriate goals, support and resources to succeed (Willis et al. 2012). This examination tool should not replace the narrative approaches to explore connections and knowledge sharing patterns within organizational units described above (Milton 2010).

KNOWLEDGE MANAGEMENT ≠ TECHNOLOGY

It is crucial to define knowledge management as being about a shift in culture and engagement, which is enabled by technology, but is not *about* technology (Davenport, Prusak and Strong 2008). Tactics to engage individuals to see this work beyond that of building websites and databases include:

Placing technology in the right context: In both proposing and implementing a knowledge initiative, it is critical to put technology in the appropriate context. Technology does not drive the change, but can support the change in culture to achieve mutual goals. Without addressing both components, culture can derail technology in clinical care and knowledge management efforts (Cusack 2008; Aarts, Doorewaard and Berg 2004; Peute et al. 2010).

Managing the expectation of what technology can do: All too often, the technology solution is expected to resolve long existing issues in an organization. When it fails to do so, members of the community blame the technology and are less receptive to using technology tools in general.

Building partnerships between different experts: To avoid creating an "us against them" or "us against technology" environment, technology experts should be aligned with implementers and content experts at all stages of the project. Assembling multidisciplinary teams can be an important strategy to build the capability for dialogue and teamwork. One technique successfully used by Motorola is the learning map process. This small group, interactive process explores specific challenges and identifies how individuals can respond to them. Learning maps can help participants in a multidisciplinary team make connections, share experiences and knowledge, and challenge assumptions in a productive way (Frame, Watson and Thomson 2008).

BUILD A CADRE OF CHAMPIONS

Building an effective and sustainable knowledge management effort requires that the right people are involved from start to finish (Davenport, De Long and Beers 1998). Reporting out to all levels of the organization can further develop an expansive cadre of champions. Tactics for enhancing the network of champions include:

Engaging leadership: Tie the knowledge management initiative to the organization's high-level strategic goals. Articulating its value in that context will help to strengthen organizational support and commitment. If the knowledge management effort can tangibly support and help accelerate progress on wider organizational strategic goals, senior management, middle managers, and implementers of activities not associated with the strategic goal could lend support.

Identifying champions: Champions are needed and can exist anywhere in the hierarchy. Nurse managers, for example, can bridge the gap between research and practice (White 2011). Managers at every level of the hierarchy can demonstrate their role as champions by rewarding those who actively support an initiative. Champions possess the tacit knowledge about what in their organization may derail or delay an initiative and use that knowledge to navigate the organizational context, connecting its importance to the values shared by the team. Individuals in the organization who are highlighted as conduits in the exploration phase may be effective champions. For example, staff who serve in coordination and administrative roles are apt to know how things work and don't work at a detailed level (Swinglehurst et al. 2011).

Soliciting team member ideas: Gathering input from team members on what they understand knowledge management to be and what it means to others with whom they interact should be designed into knowledge management development work to build opportunities for champions to emerge. Strategies to gather this knowledge include:.

- Developing and seeking opportunities to explore knowledge sharing concepts with others. This can be as simple as sharing a meal, discussing provocative journal articles, or doing in-house training and education about knowledge sharing concepts.

- Facilitating dialogues to enable shared understanding of "knowledge" and "knowledge management." Identify the common language to communicate knowledge sharing concepts with others. Demystify any jargon terms, including "knowledge management," if the term does not resonate with others.

- Networking with staff from human resources, administrative and clinical leadership, health information technology, and clinicians. Include leadership, middle managers, and staff from these cross-cutting areas (Chuang, Jason and Morgan 2011).

Trumpeting early findings/successes: Kotter suggests that even small victories can motivate interest and commitment to change – but only if they are shared (Kotter 1995). Once tracked, these early successes can be used to frame the strategy and related initiatives and recruit participants. Trumpeting early findings as they relate to broader strategic initiatives helps generate support from others who can champion the project. Regardless of the terminology used to define the project, talk about it's achievements early and often. Even the most emergent successes should be broadly shared with champions throughout the organization and, when appropriate, more publicly. Storytelling can serve as an effective tactic to spread news of success (Denning 2005).

PULL TOGETHER A MULTIDISCIPLINARY TEAM

To launch a knowledge management initiative, it is important to enable a group to work together that is small, engaged, and comfortable learning together. As Jim Collins, author of the popular book, *Good to Great* advised, first worry about who, then what (Collins 2001). Once team members have been identified, be sure to locate/co-locate them in the "right seats" on the "knowledge management bus" to optimize chances for success. To achieve this outcome, leaders should:

Build a mental model around what a team is: Make sure there is a collective understanding of leading, managing, and participating in a team. Interest in the value of teamwork in healthcare organizations is also peaking and is being used in a wide variety of quality improvement initiatives (Timmel et al. 2010). Draw from that synergy to place the development of this team within that construct.

Partner with Human Resources: Developing and sustaining a close working relationship with human resources (HR) will help achieve support for knowledge management initiatives. Enlist HR early in the process to determine ways that policies and documentation can support implementation of the project. Partnerships with HR can result in:

- *Explicit and measurable job requirements that relate to knowledge sharing behaviors/work*: Staffing issues, including role overload and inflexibility of HR policies can also undermine effective implementation of the knowledge management initiative (Chuang, Jason and Morgan 2011). To get the right people on the bus, HR can ensure that job requirements are clearly defined and that they explicitly measure and emphasize the importance of knowledge sharing and behaviors that promote knowledge sharing and accountability. This can manifest itself at the team level and as projects are implemented to support sustainability.

- *Assign accountability*: Accountability to the knowledge culture and supportive behaviors can also be reflected in job descriptions and requirements (Ellis 2001).

- *Develop policy to support knowledge sharing*: HR representatives can develop policies and procedures to support a culture of knowledge sharing. The issues with the effective use of social media and other knowledge-gathering tools external to the organization to enable learning deserve consideration. Firewalls and lagging IT policies can minimize the opportunities for learning and evidence gathering these tools present. Staff members who participate in communities of practice, email discussion groups, online education (that is, IHI Open School), Twitter, and other collaborative technologies should be empowered to participate as professionals. This strategy should be part of the overall strategy of addressing knowledge needs for the hospital. The HR representative also can help ensure that policies conform to laws to protect the privacy of clinical information, including the Health Insurance Portability and Accountability Act (HIPAA).

- *Focus orientation on tacit knowledge exchange between experienced and new providers*: Tactics could include shadowing programs and attending strategy meetings within the organization.

Articulate requirements needed to get the job done: The multidisciplinary team can identify projects that are easy to implement as well as those that may not be achievable in the short term. The team can prioritize projects with the most benefit to the organization. For example, technology projects require discussions with programmers early and often to articulate and vet project requirements. When this step is skipped programming time and effort is lost and can result in a tool or program that is not adopted or used. Instead, team members should invite the programmer to round with clinicians to understand the setting and context in which a clinician will use the technology. If this is not possible, a re-enactment or role play exercise may be useful. Clinicians and blunt end staff need to understand, at a basic level, the potential and limits of programming and system interoperability. This exchange enables the sharing of tacit knowledge through observation and dialogue to provide context to the decision making.

Provide frontline insights into the existing state: Team members representing a variety of roles and perspectives play a critical role in knowledge management initiatives. So do outsiders who can ask questions about why workflows exist in a certain way and help identify where changes can be made to improve the pathways for discovering knowledge in the workflow (Gollop et al. 2004). For example, a system to allow in-house experts to contribute to discussions on problems diagnoses or innovations (Dillings et al. 2013). The benefits of embedding this knowledge in the workflow can best be implemented, tested, and evaluated by a multidisciplinary team.

BUILD A STRATEGY EXPLICITLY CONNECTED TO MISSION AND GOALS

Aligning knowledge management improvement activities clearly with overall hospital mission and goals is important (Davenport, De Long and Beers 1998). Articulating the connection of the knowledge management work to that overarching framework can strengthen relationships with unit level champions and commitment to the hard work of change without detracting from existing organizationally defined efforts. It will deepen departmental and unit level understanding of the systemic value of improved knowledge sharing and how the work will ultimately contribute to progress and improvement. Tactics for connecting these dots include:

Creating urgency around the work by connecting it with needed improvement and safety initiatives: This sense of urgency to enable knowledge sharing behavior and culture change is paramount in moving forward, creating champions, gaining resources and sustaining the effort (Kotter 1995).

Connecting effort with areas in need of rapid attention through established metrics collected at both the sharp end and blunt ends of the organization: The knowledge needs associated with each area should be carefully determined; however, these areas should be part of an ongoing implementation process to enable a responsive knowledge sharing process. Tie the need to common goals of saving time, resources, and improving patient safety.

When aligning a knowledge management project with the hospital's mission and goals, consider how they map to existing department or unit goals that could be enhanced through knowledge sharing improvements. Tactics to identify unit level alignment include:

- Participation in regular practice council or research council meetings to learn about ongoing projects related to training and disseminating knowledge resources.

- Working with appropriate councils to identify areas ripe for partnerships.

This chapter seeks to illustrate how tacit knowledge sharing can contribute to improved safety and quality in healthcare. Given those are explicit callings for hospitals, those mission specific elements should provide the hook knowledge management leaders need to engage staff as discussed in this section.

DETERMINE OPPORTUNITIES FOR IMPROVEMENT

Multidisciplinary team members can serve as boundary spanners to help to engage both the blunt- and sharp-ends in meaningful, attainable knowledge management initiatives as they can:

Assess results of the exploration: This is an opportunity to identify how knowledge can be part of the solution to ensure quality improvement. Understanding workflows that facilitate or perpetuate knowledge gaps is an important first step in this process.

Review internal failures for knowledge gap contributors: In the case of a sentinel event, the specific improvements needed and their connection with knowledge sharing may or may not be obvious. Several areas may need attention, and prioritizing and understanding how they are interconnected may take more time than is allowed in a rapid response situation.

- If able, participate in failure mode and affects analysis or other proactive improvement opportunities. Not only will potential knowledge gaps and decision-making biases be revealed, but solutions to addressing them could be identified (Beals 2010; Zipperer and Sykes 2009).

- A less labor intensive tool to help identify the root causes of knowledge sharing problems could be the "5 Whys" process advocated by systems thinking advocates (Senge et al. 1994).

Attend meetings, programs, educational sessions to see systemic knowledge gaps (Evans and Refrow-Rutala 2010): Tacit knowledge is apt to reveal problems during informal water cooler exchanges. Situations can be strategically examined and emerging problems identified. Not only can this approach identify problems before they become normalized (Waring and Bishop 2010) but as threats are determined, the activities and participation will provide the needed return on investment.

See department and unit level activities as opportunities to generate initiative buy-in: Establish new partnerships to discover how these areas operate. As areas of common concern become more broadly known, communities of practice emerge. Training programs or regular staff meetings can be used to solicit input during the planning process. Aspects of the goals for the project may be common to other groups or departments.

Apply systems thinking tools to explore solutions and assess impact of the knowledge management initiative at an organizational level over time: A variety of prospecting tools can be used. Knowledge sharing problems and improvements may take time to materialize. Demonstrate the value of a non-siloed, multi-perspective, inter-relational approach to devising knowledge sharing efforts and their associated tools (Zipperer 2011). Two tools popularized by Senge et al. (1994) to visualize the nature of the improvements that may resonate with quality and safety improvement leaders due to a connection (Kohn, Corrigan and Donaldson 2000; Leape 1994) between a systems approach to improvement in healthcare are:

- *Delay over time graph*: This graphic device can help to manage the expectations of the time required to realize improvements. It can visualize for decision makers the need for a long term view regarding the outlay of resources needed to support the initiative.

- *Reinforcing/balancing loops*: Causal loops can illustrate the impact of an action on a related action to show both positive and negative forces on the system. They can also provide a schematic diagram to explore solutions that take into account those effects (Tompson and Zipperer 2011). The use of loop diagrams as a mechanism to illustrate decision points on the organizational effects of emphasizing an external vs internal knowledge sharing strategy is discussed in Chapter 3. Appendix 1 shows a detailed causal loop analysis of the decision.

BUILD A COMMUNICATION TOOL AND KNOWLEDGE SHARING PROCESS THAT WORKS FOR EVERYONE AND COMMIT TO USING IT

Team members, unit and organizational champions and early adopters can help recognize the viability of the selected knowledge sharing tools in real time with a connection to daily work flow. When considering tool/process development and design:

Identify and commit to a sharing process that has minimal impact on daily work: This decision should be made concurrently with the tool selection and other tactics such as sharing stories at the onset of an established weekly meeting.

Select tools that make sense: The tools should be easy to use and not require additional steps to access. This is especially true when organizations are trying something new and where buy-in is crucial to launch the change. Systems that are difficult to use, containing multiple screens and steps, are likely not to be accepted or adopted by clinicians (Campbell et al. 2008). In fact, cumbersome interfaces can obscure key information and increase the chances for errors (Shulman et al. 2005; Koppel et al. 2005). It is important to demonstrate the appropriate context for any new technology within the existing culture to avoid widespread opposition to adoption.

Leverage an existing wiki or intranet site: A central place to share stories and update progress helps team members stay informed on the progress of the implementation. While a defined mechanism to capture experience is vital, it should be augmented with regular face-to-face meetings and other explicit forms of communication (Griffith et al. 2013). Examples of tools could include knowledge maps (Call 2005; Zipperer, Gluck and Anderson 2002) or intranet sites centered on communities of practice. Whatever the technological sophistication of the method utilized, these projects are well-suited to team development and could be enriched by librarians and involvement by other boundary spanners (Bandy et al. 2009).

This multichannel strategy will enable team members to contribute to the discussion. Access to regular updates by leadership and management will provide additional motivation for the team to communicate milestones as well as challenges. Leadership should also use the tool and model the behavior accordingly. Having a place to raise awareness of the smallest successes helps validate the project and sustain a team's motivation and engagement (Kotter 1995).

BE FLEXIBLE

Knowledge is paradoxically both a thing and a flow (Snowden 2002: 102).

Knowledge morphs as it moves through an organization (Lane and Flagg 2010; Bohmer 2009). Its evolution requires that knowledge management initiatives acknowledge a certain level of complexity. In addition, teams must create a flexible process and program structure (Davenport, De Long and Beers 1998). The complexity of most healthcare organizations or units considering a knowledge management initiative requires attention to these factors:

Existing knowledge gaps may close: Events, communication patterns, and changes in behavior and personnel could address knowledge gaps, such as increase in staff members who have openness to sharing. Tactical emphases could also shift over time as the environment shifts. The flexibility of the team enables the initiative

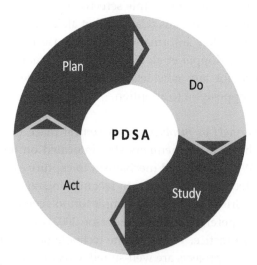

Figure 8.1   Plan-Do-Study-Act
Source: Adapted from Langley et al. 2009.

to "roll with the knowledge flow," anticipating the evolution of an initiative change over time. The complexity of the environment should be recognized as a powerful force. The non-linear, emergent nature of healthcare and the knowledge it produces cannot be underestimated. Before undertaking complex initiatives, leaders should undertake rapid prototyping using mechanisms such as Plan-Do-Study-Act (PDSA) (Morath and Turnbull 2005). These strategies have been noted as having potential in the tacit knowledge sharing tool development spectrum, although robust application has yet to be documented (Zipperer and Steward 2013; Robb and Zipperer 2009; Wheaton 2009).

Process and culture evolution should contribute to organizational learning: Staff members who are comfortable with rapid-cycle or continuous improvement concepts are essential to the success of knowledge management program implementation. Their willingness to adapt, make adjustments, design and use mechanisms for feedback and spread will not only contribute to team learning, but to the sharing of the knowledge generated by the program to ensure what is learned becomes infused in the organization's corporate memory.

Abort current program structure in favor of adopting a new direction if necessary: Open, honest discussion about how the program progresses and sharing of knowledge can assist in the development of an evidence-based, informed decision.

INFOBOX 8.1: RAPID CYCLE IMPROVEMENT

Plan-Do-Study-Act (PDSA) cycle: "[is a] Deming-inspired Model for Improvement … developed to build knowledge and to facilitate system improvements (Langley et al. 2009; Deming 2000). Initially, a PDSA cycle aims to have people test a small change idea in a 'safe' setting. The model aims to provide people with direct experience of whether or not a small change works in their setting – that is, to specifically build their understanding (combination of prediction, data, and experience) and then to start expanding the testing as their understanding grows" (Perla and Parry 2011: i26).

DEMONSTRATE KNOWLEDGE SHARING BEHAVIORS

Individual participants on teams need to demonstrate their ability to share knowledge and their interest in gaining it just as much as management/leadership. Behaviors that exhibit a knowledge sharing orientation include:

Responding to emails and other queries with knowledge, not just facts: By providing important contextual narrative, individual participants demonstrate their practiced engagement in the importance of knowledge sharing. This type of communication behavior should be rewarded.

Connecting people with knowledge, and going beyond sharing materials to link individuals: Facilitate dialogue between individuals to encourage knowledge exchange and continuing conversations about knowledge management project needs, successes, and next steps. Engaging people on a social basis can be a useful tactic to engender trust and familiarity (Collison and Parcell 2004).

Encouraging staff to share what they know in a way that enables exchange and dialogue.

Highlighting mentoring and coaching skills as knowledge transfer traits: Hire for them.

Rewarding the sharing of knowledge, although do not assume incentives or positive performance evaluations will sustain it (Zipperer 2011; Rienge 2005). Considerations for designing incentive programs include:

- Individual motivators such as relationships and professional growth, recognition, expert status and self-esteem.

- Employees' ability to learn from each other, respect each other; to grow and develop, to realize their values.

- Social motivation factors by setting knowledge sharing norms in an organization and having individuals aware of the organizational customs.

- The recognition of knowledge as a public good and the value of belonging to strong organizations can motivate knowledge workers to share what they know with others (Gu and Gu 2011).

BE REALISTIC

Juggling the commitment with other overall mission and vision-focused demands can be challenging. Initiative leaders must manage expectations to coalesce the overall planning of a knowledge management project. Here are a few steps to minimize the common pitfall of becoming overextended:

Start small: There is no such thing as a project that is too small. In fact, the smaller the project, the easier it is to define. From the beginning of project design, address areas that will not be in the scope of the project so that realistic expectations can be set. Early discussions should define how to measure progress of the project, regardless of its size. Application of the PDSA process may help with obtaining support and to test rapid improvement.

Consider the local nature of culture: The review and consideration of the culture into which knowledge management projects are explored, tested and revised needs to occur within a hospital (Huang et al. 2007; Pronovost and Vohr 2010). Culture can be markedly different from one unit to the next. The expectation that hospital units and departments are similar in culture can open the door for missteps.

Be sensitive to the role of culture: Culture can be an adversary or an ally. The often-repeated colloquialism that "culture eats strategy for lunch" is applicable in knowledge management. For example, just because practice guidelines are widely understood to improve patient safety and reduce the cost of healthcare does not ensure that they will be adopted without scrutiny. This is but one example of how culture can derail good intention (Fein and Corrato 2008). Similar forces can affect knowledge programs as well.

Test for effectiveness: Suggestions for changes to improve how knowledge is shared amongst staff can generate the buy-in needed among teams and the larger organization. PDSA and rapid improvement tools can assist in formalizing the testing process.

USE METRICS THAT TRANSLATE IMPACT

Metrics that document the impact of knowledge sharing are nascent in healthcare, although some tactics can illustrate progress (Gowen, Henagan and McFadden 2009; Zack, McKeen and Singh 2009; Kothari et al. 2011b). To address this problem when designing the initiative:

Discuss the work in terms and measures that are meaningful across the spectrum of participants both at the local and organizational level: Once identified, share evidence that improvement is happening to keep teams engaged in the work (Gollop et al. 2004).

Design metrics that work: Measures can be good enough to illustrate proof of concept and not slow improvement down. In searching for the "perfect" measure, development can be stalled or derailed. "Seek usefulness, not perfection" (Morath 1998: 122).

Devise a way of counting improvement directly related to needs that have been identified.

FACILITATE LEARNING FOR THE ORGANIZATION, THE TEAM, AND THE INDIVIDUAL

Organizational, individual, and team education opportunities can serve as mechanisms to recognize gaps and build relationships with champions and knowledge management initiative implementers. However, to facilitate learning the effort needs to go beyond training and stand-alone continuing education. In the hierarchy of actions as defined by human factors experts, there is a need to outline the tactics to support changes in human behavior to increase safety. Training alone is identified as a lower level tactic that won't result in sustainable change (Williams and Bagian 2014). Work to support a culture of learning and inquiry. Learning and inquiry as a part of daily and strategic work can be developed over time. Several suggestions for instilling a learning culture are listed opposite:

Participate in collaboratives: Collaboratives bring people together to work on a specific problem, take the expertise of the group back to their organization, test the ideas, then bring that experience back to the collaborative. The technique was incorporated into healthcare through the IHI's Breakthrough Series and its 100,000 Lives Campaign's (Sinkowitz-Cochran et al. 2012; Sorenson and Bernard 2012).

Engage in Communities of Practice: Communities of practice support internal and external learning. This concept has several definitions and metrics have yet to illustrate their impact in healthcare, yet they show promise for learning support (Li et al. 2009a; Li et al. 2009b).

Build on established interaction opportunities: Simulations, root cause analysis, failure mode and effects analysis, after action reviews and other quality improvement mechanisms can be employed as knowledge sharing occasions if staff is oriented to gathering and sharing knowledge (rather than information).

Leverage emerging and existing interprofessional education initiatives and activities: Adopt the shared language identified by these efforts to effectively communicate and lead adaptive change (Englander et al. 2013).

See external tools and experiences as illustrations of what could be done internally: Infobox 8.2 lists a few examples of programs that aim to motivate and support innovation through open sharing and discussion.

See collective work with an eye toward learning: Simply training individuals to use a new communication technology or posting an announcement on how to use it won't engender knowledge sharing. The coordination of a meeting or working session to bring peers together from within or external to an organization to share insights with a project team that has asked for help is a peer assist (Milton 2010; Collison and Parsell 2004). Examples from healthcare demonstrate a value to the process as well (Peele, Goldberg and Trompeta 2011).

While the selected examples above are primarily formal activities, the value of unstructured mechanisms for sharing knowledge should also be noted. Informal chances to tell stories and share experiences can support collective sense making, situational awareness, trust and establish conduits and boundary spanners to support a culture of safety and knowledge distribution (Wieck 1995; Waring and Bishop 2010).

INFOBOX 8.2: SELECTED KNOWLEDGE SHARING INITIATIVES

AHRQ INNOVATION EXCHANGE

The US Agency for Healthcare Research and Quality (AHRQ) built this website to support the sharing of evidence and experience in how to implement of new and improved ways to provide healthcare. The site offers a variety of opportunities to share, learn about, and ultimately adopt evidence-based innovations and tools for a variety of environments. It offers personal connections with the leaders of highlighted projects to enhance knowledge exchange (AHRQ Innovation Exchange: n.p.).

See http://innovations.ahrq.gov/

AHRQ OFFICE OF COMMUNICATIONS AND KNOWLEDGE TRANSFER (OCKT)

AHRQ has designated an office to explicitly connect innovators and experts with organizations and teams that wish to implement improvements to enable transfer of project and research experience to be spread.

See http://www.ahrq.gov/cpi/centers/ockt/

CMS INNOVATIONS CENTER

The Centers for Medicare and Medicaid Services (CMS) Innovations Center has listed as a priority the engagement of an extensive range of stakeholders to ensure the innovations submitted to its web site are infused with the knowledge in the CMS innovations community. Educational, online, and townhall-style mechanisms for collecting knowledge have been employed (CMS 2012).

See http://innovation.cms.gov/

MAYO CLINIC MODEL OF DIFFUSION

The Mayo Clinic embraced system engineering and leverage techniques to share best practice across its 24 hospitals to diffuse what it knew across its locations to ensure that preferred care processes once developed were shared and embedded in daily work (Dilling et al. 2013).

PATIENTSLIKEME®

Patient portals and sharing mechanisms have become more prevalent with the ease of access to social media. The ability of sites like PatientsLikeMe® to enable like-minded individuals to learn from one another's experience is a popular knowledge transfer strategy.

See http://www.patientslikeme.com/

Challenges: Unlucky 13 Means Opportunity

Hard evidence about barriers to the use of knowledge management in healthcare is lacking (Kothari et al. 2011b). Establishing tacit knowledge sharing initiatives is comparable to culture change and innovation efforts in safety and quality improvement. The barriers are intertwined given the complexity of the environment, knowledge sharing work in general and the manner in which knowledge migrates and transforms as it moves among an organization (Riege 2005; Bohmer 2009).

Knowledge management champions and implementation teams must be prepared for elements in the hospital environment that can work against them. When bearing in mind obstacles to knowledge sharing improvement efforts, both individual and organizational barriers should be considered (Kothari et al. 2011b).

To frame the conversation of challenges that could disrupt tacit knowledge sharing improvement initiatives, the five-point model proposed by Chuang, Jason and Morgan (2011) situates barriers in the context of a complex innovation. Chuang and colleagues submit that middle managers play a vital role in implementing complex projects and are ascribed to be problematic if they resist and don't embrace the goals of the intervention. Their study highlighted five factors (referred to here as frame points) to support to middle management engagement in complex innovation work should the implementation be centered on them.

FRAME POINT: MANAGEMENT SUPPORT

Management support is required for a change initiative to be successful (Davenport, De Long and Beers 1998). Knowledge management efforts are no different. Leaders, champions, and management backing at all levels need to be established and committed to the work and ensure success in change and innovation initiatives (Chuang, Jason and Morgan 2011; Pronovost and Vohr 2010). Challenges to achieving management support include:

Barrier 1: Lack of Influence to Negotiate Hierarchy

The hierarchy endemic in healthcare can inhibit the sharing of knowledge. Those higher in the power gradient may not pursue, or even consider, knowledge that resides at a different level. Concomitantly, those who reside at a lower level in the hierarchy may assume that their sphere of influence is nominal. This real or perceived minimization of the importance of their knowledge limits its being shared. As part of the management support for the knowledge management initiative, leadership can encourage relevant contributions from all individuals to feed into the process. This may require management to seek out those who traditionally were not included in such initiatives, but who possess knowledge that could be of value.

A frontline unit or administrative assistant, for example, who traditionally has been tasked to collect, collate, or publish relevant information regarding a particular project may be a critical asset in recognizing what knowledge exists. This individual should be encouraged by management to participate in the knowledge management initiative. Leadership should make it clear that the role brings a valued perspective to the team (Gollop et al. 2004).

Barrier 2: Lack of Champions

Frontline support for a knowledge management initiative is crucial. But if upper management doesn't support a complex innovation, middle management is less apt to participate (Chuang, Jason and Morgan 2011). Physicians also play a critical role in determining the support for improvement initiatives. Unless a strong supportive voice from the physician ranks is present, change in healthcare processes is more difficult, and often impossible, to achieve

(Pronovost and Vohr 2010). Messages must be tailored to address skepticism and reluctance to engage in the change process (Gollop et al. 2004).

Barrier 3: Lack of Sustainable Commitment to the Work

As with quality and safety improvement, if the interest and passion for the work resides with a single leader or champion, their departure could cause the project to lose momentum. The lack of a shared language can also effect long-term commitment.

FRAME POINT: FINANCIAL RESOURCE AVAILABILITY

Barrier 4: Lack of Ability to Demonstrate a "Bottom Line" Return on the Investment

An absence of the ability for the project to result in financial improvements can threaten even the most entrenched and widely recognized projects. Avenues for illustrating how knowledge management might improve the hospital's economic health should it be embraced include:

- Discussing the negative impact of lost or ineffective knowledge. Costs of lost knowledge are hidden (De Long 2004). This becomes more important with the loss of nurses and downsizings during less-robust economic times as long-term and senior staff and clinicians leave hospitals or retire (Bleich et al. 2009). Loss of corporate memory due to reorganizations, for example, was noted as a primary failure in a large scale investigation into a UK health trust (Francis 2013). The enormity of this failure alone indicates more work needs to be done in understanding this type of system breakdown.

- Exploring how a dysfunctional approach to knowledge access can become normalized. This then could result in a lack of urgency to address the issue, even when it causes financial and clinical problems.

- Raising awareness that the lack of attention to losing intellectual capital at the leadership level, and sharp and blunt ends could be a problem down the road. Time and resources should be proactively set aside to establish and sustain a process.

Barrier 5: Shortsightedness of Resource Needs

KM initiatives take time to put into place. A misunderstanding of that can limit the opportunity to acquire the resources needed to implement, record, and document the impact of knowledge sharing programs. A lack of dedicated staff, finances, materials and time to design, launch and sustain the initiative will lower commitment to the initiative and eventually the effort will not be sustained (Milton 2010).

FRAME POINT: INNOVATIONS/VALUE FIT

Changes in motivational practices are required as knowledge is intertwined with ego, hierarchy and a commitment to one's professional alignment (Davenport, De Long and Beers 1998). Extracting knowledge requires time from busy schedules to share what is known. Value can be presented as learning from failure, which resonates with patient safety improvement efforts and which can situate the effort within a strategic goal and a professional expectation. Accountability for participation may also translate from that context.

Barrier 6: Lack of Shared Mental Model Across Healthcare Disciplines About the Work and Inconsistent Communication About the Initiative

Problems with definition are important to consider to keep the program and its implementors from straying off course (Fahey and Prusak 1998).

- Acceptance can be withheld if the project is seen as too theoretical and not application oriented (Milton 2010; Gollop et al. 2004).

  Questions remain about the relationship between presenting motivational theory and purpose and the task-oriented application pieces to sustain an innovation. This conundrum could be addressed by the team's orientation to knowledge management work and the expectation that elements of the project are effectively represented.

Barrier 7: Lack of Ability to Situate Work Beyond Being Seen as Just Another "Task"

As with other quality improvement mechanisms in healthcare, busy clinicians and blunt end staff need to understand why they should alter practice and adopt change.

- Incentives to participate in knowledge sharing projects or contribute to knowledge sharing mechanisms like communities of practice need to extend beyond monetary rewards – they must be intrinsic and connected to the individual's role as a professional (Milton 2010).

- Knowledge sharing activities must integrate into daily work and add value. They cannot be perceived as simply a must do to meet a regulatory or accreditation standard.

Barrier 8: Lack of Understanding that Technology is Not the Answer

The promise of technology and its contribution to enhanced knowledge sharing is evident, but not guaranteed. Organizations should not fall victim to the belief that technology is all that is needed. Knowledge sharing initiatives can be derailed if the following foundational barriers are not addressed:

- Project focuses solely on the capture of data instead of focusing on people as the primary resource (De Long 2004; Fahley and Prusak 1998).

- Project begins and ends with a shared drive. Creating a shared drive for access by individuals on a team or project is an ineffectual method for sharing information (Carthey et al. 2011). Carthey's discussion of the example of the National Health Service unsuccessfully using a shared drive could illustrate the short-sightedness of an approach that takes on a "build it and they will come" approach to inform knowledge sharing improvement efforts.

- Technology overwhelms the effort. A wide array of gizmos and gadgets can potentially derail a knowledge management initiative by adding choices, complexity and unnecessary functions that bog the process down. A technology solution could be state of the art, but if it's underused, it may therefore be unsuccessful (Call 2005). For example, passwords, needed to ensure privacy and security, can block members in the organization from using knowledge sharing tools. If users are frustrated by managing multiple passwords to access an in-house expertise directory, a knowledge management initiative tool could include an effort to promote secure single sign on for accessing clinical systems.

- Technology replaces human contact. Quick-fix technologies garner resources for their program but lack the ability for people to share the knowledge process. The lack of sensitivity that human connections are important to the success of sharing what is learned, what didn't work, and what could work (Fahley and Prusak 1998).

FRAME POINT: IMPLEMENTATION POLICIES AND PROCEDURES

Knowledge management needs to be seen as a continuous process. Teams should be designed and linked to share what they know before, during and after a project or initiative (Milton 2010; Dixon 2000). Polices that enable sharing over time should be hardwired into how teams and units function. In healthcare, mechanisms such as unit huddles and team meetings should be resourced and reviewed with these goals in mind.

Barrier 9: Lack of Integration in to the Daily Work of Staff at Many Levels

The knowledge sharing process needs to be reliable, useful, and flexible enough to fit into the daily work of the contributors and users of the system. Hardwiring changes into how work is done is an important element of sustaining change initiatives (Sinkowitz-Cochran et al. 2012).This concern plays out in knowledge management improvements as well. The organization that convenes a committee with no regard to the impact of the program on process, technology, and administrative activities is likely to fail.

Barrier 10: Lack of Effective Policies and Process to Guide the Initiative

The lack of a clear scope and defining mechanisms for the innovation will hamper the ability of implementers and contributors. Although process steps don't necessarily need to be defined (Davenport, DeLong and Beers 1998) tools and processes must be enabled to guide middle managers in their implementation role as boundary spanners (Chuang, Jason and Morgan 2011). This is a challenge as the terminology for knowledge management and the elements therein lack a consistent definition or are interpreted differently by the groups that need to work together to achieve success.

Barrier 11: Lack of Sensitivity to Complexity of the Work Environment

The value of seeing knowledge management improvement work through the prism of organizational learning culture and complexity has been discussed throughout this text. Other elements that create problems if not considered are operational, and include:

- A lack of team participation due to fluctuation in the workforce. This is more problematic at the sharp end of healthcare, where there is recognition by the initiative leaders about the time needed to understand and adopt the initiative.

- The need for repetitive education as to the objectives and processes for the initiative.

- The ability to implement an easily usable feedback loop and the resources needed to implement revisions to the initiative.

- A dark side to tacit knowledge sharing exists and can enable normalization of deviance. A popular culture example of this phenomenon exists in the character of Gregory House, MD, who was featured in the popular television show "House." Characterized as a superlative diagnostician, House embodies many insidious, deceitful behaviors that he tacitly and explicitly encourages his students to embrace. Episodes detail his repeated ability to solve problems and often save lives despite his disruptive and sometimes unethical actions.

    Real-world examples permeate medical education, where residents absorb behaviors that can hover toward the disruptive (National Patient Safety Foundation 2010). This type of knowledge sharing and the conduits at both the sharp and blunt ends that enable it can help facilitate success overall and minimize derailment that can be associated with change efforts.

FRAME POINT: IMPLEMENTATION CLIMATE

Change projects in general require cultural alignment to be successful (Davenport, De Long and Beers 1998). However, hierarchy, blame, silos, and secrecy can obstruct the cultural alignment that is needed to support knowledge sharing – which in turn minimizes organizational learning from failure (Walsh and Offen 2001; Weick and Sutcliff 2003, Milton 2010). These cultural barriers don't support the sharing of information on failures, let alone the tacit knowledge of the individuals involved in an incident. A narrow tolerance for failure exists where failure can be synonymous with harm as in healthcare and other high risk industries, thusly raising it as a concern in hospitals that seek to implement knowledge management programs.

Barrier 12: Lack of Time (Perceived or Real)

Time is an undervalued element in knowledge sharing work. Due to change fatigue, overburdened staff and managers are reluctant to embrace an effort that they perceive will add to inefficiencies without a direct benefit to their daily work (De Long 2004). For example:

- Management and leadership cannot see allocating the time to a large initiative without measurable impact on the bottom line or a sense of urgency calling for the initiative to be installed (Kothari et al. 2011b).

- If the urgency of situation isn't reinforced by influencers and forces – that is, the blunt-blunt end – to enable work redesign and realignment, lack of commitment and cynicism will result (Gollop et al. 2004). Allocating the time towards knowledge management improvement will suffer without an articulated connection to a strategic goal and a trigger episode (Griffiths and Moon 2011).

The question arises as to whether it will take a sentinel event exploration that includes tacit knowledge management concepts and terminology to generate action and allocate resources including staff time to the program. Until that lesson is outlined, other time, energy, and urgency barriers can block knowledge sharing improvements in healthcare.

Barrier 13: Lack of Individuals Seeing a Reward on Investing Time and Effort to Share What They Know

- Problems occur when the incentives of the tacit knowledge sharing project are not aligned. If goals, action, and commitment are seen as self-serving without broader application to the organization, individuals and leadership could become skeptical of its intent and usefulness. For example, if the IT department, education office or library is facing budget cuts and they include "knowledge management" as a "buzzword" to promote a service offered in an effort to gain visibility and don't fully embrace the work involved beyond that of existing information or training services, a lack of overall support for the initiative could result.

- Competing priorities within organization. A lack of understanding of the pressures and priorities of the organization can make the timing and placement of a knowledge management initiative ill advised. Connecting with strategic goals and cultivating a systemic sense of what is happening, who is involved and why they should help, can present the knowledge management improvement effort as a collaborative project. A systems-thinking approach to knowledge management can help nullify this misstep and barrier (Tompson and Zipperer 2011).

As with any complex system-oriented effort, barriers do not exist independently of one another. They affect the other, as efforts to address them on the blunt end can create both positive and negative impacts on the sharp end or at any points along the continuum. Use of analysis tools such as loop diagrams (see Appendix 1) may help expose potential impacts of changes and illustrate how one affects the other.

Facilitating an Informed Organizational Future

In designing the knowledge management initiative, leaders, champions and planners must effectively communicate the rationale for the initiative and its expected outcome for it to be successful. As part of the initial plan kick-off, the participants must be confident that the project will lead to the anticipated outcome, the outcome is worth the time and effort required to achieve it, and the leaders will support the participants as barriers are encountered.

"Knowledge management does not provide you with the answer to your problem, rather it facilitates the learning of the answer" (Call 2005: 20).

Knowledge management does not provide you with the answer to your problem; rather it facilitates the learning of the answer (Call 2005: 20). Through a knowledge management initiative, an organization begins to gather and understand the tacit knowledge that already exists within it; knowledge that can be used to facilitate patient safety and quality improvement opportunities. The sociotechnical approach supported by the elements described here has the potential to promote both knowledge sharing and the value of changes associated with organizational learning (Orzano et al. 2008). Through this process, an organization – whether a hospital, health system or other care setting – can acquire the attributes of a learning culture. Such a culture celebrates knowledge, actively seeks to understand its shortcomings or failures, values the lessons to be learned from them, and then utilizes that knowledge to continually improve the quality of its care.

KEY TAKE-AWAYS
- Knowledge management initiatives are large complex endeavors and need to be approached through change management and complexity lenses to be implemented successfully.
- Elements of implementing quality and safety improvements parallel tacit knowledge sharing program implementation and offer alignments that would benefit each area of work over time.

Suggested Reading

Collison, C. and Parcell, G. 2004. *Learning to Fly – Practical Knowledge Management from Leading and Learning Organizations.* Chichester: Capstone.

Davenport, T.H., De Long, D.W. and Beers, M.C. 1998. "Successful Knowledge Management Projects." *Sloan Management Review*, 39(2), 43–57.

Stewart, T.A. 2007. *The Wealth of Knowledge: Intellectual Capital and the Twenty-first Century Organization.* New York, NY: Random House Inc.

Wickramasinghe, N., Bali, R.K., Lehaney, B., Schaffer, J. and Gibbons, M.C. 2009. *Healthcare Knowledge Management Primer.* New York, NY: Routledge.

9

Strategies for Knowledge Sharing: Lessons from Improvisation

Geri Amori, Jan Chindlund and Lorri Zipperer

> *Improvising is wonderful. But, the thing is that you cannot improvise unless you know exactly what you're doing (Christopher Walken 2004, see http://www.blackfilm.com/ 20041001/features/chriswalken.shtml).*

Applying What is Known While Learning

The bright lights shine squarely on the individuals poised to play their roles. Someone in the room shouts a phrase that provides a jumping off point for the action to follow. The key players quickly huddle to decide and agree on how each of them will interpret the audience member's command. Within moments, it's time to begin.

Where is this action taking place? Could it be a hospital operating room? Or it could be on the stage of the famed improvisation Second City troupe in Chicago? It could be either.

Theatrical improvisation, like healthcare practice, is a highly skilled art form. Each relies on time-honored rules and standards that demand repeated practice to prepare for successful execution in real time. To the casual observer, improvisation looks spontaneous and free-form. To the person on stage, however, improvisation is considered one of the most difficult types of performance art. Only the most psychologically available, responsive, and alert improvisers – referred to as "actors" herein – can reap the rewards of a brilliant performance earned through effective knowledge sharing before a live audience. For this to happen, each member of the troupe must assume complete responsibility for the success of the performance.

While the analogy of theatrical improvisation and healthcare delivery has obvious limits, the common themes of trust, routine, knowledge, respect, sensemaking, and skill offer clear parallels.

For example, in healthcare, the operating room was historically called the operating "theatre." Not only was it built in such a way to facilitate observation and learning by students and colleagues, but the action on the "stage" was also often dramatic. The theatre of the operating room requires individuals to be sensitive to non-verbal and verbal interaction to gather knowledge, assert understanding, and use specific skills that facilitate successful action.

Healthcare operates from a similar vantage point. Unlike car mechanics who assume each car of a certain year, make, and model has standard parts and similar vulnerabilities, healthcare providers must regard each patient as an individual with unique strengths and weaknesses. Each patient's care has as great a chance of failure or success if the providers are not keenly attentive to the patient's immediate needs. Each provider must be alert to the patient's unique circumstances, reveal their perspectives, and be ready to share knowledge. Each member of the team must be fully accountable for the outcome of care. While members of formal healthcare teams feel increasing accountability for the outcome of the patients, healthcare is moving to establish broader accountability for patients through the development of a culture of safety and individual engagement (see Infobox 9.1).

INFOBOX 9.1: A STORY OF CULTURE AND TEAM ORIENTATION

One of the chapter authors visited a hospital in a large city where she happened to get a ride from a shuttle driver. Since she was the only passenger, she asked the driver, "What is it like to work here?" Given he had no idea who she was she figured she'd get an honest reply.

"I am so proud to work here!" he exclaimed.

"Really?" she responded. "what makes you so proud?"

"I may be the shuttle driver, but I know I'm part of the team that takes care of patients."

"How do you know that?" she queried.

"Not only did they tell us at orientation, but they show they mean it," he said. "I get emails regularly telling me about things going on that are important for me to know. I am regularly trained on the things I might see that need fixing, and how to let people know. And when I do let people know, I hear about what they did. Everyone on the staff talks to me like an equal. I am not only told, but treated, like an important part of what happens to every patient we take care of. Moreover, I'm told I can do anything for a patient if it seems like the right thing to do. And I'm supported when I do it!"

A shared commitment and accountability is required for knowledge sharing to promote and sustain high-quality healthcare. The effective communication and knowledge sharing that takes place during theatrical improvisation can be used in a similar way in a healthcare organization. Despite this potential, effective knowledge sharing in healthcare is the exception rather than the rule. Instead, communication remains prone to error and often beholden to power. In this chapter, the concept and application of theatrical improvisation will help visualize the future of tacit knowledge management as it could be applied in healthcare organizations.

Reliability of Action while Allowing for Improvisation

The salient difference between acting from a script and improvising is that one has to be not less but far more keenly attentive to what is given by the other actors and by the situation. You cannot get away with doing anything by rote; you must be actively aware and responsive at every moment (Martha Nussman, quoted in Yanow 2001: 61).

Yanow (2001) believes that the collective philosophy of improvisation supports collaborative creation of new results in real time within the limitations of what the team has available to them. Spolin (1963) further asserts that improvisation involves being open to using everything in the environment as a resource when teams or individuals work to resolve a problem. Nussman reflects that improvisation has a culture that is not, as popularly thought, where anything goes. In fact, "There are ground rules!" (Vera and Crossan 2004: 739). Three key factors describe improvisation by its finest practitioners:

1.   Each participant is completely accountable for everything that happens during the performance. Whether actively contributing to

the interaction at a given moment, each person has the responsibility to be engaged and to contribute whatever knowledge and skill they have to inform the process.

2.   Each participant understands that working in real time is complex in that the information, situations, conditions, and demands upon the actor will change constantly.

3.   Each participant is required to know and understand the rules of participating in an art form that embraces the creation of a high standard of performance in real time.

Essential Factor No. 1 – Be accountable: Theatre is a team activity. Actors are taught at an early stage that each individual is responsible for the success of the team, even when not on stage. Part of the actor's craft is learning to watch other participants, the audience, the safety concerns on the stage (from loose equipment, flash bulbs and unsecure props), the lighting and sound, or other unanticipated conditions. They recognize they will have to respond in a natural, organic way to address issues before they affect the quality of the performance. Actors are trained to respond to heat, cold, fellow actors' mistakes, or malfunctions in scenery or wardrobe. No actor is so important that they are not responsible for the success of the production, nor is any actor so unimportant that their needs don't count.

Essential Factor No. 2 – Participate in real-time learning: Another factor in quality improvisation is the real-time nature of interaction. The spontaneity that exists in improvisation (and also in effective scripted theatre) can't be faked. It is based upon a genuine appreciation that each scene and interaction is unique and the outcome isn't necessarily prescribed. Each improvisation episode must be viewed as a new opportunity to share and apply knowledge and creativity to enhance the outcome. This attitude leads to vitality of the performance and a heightened sense of alertness throughout.

Essential Factor No. 3 – Follow the rules for engagement: Successful improvisation relies on rules of engagement that create an infrastructure for the free-form action that will follow. Those rules are not only part of the actor's training, but are the standards of measurement for members of the troupe. Instead of the number of laughs or level of applause any individual actor receives, success is determined by how the actor participates as a member of the team. The standard rules of engagement are: Agree, Be Aware, Draw on Ready-Mades, and Collaborate (Vera and Crossan 2004: 739).

Rigor alone is paralytic death, but imagination alone is insanity (Bateson 1979: 242).

Rule No. 1 – Agree: The contributions of other actors should not be denied but work to "advance the game" (Gale 2004). Young actors are taught to always respond with a "Yes, and … " , not "No" or "but." Positive statements can keep the momentum of a scene going, but few avenues exist to build upon a negative interaction. An actor attempting to respond to "no" is forced to rethink and re-direct action toward the goal. If a suggestion appears to be headed to a dead end, the actor can re-frame the action to begin in another direction.

Rule No. 2 – Be Aware: Actors should strive to remain in the moment and be mindful about what is being said. A closely synchronized mind and body allows an actor to quickly respond to what is happening in real time. When actors allow themselves to be distracted by what they are going to say or do next, important information is missed and knowledge is not available for others to draw from. Active listening is not optional; it is essential. Actors who are unable to develop that concentration can create a siloed reality that does not fully reflect the onstage activity and is devoid of contextual insights.

Rule No. 3 – Draw on Ready-Mades (or bricolage): The effective use of the total environment as part of the creative process is another key feature of effective improvisation. A typical improvisation scene will see actors using any prop available to them, such as tables, chairs, glasses, or flowers in a vase. Actors see everything – props, each other, the audience – as potential mechanisms to inform their knowledge and action. All input is respected and viewed as worthwhile.

Rule No. 4 – Collaborate: Improvisation teams must work well together, giving full support to collaboration and trust to achieve a common goal. Successful actors perceive themselves as part of a team process and prepare themselves accordingly. The preparation work focuses on the elimination of silo mentality, jealousy, trying to look better or more cleverer than the others in troupe, or trying to prevent others from looking good. They also help others succeed by giving them lines that they can work with effectively to produce a better outcome for the entire team. For collaboration to succeed, actors must also trust each other's intent, words, and actions.

In reviewing improvisation's secrets for success, its relationship to knowledge sharing that supports high-quality healthcare becomes increasingly clear.

Improvisation as a Guide for Tacit Knowledge Sharing

Could a healthcare system based on improvisational theatre's precepts of accountability, real-time learning, and rules of engagement reliably share tacit knowledge?

Applying this model to a healthcare organization could bring forth the following characteristics.

ACCOUNTABLE FOR SHARING KNOWLEDGE

In an accountable organization, every person feels like part of the team, shares what they know with others and trusts that others will do the same. A collective accountability exists throughout the organization as individuals recognize the value to sharing and receiving tacit knowledge. Everyone from housekeeping to executive staff supports this philosophy and practice.

Tacit knowledge sharing is part of the organization's culture, not relegated only to education programs and teamwork improvement initiatives. In an accountable organization, employees are evaluated on their commitment to acting in the best interests of patients and colleagues. Simply verbalizing patient safety concerns is not enough.

This commitment extends into sharing what is known, creating opportunities to disseminate what is known, and acting on what is surfaced through coaching, feedback or improvement mechanisms. This type of cultural environment is not created by a program per se, but by a fundamental shift in how organizational silos are preserved, hierarchy is reinforced, and how knowledge is shared and traded as a mechanism to preserve power.

Healthcare employees who felt pride and responsibility for the care provided to patients are more likely to share knowledge (see Infobox 9.1). This story illustrates how all employees in a healthcare organization can believe that he or she is an essential part of patients' well-being.

COMMIT TO REAL-TIME LEARNING

> *... look at learning, say, a dance troupe learning a dance. There's a choreographer who comes and the first time they do it, they just walk through one, two, three, step, turn. And they're having to actually do everything and it's not art, a long way from it. And it's painful and people get it wrong and people turn the wrong way and they collide into each other. And then gradually this, through practice, repetition, anticipation, flow, kinesthetics, all sorts of stuff, this becomes effortless. And then the dance emerges and then the art happens. And it's really simply about learning and immersing in this thing and making it part of you and you become part of it and you're working out, mostly in a tacit mode (Interview 5/146–159).*

In team training, healthcare providers are taught situational awareness, huddle, and communication skills. Leadership is encouraged to use storytelling as a strategic change management technique (Institute for Safe Medication Practices 2011). The challenge is that these skills are often taught in the context of an environment that reflects hierarchical patterns of interactions and reliance on evidence-based management (Kothari et al. 2011b). Another challenge is the need to "unlearn" old behaviors (ineffective or destructive tacit knowledge) that prevent acceptance of new behaviors. Skills that support real-time learning through tacit knowledge sharing in both improvisation and healthcare include:

Leading by example: By paying attention to knowledge sharing, stimulating curiosity, encouraging storytelling and learning through questions, leaders can establish a mechanism to engrain knowledge sharing culture. By combining tacit knowledge sharing with a passion for patient care, being authentic, being hungry for learning, and by caring and trusting (from Chapter 2), leadership can illustrate effective knowledge sharing behaviors. Establishing knowledge sharing as a core value, like improvisation, requires "dynamic visionaries whose belief is unwavering" (Kanter 2002: 79).

Speaking up: Everyone recognizes that each individual is a member of the team or organization has a responsibility share what they know. Individuals recognize that the other people are at risk if knowledge is not shared.

Listening: While healthcare organizations seek to ensure that employees and patients understand the information that is being communicated, that goal is often not achieved. In fact, breakdown in communications occur in two-thirds of interactions that result in sentinel events (Joint Commission 2012). Efforts to correct communication often result in even more communication. Effective communication is based upon listening to verify, to expound, to gain context, to explain. Improvisation requires listening to your team partner to build upon what is being offered with one's own knowledge and skills. It is knowledge that creates the opportunity for the information communicated to be most useful.

> *Listeners actively participate in thinking through and understanding the story as each listener often becomes another teller (Gale 2004: n.p.).*

Seeing with fresh eyes: Healthcare workers go to jobs each day, take care of patients, and begin the same process the next day. Not surprisingly, employees can become lulled into boredom, inattention or diminished observance. This is precisely when borderline unsafe situations can become accepted as the norm. Seeing such situations with fresh eyes helps employees recognize the subtle changes, hints, the slight variations that can make the difference between an unsafe and a safe care environment.

Considering all input: Accountability for every patient belongs to everyone who works in the hospital. Each person has a responsibility to both speak up and to consider all input, regardless of whether it comes from a physician, librarian, or shuttle bus driver (see Infobox 9.1). "Collective intelligence assumes that different agents have different forms of expertise (knowledge, information, skills)" (Heylighen 2011: 11). Each individual brings a different perspective, which helps to bring together a wide range of pertinent information and knowledge.

Creating safe rooms/space: While improvisation theaters have rehearsal rooms where actors do improvisational warm up exercises before they gather onstage, healthcare organizations lack a similar work environment to foster knowledge sharing in an organic way. While protecting patient privacy is essential, safety could be enhanced by creating dedicated areas where healthcare workers can share observations and gain from the experience of others. Simulation experiences can provide an opportunity to use external stimuli to develop and share knowledge through action and debriefing (Schmidt et al. 2013).

Participating in an "Open Source" culture: Tacit knowledge sharing is supported by an "open source" culture, one in which inputs come from everywhere and are used to create new solutions. Open source implies that change is the norm, the status is in flux and people learn to live and thrive in this dynamic environment.

FOLLOW THE RULES OF ENGAGEMENT

If healthcare is to move beyond silo mentality to true teamwork, a different type of belief system about the meaning of team will have to emerge. This shift in thinking is bound to affect how tacit knowledge is shared if all are committed to the standard rules of engagement: agree, be aware, draw on ready-mades, and collaborate (Vera and Crossan 2004: 739):

> *Structure provides a framework for improvisation (Stamatopolos 2009: 66).*

Rule No. 1 – Agree: Much of what occurs in silo and hierarchical organizations is a desire among individuals or groups to hold the correct answer. This is reflected in healthcare's reliance on specialty care, where a highly detailed understanding of a specific illness is favored over a comprehensive view of the patient as a physical, spiritual, and emotional being. In hierarchical systems, disagreement and proving the accuracy of one's insight is favored over a group evolution of a diagnosis. Nowhere is this more true than in the dynamic interactions between physicians and experienced nurses, both of whom bring extensive experience to diagnosis and treatment. What if the input of every person who has contact with the patient was considered in the direction of care planning – before, during and after a patient's hospital stay? What if there were a system that valued the observations and interactions of aides, dietary assistants, transporters, housekeepers as well as therapists, nurses and physicians? What if there was a mechanism by which those observations and what the observers thought about those observations could be recorded and shared? While some fear this could cause chaos, some errors that occur as a result of not listening to families or non-clinical observations may be avoided. Honesty and latitude are prerequisites if "everyone in a healthcare system, from housekeepers to senior physicians feel safe to raise their hand and voice a concern" (Chapter 2).

Rule No. 2 – Be Aware: A team member cannot be accountable if they function solely in the tunnel of their job and focus on making it through the day. This closed-minded approach serves to protect the individual from unrealistic demands, feeling overwhelmed, feeling unduly measured or held responsible for something over which they have no control. Consequently, the concept of being aware will only work if the organization supports the individual and ensures they will not be penalized for expanding the view of the organization in the care of patients and colleagues. Awareness is a prerequisite for improvisation and knowledge sharing in healthcare and mindfulness may be one of the added benefits in helping people to "'connect the dots' in ways not coupled before" (Chapter 4).

Rule No. 3 – Draw on Ready-Mades: Routines serve as the bases for ready-mades. Routines are not the enemy of creativity, but the framework upon which it is based. Routine is the discipline that allows the room for seeing what is distinctly different in any given situation through the application of tacit knowledge. One interviewee told a story about how tacit knowledge helped them to recognize what was abnormal. Routine enables improvisation to emerge (Batista and Cunha 2008, 27; Stamatopolos 2009). Without routine, creativity can become chaos. With routine, unique knowledge has parameters and can be implemented safely. However, routine can also curtail tacit knowledge sharing in a chaotic healthcare setting, where tacit knowledge can be disregarded in favor of evidence and scientific information. The new approach to knowledge sharing in healthcare is embracing both evidence and tacit knowledge to ensure that no bit of information, evidence, or subtle implication is overlooked.

INFOBOX 9.2: EXPERIENCE = TACIT KNOWLEDGE

In healthcare, data and evidence are valued. A friend of one of the authors told her about his grandfather, an old-time family practitioner, who was training a young physician a few years ago. According to the older man, the young physician was ordering all kinds of lab tests and exams. The older man looked at the patient, went over and smelled his breath, looked at the young physician and said, "diabetes." Tacit knowledge gained from experience can be lost when "information" is solely relied upon.

Rule No. 4 – Collaborate: Collaboration implies that each participant trusts, appreciates, needs and supports the knowledge and the experience of the others. Tacit knowledge is more likely shared within groups that feel and function like teams. Also, the sharing of tacit knowledge takes place in informal, face-to-face interactions. This means that the unit, the division, or the work team is the most likely place the sharing of tacit knowledge can occur and where the most improvisational collaboration can be

"The new approach to knowledge sharing in healthcare is embracing both evidence and tacit knowledge to ensure that no bit of information, evidence, or subtle implication is overlooked."

found. From the sharp end to the blunt end, communication based on trust enables the sharing of tacit knowledge. As pointed out in Chapter 4, this sharing across the boundaries is especially important as "less experienced people" are "working in increasingly sophisticated environments."

Improvisation on the Sharp End: Fluid Use of Knowledge can Enhance Teamwork

Studying improv could make me a better doctor (Watson 2011: 1260).

What if improvisation were routinely taught as part of training in healthcare? Watson (2011) and Gale (2004) have explored how it raises an awareness of understanding professional relationships, increases ability to adjust to the complexity and fluidity of the therapeutic environment, hones listening and communication skills and improves the ability to rapidly adjust to verbal and non-verbal cues. What would it look like and would it foster cultural expansion, teamwork and awareness?

Table 9.1   Improvisation and Knowledge Sharing Synergies

	Improvisation	Knowledge Sharing
	No script, but conventions, memory, ground rules, props, and audience provide the knowledge to act. Structured not scripted (Watson 2011).	Standards, routines, rules, policies and procedures may not always be the answer.
WHY	Vision: to collaboratively create new work in real time within the constraints of what is available.	Vision: to collaboratively arrive at the best solution for patient care in real time within the constraints of what is known.
HOW	Culture: "Agree, Be Aware, Draw on Ready-Mades, and Collaborate," trust, listening, all input used, fresh eyes, Bricolage – making use of what is available, props, audience, "open source" culture.	Culture: trust, "speak up," listening, all input considered; creating safe rooms/space, fresh eyes, Bricolage – making use of what is available, props, equipment in environment, other people, "open source" culture
WHAT	Source of knowledge: remembering, drawing on experience memory, routines, risk taking, novel combination of previous knowledge. Enhances awareness of nonverbal cues (Watson 2011).	Source of knowledge: remembering, drawing on experience, memory, routines, standards, rules, testing the knowledge by trial and error (but safely), where is information to initiate knowledge exchange stored. Enhances awareness of nonverbal cues (Watson 2011).
WHEN	Timing: in the moment; just-in-time supports rapid cognition for sophisticated decision making. (Gladwell 2005).	Timing: in the moment; just-in-time supports rapid sharing of what is known.

Improvisation on the Blunt End: Nimble Use of Knowledge Can Drive Improvement

> *To improvise, you take a group of people and enter a situation with*
> *their collective knowledge with the best information you have to date,*
> *knowing that the second you enter, change begins (Robin McCulloch,*
> *as quoted by Kanter 2002: 79).*

Healthcare leadership would benefit from using improvisation skills as well. The mental model that is developed during the course of a career in upper management most likely does not include improvisation techniques or concepts. As improvisation pioneer Virginia Spolin once noted, to direct action stifles learning from experience. Instead setting up contexts for the actors – in healthcare leadership's case – their teams and direct reports – to make appropriate choices enables new types of interactions to emerge (Gale 2004).

> *I think that need for control makes it very difficult for a lot of managers*
> *to allow their frontline staff to become creative and use knowledge that*
> *exists, but is outside of the scope of what they do (Interview 10/299–301).*

> *You can't micromanage a situation and have tacit knowledge. You got*
> *to let some things just happen (Interview 20/346–347).*

Improvisation techniques can influence knowledge sharing at both the sharp end and blunt end. Leaders need to enable improvisation to address plans for improvement to enable a culture to share knowledge in support of safe, high quality reliable patient care. Just as the head of a theater troupe must be nimble in responding to loss of space, funding and performance venue rules, hospital and blunt-blunt end leadership could apply improvisation strategies to enable their staff and the clinical teams to respond to the complexity of their environment and enable effective performance for patient care.

> *… clinical practice is inherently a team activity, but doctors, in*
> *particular, continue to be socialized primarily as autonomous agents;*
> *serious, formal rehearsing in multidisciplinary groups is the exception*
> *… unless the training and practice of all health professionals seriously*
> *comes to grip with [this] reality, medical care will continue to be shot*
> *through with unnecessary and disruptive cacophony (Pronovost and*
> *Freischlag 2010, as quoted by Davidoff 2011: 428).*

What Type of Culture is Necessary to Make this Performance Possible?

Healthcare is ripe for improvisational techniques that can encourage and support system-wide knowledge sharing.

Table 9.2   How Elements of Improvisational Theater can Optimize Knowledge Sharing for Quality Care

Six elements of strategic improvisation (Kanter 2002)	Opportunities informed by tacit knowledge use on the blunt end or blunt-blunt end
1) Themes	Importance of infusing quality and safety improvement efforts with knowledge and experience to gain buy-in and momentum for the culture change to take place in rapid time.
2) Theaters	Structure for sharing knowledge to generate ideas and opportunities for knowledge to be shared to support high quality care.
3) Actors	Leadership role; understanding how to nurture leaders as knowledge disseminators and boundary spanners to drive improvement and engagement in the knowledge sharing culture. Seeing individuals as knowledge conduits and allowing them to think on their feet and appropriately multitask to gather apply and share knowledge rapidly.
4) Audiences	Important to actively involve all to gain the best tacit knowledge to enhance improvement solutions shored up by evidence, information and data during the process of improvement, not as an afterthought or only at the onset.
5) Suspense	Comfort with ambiguity; trust in the players that they'll participate appropriately without too many rules and constraints. This ability to be nimble and rapidly process what is created can enable rapid spread and intelligent innovation rather than seeing unproven "sexy" tactics as the way to go or effective approaches grown moldy with age (Dixon-Woods et al. 2011).
6) Successive Versions	• Willingness and ability to accept rapid improvements and planned failures as tacit knowledge generating opportunities to inform action. Use of Plan-Do Study Act for knowledge generation to enable quality improvement. • After action reviews help generate new realities as goals and values can become apparent though discussion of group actions to supercharge action (Barrett 2012). • Application of revisions to use checklists infused with knowledge so they work on the frontline (Pronovost and Vohr 2010). • See unplanned failure as learning opportunity and revise process in real time to reduce failure occurrence.

For more than a decade, healthcare organizations have committed themselves to learn from mistakes, share learning about errors, and become accountable for outcomes. Movements have been launched to instill "learning culture," "safety culture," "just culture" and more (Kohn, Corrigan and Donaldson 2000; Marx 2001). In reality, each of these types of cultural elements is a subculture of a larger organizational culture. Each of these elements implies a way of approaching work and relationships within the organization.

Tacit knowledge management and tacit learning transcend various organizational subcultures. A culture that values knowledge sharing encourages an environment that facilitates the informal, face-to-face sharing of organizational norms, and informal information about contributing to safe patient care.

To create a culture where knowledge sharing is valued, organizational silos must be viewed as a limitation, not a source of prestige. Likewise, chains of command and hierarchy must be seen as restrictive rather than imperative. Open discussion among professionals about problems and concerns must be encouraged rather than viewed as a breach of secrecy (Waring and Bishop 2010).

The Future of Knowledge Management in Healthcare: Yes and ... ?

Watson (2011) highlights how improvisation helped inner-city and immigrant children cope with their often difficult surroundings. Can healthcare use the creative but essential principles of improvisation to routinely yield tacit knowledge that can drive quality improvement? To rehearse for this new production, novel ways of assessing and measuring the effectiveness of knowledge sharing – based on agreement, awareness, ready-mades and collaboration – should be tested and practiced. Research could enable the results of this work to be spread reliably and improvised at the organizational, unit and team level.

Many questions remain unanswered about how healthcare organizations would respond to a cultural shift of this magnitude. To help prepare themselves for this process, healthcare organizations might explore these questions:

Can free spaces for hospital employees be designed that encourage the exchange of knowledge about patients, their care needs and the practice supporting that care?

Yes, and …

Can healthcare support and sustain an "open source" culture that values the input of anyone who comes into contact with the patient, or who designs services to help those who do and builds on shared knowledge?

Yes, and …

Can workflow be designed to enable interaction that encourages knowledge sharing without organization siloes?

Yes, and …

Can leaders value knowledge sharing beyond the confines of information technology and build it into the relationships of all employees?

Yes, and …

Can metrics be developed that value impact of knowledge exchange over numbers that illustrate activity that lacks connection with patient outcomes?

Yes and …

Can healthcare's blunt end become engaged in knowledge exchange that permits tacit knowledge sharing and its effect on patient care?

Yes and …

Can patients be safer and have a better experience because tacit knowledge has been reliably shared?

Yes.

Improvisation teams pay attention to each other and work to engage and provide a quality outcome to their audience. The audience is not only the receiver of the performance, but they play a role in the performance. Mindfulness, trust, respect, and willingness of all to participate, contribute, and share knowledge leads to effective innovation, improvisation and improvement. In the same way, healthcare organizations, their diverse staff and "audience" should learn new ways of being engaged, encouraged and enabled to share what they know. The collective performance be stronger and produce greater benefits for all.

　　All the world's a stage.

KEY TAKE-AWAYS

- Improvisation provides lessons to apply to efforts to improve both team and organizational-level knowledge sharing.
- An orientation to improvisation relies on transparent sharing of what one knows and an openness to gather knowledge from others.
- Improvisational techniques build on teamwork skills currently being emphasized in healthcare to enhance care delivery

---

Suggested Reading

Barrett, F.J. 2012. *Say Yes to the Mess: Surprising Leadership Lessons from Jazz.* Boston, MA: Harvard Business School Press.

Davidoff, F. 2011. "Music Lessons: What Musicians Can Teach Doctors (and Other Health Professionals)." *Annals of Internal Medicine,* 154(6), 426.

Gladwell, M. 2005. *Blink.* New York, NY: Little Brown.

References

Aarts, J., Doorewaard, H. and Berg, M. 2004. "Understanding Implementation: The Case of a Computerized Physician Order Entry System in a Large Dutch University Medical Center." *Journal of the American Medical Informatics Association*, 11(3), 207–16.

Abidi, S.S.R. 2007. "Healthcare Knowledge Sharing: Purpose, Practices, and Prospects." In *Healthcare Knowledge Management*, edited by R. Bali and A.N. Dwivedi, 67–86. New York: Springer.

Ackoff, R.L. 1989. "From Data to Wisdom, Presidential Address to ISGSR, June 1988." *Journal of Applied Systems Analysis*, 16, 3–9.

Acting Locally: Working in Clinical Microsystems [CD-ROM]. 2005. Oakbrook Terrace, IL: Joint Commission Resources.

Agency for Healthcare Research and Quality (AHRQ). "Patient Safety Network Glossary." Available at: http://psnet.ahrq.gov/glossary.aspx.

Agency for Healthcare Research and Quality (AHRQ). "Patient Safety Organization." Available at: http://www.pso.ahrq.gov.

Agency for Healthcare Research and Quality (AHRQ). 2012. "Safety Culture Primer." *AHRQ Patient Safety Network*, October. Available at: http://psnet.ahrq.gov/primer.aspx?primerID=5

Aitken, E.M., Powelson, S.E., Reaume, R.D. and Ghali, W.A. 2011. "Involving Clinical Librarians at the Point of Care: Results of a Controlled Intervention." *Academic Medicine*, 86(12), 1508–12.

Anderson, J.A. and Willson, P. 2009. "Knowledge Management: Organizing Nursing Care Knowledge." *Critical Care Nursing Quarterly*, 32(1), 1–9.

Antweiler, C. 1998. "Local Knowledge and Local Knowing. An Anthropological Analysis of Contested "Cultural Products' in the Context of Development." *Anthropos*, 93(4/6), 469–94.

Argyris, C. 1999. "Tacit Knowledge and Management." In *Tacit Knowledge in Professional Practice*, edited by R.J. Sternberg and J.A. Horvath. Mahwah, NJ: Lawrence Erlbaum Associates, 123–40.

Aune, B. 1970. *Rationalism, Empiricism, and Pragmatism*. New York, NY: Van Nostrand.

Balik, B. 2011. "Leaders' Role in Patient Experience." *Healthcare Executive*, 26(4), 76–7.

Balik, B. and Gilbert, J. 2010. *The Heart of Leadership: Inspiration and Practical Guidance for Transforming Your Healthcare Organization*. Chicago, IL: American Hospital Association Press.

Balik, B., Conway, J., Zipperer, L. and Watson, J. 2011. *Achieving an Exceptional Patient and Family Experience of Inpatient Hospital Care*. Cambridge, MA: Institute for Healthcare Improvement.

Bandy, M., Katherine, R., Frumento, S. and Langman, M.M. 2009. *Role of Health Sciences Librarians in Patient Safety Position Statement*. Chicago, IL: Medical Libraries Association.

Banja, J. 2010. "The Normalization of Deviance in Healthcare Delivery." *Business Horizons*, 53(2), 139–48.

Banks, D.E., Shi, R., Timm, D.F., Christopher, K.A., Duggar, D.C., Comegys, M. and McLarty, J. 2007. "Decreased Hospital Length of Stay Associated with Presentation of Cases at Morning Report with Librarian Support." *Journal of the Medical Library Association*, 95(4), 381–7.

Barrett, F.J. 2012. *Say Yes to the Mess: Surprising Leadership Lessons from Jazz*. Boston, MA: Harvard Business School Press.

Bartholomew, D. 2005. *Sharing Knowledge*. Available at: http://www.usable buildings.co.uk/Pages/Unprotected/SpreadingTheWord/SharingKnowledge. pdf [accessed March 12, 2012].

Batalden, P. and Davidoff, F., (eds). 2011. "Knowledge for Improvement." *BMJ Quality and Safety*, 20(1), 1–105.

Batista, M.G. and Cunha, M.P. 2008. "Improvisation in Tightly Controlled Work Environments: The Case of Medical Practice." Universidade Nova de Lisboa, Faculdade de Economia in its series FEUNL Working Paper Series; wp537. Available at: http://fesrvsd.fe.unl.pt/WPFEUNL/WP2008/wp537.pdf [accessed April 23, 2013].

Bateson, G. 1979. *Mind and Nature: A Necessary Unity*. New York, NY: Dutton.

Beales, D. 2010. "Medical Librarianship as a Risk Management Strategy: Case Files and Discussion." *Journal of Hospital Librarianship*, 10(4), 329–40.

Becher, E.C. and Chassin, M.R. 2001. "Improving the Quality of Health Care: Who Will Lead?" *Health Affairs*, 20(5), 164–79.

Beesley, L.G.A. and Cooper, C. 2008. "Defining Knowledge Management (KM) Activities: Towards Consensus." *Journal of Knowledge Management*, 12(3), 48–62.

Bellinger, G., Castro, D. and Mills, A. 2004. "Data, Information, Knowledge, and Wisdom." Available at: http://www.systems-thinking.org/dikw/dikw. htm [accessed October 1, 2011].

Benham-Hutchins, M.M. and Effken, J.A. 2010. "Multi-Professional Patterns and Methods of Communication During Patient Handoffs." *International Journal of Medical Informatics*, 79(4), 252–67.

Benner, P. 1984. *From Novice to Expert: Excellence and Power in Clinical Nursing Practice*. Menlo Park, CA: Addison-Wesley.

Benner, P., Hughes, R.G. and Sutphen, M. 2008. "Clinical Reasoning, Decision Making, and Action: Thinking Critically and Clinically." In *Patient Safety and Quality: An Evidence-Based Handbook for Nurses*, edited by R.G. Hughes, Chapter 6. Rockville, MD: Agency for Healthcare Research and Quality.

Berger, P.L. and Luckman, T. 1966. *The Social Construction of Reality: A Treatise in the Sociology of Knowledge*. New York, NY: Penguin Books.

Berwick, D. 1999. "2020 Visions. Knowledge Always on Call." *Modern Healthcare*. September 27, 29(39), suppl 2–4.

Berwick, D.M. 2002. *Escape Fire: Lessons for the Future of Health Care*. New York, NY: The Commonwealth Fund.

Bleakley, A. 2006. "Broadening Conceptions of Learning in Medical Education: The Message from Teamworking." *Medical Education*, 40(2), 150–57.

Bleich, M.R., Cleary, B.L., Davis, K., Hatcher, B.J., Hewlett, P.O. and Hill, K.S. 2009. "Mitigating Knowledge Loss: A Strategic Imperative for Nurse Leaders." *Journal of Nursing Administration*, 39(4), 160–64.

Bohmer, R.M.J. 2009. *Designing Care*. Boston, MA: Harvard Business Press.

Bohmner, R.M.J. 2009. "Care Processes and Knowledge Types." In *Designing Care*, edited by R.M.J. Bohmner. Boston, MA: Harvard Business Press.

Boisnier, A. and Chatman, J.A. 2002. "The Role of Subcultures in Agile Organizations." Available at: http://faculty.haas.berkeley.edu/chatman/papers/20_CulturesSubculturesDynamic.pdf.

Bontis, N. 1998. "Intellectual Capital: An Exploratory Study that Develops Measures and Models." *Management Decision*, 36(2), 63–76.

Braithwaite, J., Runciman, W.B. and Merry, A.F. 2007. "Towards Safer, Better Healthcare: Harnessing the Natural Properties of Complex Sociotechnical Systems." *Quality and Safety in Healthcare*, 18(1), 37–41.

Braithwaite, J., Westbrook, J.I., Ranmuthugala, G., Cuningham, F., Plumb, J., Wiley, J., Ball, D., Huckson, S., Hughes, C., Johnston, B., Callen, J., Creswick, N., Geogiou, A., Betbeder-Matibet, L. and Debono, D. 2009. "The Development, Design, Testing, Refinement, Simulation and Application of an Evaluation Framework for Communities of Practice and Social-Professional Networks." *BMC Health Services Research*, 9, 162.

Call, D. 2005. "Knowledge Management, Not Rocket Science." *Journal of Knowledge Management*, 9(2), 19–30.

Campbell, E.M., Guappone, K.P., Sitting, D.F., Dykstra, R.H. and Ash, J.S. 2008. "Computerized Provider Order Entry Adoption: Implications for Clinical Workflow." *Journal of General Internal Medicine*, 24(1), 21–6.

Capozzi, M.M., Lowell, S.M. and Silverman, L. 2003. "A Closing View: Knowledge Management Comes to Philanthropy." *McKinsey Quarterly*, 3, 89–91.

Carr, S. 2009. *Disclosure and Apology: What's Missing? Advancing Programs that Support Clinicians.* Chestnut Hill, MA: Medically Induced Trauma Support Services.

Carthey, J., Walker, S., Deelchand, V., Vincent, C. and Griffiths, W.H. 2011. "Breaking the Rules: Understanding Non-Compliance with Policies and Guidelines." *British Medical Journal*, 343, d5283.

Centers for Medicare and Medicaid Services (CMS) and Center for Medicare and Medicaid Innovation. 2012. *Report to Congress (December 2012).* Available at: http://innovation.cms.gov/Files/reports/RTC-12-2012.pdf.

Chan, P.S., Jain, R., Nallmothu, B.K., Berg, R.A. and Sasson, C. 2010. "Rapid Response Teams: A Systematic Review and Meta-Analysis." *Archives of Internal Medicine*, 170(1), 18–26.

Chang, C.W., Huang, H.C., Chiang, C.Y., Hsu, C.P. and Chang, C.C. 2012. "Social Capital and Knowledge Sharing: Effects on Patient Safety." *Journal of Advanced Nursing*, 68(8), 1793–803.

Choo, C.W. 1996. "The Knowing Organization: How Organizations Use Information to Construct Meaning, Create Knowledge and Make Decisions." *International Journal of Information Management*, 16(5), 329–40.

Choo, C.W. 2002. *Information Management for the Intelligent Organization: The Art of Scanning the Environment.* 3rd Edition. Medford, NJ: Information Today.

Chou, L.F., Wang, A.C., Wang, T.Y., Huang, M.P. and Cheng, B.S. 2008. "Shared Work Values and Team Member Effectiveness: The Mediation of Trustfulness and Trustworthiness." *Human Relations*, 61(12), 171342.

Chuang, E., Jason, K. and Morgan, J.C. 2011. "Implementing Complex Innovations: Factors Influencing Middle Manager Support." *Health Care Manage Review*, 36(4), 36979.

Clarke, C.L. and Wilcoxson, J. 2002. "Seeing Need and Developing Dare: Exploring Knowledge for and from Practice." *International Journal of Nursing Studies*, 39(4), 398.

Classen, D.C., Resar, R., Griffin, F., Federico, F. and Frankel, T. 2011. "Global Trigger Tool' Shows that Adverse Events in Hospitals May Be Ten Times Greater than Previously Measured." *Health Affairs*, 30(4), 5819.

Cohen, M.D., Hilligoss, B. and Kajdacsy-Balla Amaral, A.C. 2012. "A Handoff is Not a Telegram: An Understanding of the Patient is Co-constructed." *Critical Care*, 16(1), 303.

Cohen, M.R. (ed.) 2006. *Medication Errors*. 2nd Edition. Washington, DC: American Pharmaceutical Association.

Coiera, E. 2000. "When Conversation is Better than Computation." *Journal of the American Medical Informatics Association*, 7(3), 277–86.

Collins, J. 2001. *Good to Great: Why Some Companies Make the Leap and Others Don't*. New York, NY: Harper Business.

Collison, C. and Parcell, G. 2004. *Learning to Fly: Practical Knowledge Management from Leading and Learning Organizations*. Chichester: Capstone.

Committee on Quality of Health Care in America, Institute of Medicine. 2001. *Crossing the Quality Chasm: A New Health System for the 21st Century*. Washington, DC: National Academies Press.

Conway, J. 2008. "Could It Happen Here? Learning from Other Organizations' Safety Errors." *Healthcare Executive*, 23(6), 64–7.

Cox, L.M. and Logio, L.S. 2011. "Patient Safety Stories: A Project Utilizing Narratives in Resident Training." *Academic Medicine*, 86(11), 1473–8.

Cronin, G. and Andrews, S. 2009. "After Action Reviews: A New Model for Learning." *Emergency Nurse*, 17(3), 32–5.

Croskerry, P. 2009. "Context is Everything or How Could I Have Been that Stupid?" *Healthcare Quarterly*, 12(Spec No), e171–6.

Cross, R.L., Singer, J., Sally Colella, S., Thomas, R.J. and Silverstone, Y. 2010. *The Organizational Network Fieldbook: Best Practices, Techniques and Exercises to Drive Organizational Innovation and Performance*. San Francisco, CA: Jossey-Bass.

Cunningham, F.C., Ranmuthugala, G., Plumb, J., Georgiou, A., Westbrook, J.I. and Braithwaite, J. 2012. "Health Professional Networks as a Vector for Improving Healthcare Quality and Safety: A Systematic Review." *British Medical Journal of Quality and Safety*, 21, 239–49.

Currie, G., Waring, J. and Finn, R. 2008. "The Limits of Knowledge Management for UK Public Services Modernization: The Case of Patient Safety and Service Quality." *Public Administration*, 86(2), 363–85.

Cusack, C.M. 2008. "Electronic Health Records and Electronic Prescribing: Promise and Pitfalls." *Obstetrics and Gynecology Clinics of North America*, 35(1), 63–79.

Davenport, T.H. 2005. *Thinking for a Living*. Boston, MA: Harvard Business School Press.

Davenport, T.H. and Prusak, L. 1998. *Working Knowledge: How Organizations Manage What They Know*. Boston, MA: Harvard Business School Press.

Davenport, T.H., De Long, D.W. and Beers, M.C. 1998. "Successful Knowledge Management Projects." *Sloan Management Review*, 39(2), 43–57.

Davenport, T.H., Prusak, L. and Strong, B. 2008. "Putting Ideas to Work." *Sloan Management Review*. Available at: http://ai.arizona.edu/mis480/other_materials/4_Putting-Ideas-to-Work.pdf.

Davidoff, F. 2011. "Music Lessons: What Musicians Can Teach Doctors (and Other Health Professionals)." *Annals of Internal Medicine*, 154(6), 426.

Davidoff, F. and Florance, V. 2000. "The Informationist: A New Health Profession?" *Annals of Internal Medicine*, 132(12), 996–8.

Davidoff, F. and Miglus, J. 2011. "Delivering Clinical Evidence Where it's Needed: Building an Information System Worthy of the Profession." *Journal of the American Medical Association*, 305(18), 1906–7.

Davies, S., Donaher, C., Hatfield, J. and Zeitz, J. 2011. "Making the Semantic Web Usable: Interface Principles to Empower the Lay Person." *Journal of Digital Information*, 12(1).

Davison, G., and Blackman, D. 2005. "The Role of Mental Models in the Development of Knowledge Management Systems." *International Journal of Organisational Behaviour*, 10(6), 757–69.

De Brun, C. 2005. "ABC's of Knowledge Management." Available at: http://thiqaruni.org/medcine/13.pdf.

De la Mothe, J. and Foray, D. 2001. *Knowledge Management in the Innovation Process*. Portland, OR: Book News.

De Long, D.W. 2004. *Lost Knowledge: Confronting the Threat of an Aging Workforce*. New York, NY: Oxford.

Delen, D. and Al-Hawamdeh, S. 2009. "A Holistic Framework for Knowledge Discovery and Management." *Communications of the ACM*, 52(6), 141–5.

Deming, W.E. 2000. *The New Economics for Industry, Government, Education*. 2nd edition. Boston, MA: MIT Press.

Denning, S. 2004. "Telling Tales." *Harvard Business Review*, 82(5), 122–9, 152.

Denning, S. 2006. "Effective Storytelling: Strategic Business Narrative Techniques." *Strategy and Leadership*, 34(1), 42–8.

Dilling, J.A., Swensen, S.J., Hoover, M.R., Dankbar, G.C., Donahoe-Anshus, A.L., Murad, M.H, and Mueller, J.T. 2013. "Accelerating the Use of Best Practices: The Mayo Clinic Model of Diffusion." *Joint Commission Journal on Quality and Patient Safety*, 39(4), 167–76.

Dixon, N.M. 2000. *Common Knowledge: How Companies Thrive by Sharing What They Know*. Boston, MA: Harvard Business School Press.

Dixon-Woods, M., Amalberti, R., Goodman, S., Bergman, B. and Glasziou, P. 2011. "Problems and Promises of Innovation: Why Healthcare Needs to Rethink its Love/Hate Relationship with the New." *BMJ Quality and Safety*, 20(Suppl 1), i47–51.

Dixon-Woods, M., Bosk, C.L., Aveling, E.L., Goeschel, C.A. and Pronovost, P.J. 2011. "Explaining Michigan: Developing an Ex Post Theory of a Quality Improvement Program." *Milbank Quarterly*, 89(2), 167–205.

Dominguez, C., Uhlig, P., Brown, J., Gurevich, O., Shumar, W., Stahl, G., Zemel, A. and Zipperer, L. 2005. "Studying and Supporting Collaborative Care

Processes." *Proceedings of the Human Factors and Ergonomics Society Annual Meeting*, 49, 1074–8.

Dominguez, C., Uhlig, P., Brown, J., Gurevich, O., Shumar, W., Stahl, G., Zemel, A., Zipperer, L. 2005. Studying and Supporting Collaborative Care Processes. Presentation at the Human Factors and Ergonomic Society Conference, September 30, 2005.

Donaldson, L. 2000. *An Organisation with a Memory: Report of an Expert Group on Learning from Adverse Events in the NHS Chaired by the Chief Medical Officer*. London: The Stationery Office.

Drucker, P.F. 1969. *The Age of Discontinuity: Guidelines to Our Changing Society*. New York, NY: Harper and Row.

Edgman-Levitan, S. 2004. "Involving the Patient in Safety Efforts." In *Achieving Safe and Reliable Healthcare – Strategies and Solutions*, by M. Leonard, A. Frankel and T. Simmonds. Chicago, IL: Health Administration Press, 81–92.

Edmondson, A. 1999. "Psychological Safety and Learning Behavior in Work Teams." *Administrative Science Quarterly*, 44(4), 350–83.

Edmondson, A.C. 2003. "Speaking Up in the Operating Room: How Team Leaders Promote Learning in Interdisciplinary Action Teams." *Journal of Management Studies*, 40(6), 1419–52.

Edmondson, A.C. 2011. "Strategies for Learning from Failure." *Harvard Business Review*, 89(4), 48–55.

Englander, R., Cameron, T., Ballard, A.J., Dodge, J., Bull, J. and Aschenbrener, C.A. 2013. "Toward a Common Taxonomy of Competency Domains for the Health Professions and Competencies for Physicians." *Academic Medicine*, 88(8), August 2013, 1088–94.

Ellis, K. 2001. "Dare to Share." *Training*. Available at: http://www.trainingmag.com/article/dare-share-1.

Epstein, R.M. 1999. "Mindful Practice." *Journal of the American Medical Association*, 282(9), 833–9.

Evans, A. and Refrow-Rutala, D. 2010. "Medico-Legal Education: A Pilot Curriculum to Fill the Identified Knowledge Gap." *Journal of Graduate Medical Education*, 2(4), 595–9.

Fahey, L. and Prusak, L. 1998. "The Eleven Deadliest Sins of Knowledge Management." *California Management Review*, 40(3), 265–76.

Fein, I.A. and Corrato, R.R. 2008. "Clinical Practice Guidelines: Culture Eats Strategy for Breakfast, Lunch, and Dinner." *Critical Care Medicine*, 36(4), 1360–61.

Frame, J., Watson, J. and Thomson, K. 2008. "Deploying a Culture Change Programme Management Approach in Support of Information and

Communication Technology Developments in Greater Glasgow NHS Board." *Health Informatics Journal*, 14(2), 125–39.

Francis, R. 2013. *Report of the Mid Staffordshire NHS Foundation Trust: Public Inquiry*. London: The Stationary Office.

Frankel, A., Graydon-Baker, E., Neppl, C., Simmonds, T., Gustafson, M., Gandhi, T.K. 2003. "Patient Safety Leadership WalkRounds." *Joint Commission Journal on Quality Improvement*, 29(1), 16–26.

Frankel, A., Grillo, S.P., Baker, E.G., Huber, C.N., Abookire, S., Grenham, M., Console, P., O'Quinn, M., Thibault, G. and Gandhi, T.K. 2005. "Patient Safety Leadership WalkRounds at Partners Healthcare: Learning from Implementation." *Joint Commission Journal on Quality and Patient Safety*, 31(8), 423–37.

Frankel, A.S. Leonard, M.W. and Denham, C.R. 2006. "Fair and Just Culture, Team Behavior and Leadership Engagement." *Health Services Research*, 41(4 pt. 2), 1690–708.

Fritz, R. 2011. "The Learning Organization Revisited." *The Systems Thinker*, 22(5), 8 – 10.

Frush, K., Leonard, M., Frankel, A. 2013. "Effective Teamwork and Communication." In *The Essential Guide for Patient Safety Officers*, edited by M. Leonard, A. Frankel, F. Federico, K. Frush, and C. Haraden. Second edition. Oakbrook Terrace, IL: Joint Commission Resources, Institute for Healthcare Improvement.

Furnham, A.F. 1986. "Medical Students' Beliefs about Nine Different Specialties." *British Medical Journal (Clinical Research Edition)*, 293(6562), 1607–10.

Gale, J. 2004. "Experiencing Relational Thinking: Lessons from Improvisational Theater." *Context*, 75, 10–12.

Garcia, J.L., and Wells, K.K. 2009. "Knowledge-based Information to Improve the Quality of Patient Care." *Journal of Healthcare Quality*, 31(1), 30–35.

Garfield, S. 2007. *Identifying Objectives*. Available at: http://sites.google.com/site/stangarfield/IK_May07_Masterclass_Identifyingobje.pdf.

Garvin, D.A. 1993. "Building a Learning Organization." *Harvard Business Review*, 71(4), 78–91.

Garvin, D.A., Edmondson, A.C. and Gino, F. 2008. "Is Yours a Learning Organization?" *Harvard Business Review*, 86(3), 109–16.

Gherardi, S. 2006. *Organizational Knowledge: The Texture of Workplace Learning*. Oxford: Blackwell Publishing.

Gladwell, M. 2005. *Blink*. New York, NY: Little Brown.

Glassman, P. 2013. "Clinical Pharmacist's Role in Preventing Adverse Drug Events: Brief Update Review." In *Making Health Care Safer II: An Updated Critical Analysis of the Evidence for Patient Safety Practices*, edited by P.G.

Shekelle, R.M. Wachter, and P.J. Pronovost. Rockville, MD: Agency for Healthcare Research and Quality; March 2013. AHRQ Publication No. 13-E001-EF. Available at: http://www.ahrq.gov/research/findings/evidence-based-reports/patientsftyupdate/ptsafetyIIchap4.pdf.

Gluck, J.C. 2004. "The Contribution of Hospital Library Services to Continuing Medical Education." *Journal of Continuing Education in the Health Professions*, 24(2), 119–23.

Goldman, G.M. 1990. "The Tacit Dimension of Clinical Judgment." *Yale Journal of Biology and Medicine*, 63(1), 47–61.

Gollop, R., Whitby, E., Buchanan, D. and Ketley, D. 2004. "Influencing Sceptical Staff to Become Supporters of Service Improvement: A Qualitative Study of Doctors' and Managers' Views." *Quality and Safety in Health Care*, 13(2), 108–14.

Gowen, C.R., Henagan, S.C. and McFadden, K.L. 2009. "Knowledge Management as a Mediator for the Efficacy of Transformational Leadership and Quality Management Initiatives in U.S. Health Care." *Health Care Management Review*, 34(2), 129–40.

Graham, I.D., Logan, J., Harrison, M.B., Straus, S.S., Tetroe, J., Caswell, W. and Robinson, N. 2006. "Lost in Knowledge Translation: Time for a Map?" *Journal of Continuing Education in the Health Professions*, 26(1), 13–24.

Gray, M. 2011. *Report for the Mid Staffordshire Inquiry on the Benefits of Knowledge Management*, 19 October. Available at: http://www.midstaffspublicinquiry.com/sites/default/files/uploads/Sir_Muir_Gray_paper.pdf

Green, P.L. and Plsek, P.E. 2002. "Coaching and Leadership for the Diffusion of Innovation in Health Care: A Different Type of Multi-Organization Improvement Collaborative." *Joint Commission Journal on Quality Improvement*, 28(2), 55–71.

Greenhalgh, J., Flynn, R., Long, A. F. and Tyson, S. 2008. "Tacit and Encoded Knowledge in the Use of Standardized Outcome Measures in Multidisciplinary Team Decision Making: A Case Study of In-patient Neurorehabilitation." *Social Science and Medicine*, 67(1), 183–94.

Grefsheim, S.F., Whitmore, S.C., Rapp, B.A., Rankin, J.A., Robison, R.R. and Canto, C.C. 2010. "The Informationist: Building Evidence for an Emerging Health Profession." *Journal of the Medical Library Association*, 98(2), 147–56.

Griffith, J.R., Fear, K.M., Lammers, E., Banaszak-Holl, J., Lemak, C.H. and Zheng, K. 2013 "A Positive Deviance Perspective on Hospital Knowledge Management: Analysis of Baldrige Award Recipients 2002–2008." *Journal of Healthcare Management*, 58(3), May–June, 187–203, discussion, 203–4.

Griffiths, D., and Moon, B. 2001. "The State of Knowledge Management." *KM World*, 20(10), 16–17, 28.

Gu, Q. and Gu, Y. 2011. "A Factorial Validation of Knowledge-Sharing Motivation Construct." *Journal of Service Science and Management*, 4(1), 59–65.

Gupta, V. and Lehal, G.S. 2009. "A Survey of Text Mining Techniques and Applications." *Journal of Emerging Technologies in Web Intelligence*, 1(1), 60–76.

Haig, K.M., Sutton, S. and Whittington, J. 2006. "SBAR: A Shared Mental Model for Improving Communication between Clinicians." *Joint Commission Journal of Quality and Patient Safety*, 32(3), 167–75.

Harvey, S. and Kou, C.Y. 2011. "Collective Engagement: Exploring Creative Processes in Groups." *Academy of Management Annual Meeting Proceedings 2011*, 1–6.

Hatcher, B.J., Bleich, M.R., Connolly, C., Davis, K., Hewlett, P.O. and Hill, K.S. 2006. *Wisdom at Work: The Importance of the Older and Experienced Nurse in the Workplace.* Available at: http://www.rwjf.org/files/publications/other/wisdomatwork.pdf [accessed December 18, 2011].

Haynes, A.B., Weiser, T.G., Berry, W.R., Lipsitz, S.R., Breizat, A.H., Dellinger, E.P., Herbosa, T., Joseph, S., Kibatala, P.L., Lapitan, M.C., Merry, A.F., Moorthy, K., Reznick, R.K., Taylor, B., Gawande, A.A. and Safe Surgery Saves Lives Study Group. 2009. "A Surgical Safety Checklist to Reduce Morbidity and Mortality in a Global Population." *New England Journal of Medicine*, 360(5), 491–9.

Hazlett, S.A., McAdam, R. and Beggs, V. 2008. "An Exploratory Study of Knowledge Flows: A Case Study of Public Sector Procurement." *Total Quality Management*, 19(1/2), 57–66.

HERO (Health & Environmental Research Online) Glossary. Available at: http://hero.epa.gov/index.cfm

Heylighen, F. 2013. "Self-Organization in Communicating Groups: The Emergence of Coordination, Shared References and Collective Intelligence." In, *Complexity Perspectives on Language, Communication, and Society*, edited by A. Massip-Bonet and A. Bastardas-Boada. New York: Springer, 117–50.

Hicks, R.C., Dattero, R. and Galup, S.D. 2006. "The Five-Tier Knowledge Management Hierarchy." *Journal of Knowledge Management*, 10(1), 19–31.

Hoss, R. and Schlussel, A. 2009. "How Do You Measure the Knowledge Management (KM) Maturity of Your Organization? Metrics that Assess an Organization's KM State." Available at: http://www.digitalgovernment.com/media/Downloads/asset_upload_file66_2654.pdf.

Huang, D.T., Clermont, G., Sexton, J.B., Karlo, C.A., Miller, R.G., Weissfeld, L.A., Rowan, K.M. and Angus, D.C. 2007. «Perceptions of Safety Culture Vary Across the Intensive Care Units of a Single Institution.» *Critical Care Medicine*, 35(1), 165–76.

Hurley, T.A. and Green, C.W. 2005. "Knowledge Management and the Nonprofit Industry: A Within and Between Approach." *Journal of Knowledge Management Practice*. Available at: http://www.tlainc.com/articl79.htm.

Hylton, A. 2002. "Measuring and Assessing Knowledge-Value and the Pivotal Role of the Knowledge Audit." Available at: http://www.providersedge. com/docs/km_articles/Measuring_%26_Assessing_K-Value_%26_Pivotal_ Role_of_K-Audit.pdf.

Institute for Healthcare Improvement. 2004. *Safety Briefings*. Available at: http://www.ihi.org/knowledge/Pages/Tools/SafetyBriefings.aspx [accessed December 31, 2011].

Institute for Safe Medication Practices (ISMP). 2011. "Telling True Stories is an ISMP Hallmark. Here's Why You Should Tell Stories, Too." *ISMP Medication Safety Alert, Acute Care Edition*. Available at: http://www.ismp.org/ Newsletters/acutecare/showarticle.asp?ID=4 [accessed September 8, 2011].

Institute for Safe Medication Practices. 2008. "Using External Errors to Signal a Clear and Present Danger." *ISMP Medication Safety Alert! Acute Care Edition*. Available at: http://www.ismp.org/Newsletters/acutecare/articles/20081106. asp.

Institute of Medicine, Committee on the Work Environment for Nurses and Patient Safety, Board on Health Care Services. 2004. *Keeping Patients Safe: Transforming the Work Environment of Nurses*. Washington, DC: National Academies Press.

Joint Commission. 2012. *Sentinel Event Statistics: Q1 2012*. Available at: http:// www.jointcommission.org/assets/1/18/Root_Causes_by_Event_Type_2004- 1Q2012.pdf

Joint Commission. 2012. *Speak Up Campaign*. Available at: http://www. jointcommission.org/speakup.aspx.

Kaboli, P.J., Hoth, A.B., McClimon, B.J. and Schnipper, J.L. 2006. "Clinical Pharmacists and Inpatient Medical Care: A Systematic Review." *Archives of Internal Medicine*, 166(9), 955–64.

Kanan, G. and Albur, W.G. 2004. "Intellectual Capital: Measurement Effectiveness." *Journal of Intellectual Capital*, 5(3), 389–413.

Kanter, R.M. 2002. "Strategy as Improvisational Theater." *Sloan Management Review*, 43(2), 76–81.

Kaplan, G.S. 2013. "Foreword." In *The Essential Guide for Patient Safety Officers*, edited by M. Leonard, A. Frankel, F. Federico, K. Frush and C. Haraden. Second edition. Oakbrook Terrace, IL: Joint Commission Resources, Institute for Healthcare Improvement.

Kelly, T. 2010. "A Positive Approach to Change: The Role of Appreciative Inquiry in Library and Information Organizations." *Australian Academic and Research Libraries*, 41(3), 163–77.

Klinger, D.W., and Hahn, B.B. 2003. *Handbook of Team CTA* (Manual developed under prime contract F41624-97-C-6025 from the Human Systems Center, Brooks AFB, TX). Fairborn, OH: Klein Associates Inc.

Kohn, L., Corrigan, J. and Donaldson, M. (eds). 2000. *To Err Is Human: Building a Safer Health System*. Washington, DC: National Academies Press.

Koppel, R., Metlay, J.P., Cohen, A., Abaluck, B., Localio, A.R., Kimmel, S.E. and Strom, B.L. 2005. "Role of Computerized Physician Order Entry Systems in Facilitating Medication Errors." *Journal of the American Medical Association*, 293(10), 1197–203.

Kothari, A.R., Bickford, J.J., Edwards, N., Dobbins, M.J. and Meyer, M. 2011a. "Uncovering Tacit Knowledge: A Pilot Study to Broaden the Concept of Knowledge in Knowledge Translation." *BMC Health Services Research*, 11(1), 198.

Kothari, A.R., Hovanec, N., Hastie, R. and Sibbald, S. 2011b. "Lessons from the Business Sector for Successful Knowledge Management in Health Care: A Systematic Review." *BMC Health Services Research*, 11(1), 173.

Kotter, J.P. 1995. "Leading Change: Why Transformation Efforts Fail." *Harvard Business Review*, 73(2), 59–67.

Kouzes, J. and Posner, B. 2007. *The Leadership Challenge*. San Francisco, CA: Jossey-Bass.

Krause, T.R. 2005. *Leading with Safety*. Hoboken, NJ: Wiley-Interscience.

Lane, J.P. and Flagg, J.L. 2010. "Translating Three States of Knowledge: Discovery, Invention, and Innovation." *Implementation Science*, 5(1), 9.

Lane, J.P. and Rodgers, J.D. 2011. "Engaging National Organizations for Knowledge Translation: Comparative Case Studies in Knowledge Value Mapping." *Implementation Science*, 6(1), 106.

Langley, G.J., Moen, R., Nolan, K.M., Nolan, T.W., Norman, C.L. and Provost, L.P. 2009. *The Improvement Guide: A Practical Approach to Enhancing Organizational Performance*. 2nd edition. San Francisco, CA: Jossey-Bass.

Leach, D.C. and Batalden, P.B. 2007 "Preparing the Personal Physician for Practice (P(4)): Redesigning Family Medicine Residencies – New Wine, New Wineskins, Learning, Unlearning, and a Journey to Authenticity." *Journal of the American Board of Family Medicine*, July–August, 20(4), 342–7; discussion 329–31.

Leape, L.L. 1994. "Error in Medicine." *Journal of the American Medical Association*, 272, 1851–7.

Leape, L.L. and Berwick, D.M. 2005. "Five Years After 'To Err is Human': What Have We Learned?" *Journal of the American Medical Association*, 293(19), 2384–90.

Leape, L.L., Cullen, D.J., Clapp, M.D., Burdick, E., Demonaco, H.J., Erickson, J.I. and Bates, D.W. 1999. "Pharmacist Participation on Physician Rounds and Adverse Drug Events in the Intensive Care Unit." *Journal of the American Medical Association*, 282(3), 267–70. [Erratum in JAMA, 283, 1293].

Leape, L.L., Kabcenell, A., Gandhi, T.K., Carver, P., Nolan, T.W. and Berwick, D.M. 2000. "Reducing Adverse Drug Events: Lessons from a Breakthrough Series Collaborative." *Joint Commission Journal on Quality Improvement*, 26(6), 321–31.

Leape, L.L., Rogers, G., Hanna, D., Griswold, P., Federico, F., Fenn, C.A., Bates, D.W., Kirle, L. and Clarridge, B.R. 2006. "Developing and Implementing New Safe Practices: Voluntary Adoption through Statewide Collaboratives," *Quality and Safety in Health Care*, 15(4), 289–95.

Leapfrog Group. 2011. *ICU Physician Staffing (IPS). Fact Sheet.* Washington, DC: The Leapfrog Group. Available at: http://www.leapfroggroup.org/media/file/FactSheet_IPS.pdf.

Leonard, M., Frankel, A. and Simmonds, T. 2004. *Achieving Safe and Reliable Healthcare: Strategies and Solutions.* Chicago, IL: Health Administration Press.

Leonard, N. and Insch, G.S. 2011. "Tacit Knowledge in Academia: A Proposed Model and Measurement Scale." *Journal of Psychology*, 139(6), 495–512.

Li, L.C., Grimshaw, J.M., Nielsen, C., Judd, M., Coyte, P.C. and Graham, I.D. 2009. "Use of Communities of Practice in Business and Healthcare Sectors: A Systematic Review." *Implementation Science*, 4(27), 1–9.

Li, L.C., Grimshaw, J.M., Nielsen, C., Judd, M., Coyte, P.C. and Graham, I.D. 2009. "Evolution of Wenger's Concept of Community of Practice." *Implementation Science*, 4(1), 11.

Liebowitz, J. 2005. "Linking Social Network Analysis with the Analytic Hierarchy Process for Knowledge Mapping in Organizations." *Journal of Knowledge Management*, 9(1), 76–86.

Liebowitz, J. 2007. "The Hidden Power of Social Networks and Knowledge Sharing in Healthcare." In *Healthcare Knowledge Management: Issues, Advances, and Successes*, edited by R.K. Bali and A.N. Dwivendi. New York, NY: Springer, 104–11.

Liebowitz, J. and Suen, C.Y. 2000. "Developing Knowledge Management Metrics for Measuring Intellectual Capital." *Journal of Intellectual Capital*, 1(1), 54–67.

Lindberg, C., Nash, S., and Lindberg, C. 2008. *On the Edge: Nursing in the Age of Complexity.* Bordentown, NJ: PlexusPress.

Lorenzi, N.M., Kouroubali, A., Detmer, D.E., Bloomrosen, M. 2009 "How to Successfully Select and Implement Electronic Health Records (EHR) in Small Ambulatory Practice Settings." *BMC Medical Informatics and Decision Making.* Available at: http://www.ncbi.nlm.nih.gov/pubmed/19236705

Lim, B.C. and Klein, K.J. 2006. "Team Mental Models and Team Performance: A Field Study of the Effects of Team Mental Model Similarity and Accuracy." *Journal of Organizational Behavior*, 27(4), 403–18.

Lundgrén-Laine, H., Kontio, E., Perttilä, J., Korvenranta, H., Forsström, J. and Salanterä, S. 2011. "Managing Daily Intensive Care Activities: An Observational Study Concerning Ad Hoc Decision Making of Charge Nurses and Intensivists." *Critical Care*, 15(4), R188.

Lynn, J. 2011. "Building an Integrated Methodology of Learning that Can Optimally Support Improvements in Healthcare." *BMJ Quality Safety*, 20(Suppl 1), i58–61.

MacIntosh-Murray, A. and Choo, C.W. 2005. "Information Behavior in the Context of Improving Patient Safety." *Journal of the American Society for Information Science and Technology*, 56(12), 1332–45.

Maggio, L.A. and Posley, K.A. 2011. "Training the Trainers: Teaching Clinician Educators to Provide Information Literacy Skills Feedback." *Journal of the Medical Library Association*, 99(3), 258–61.

Matney, S.A., Maddox, L.J. and Staggers, N. 2013 Nurses As Knowledge Workers: Is There Evidence of Knowledge in Patient Handoffs? *Western Journal of Nursing Research*, July 25. [Epub ahead of print].

Marx, D. 2001. *Patient Safety and the "Just Culture": A Primer for Health Care Executives*. New York, NY: Columbia University.

Massoud, M.R., Nielsen, G.A., Nolan, K., Schall, M.W. and Sevin, C. 2006. "A Framework for Spread: From Local Improvements to System-Wide Change." *IHI Innovation Series White Paper*. Cambridge, MA: Institute for Healthcare Improvement.

McCannon, C.J. and Perla, R.J. 2009. "Learning Networks for Sustainable, Large-Scale Improvement." *Joint Commission Journal on Quality and Patient Safety*, 35(5), 286–91.

McComb, S. and Simpson, V. 2013. "The Concept of Shared Mental Models in Healthcare Collaboration." *Journal of Advanced Nursing*. [Epub ahead of print].

McDermott, R. 1999. "Why Information Technology Inspired but Cannot Deliver Knowledge Management." *California Management Review*, 41(4), 103–17.

McDermott, R. 2001. *Knowing in Community: 10 Critical Success Factors in Building Communities of Practice*. Available at: http://www.co-i-l.com/coil/knowledge-garden/cop/knowing.shtml [accessed December 21, 2011].

McDonald, P.W. and Viehbeck, S. 2007. "From Evidence-Based Practice Making to Practice-Based Evidence Making: Creating Communities of Research and Practice." *Health Promotion Practice*, 8(2), 140–44.

Meadows, D.H. 2008. *Thinking in Systems: A Primer*. White River Junction, VT: Chelsea Green Publishing.

Mengis, J. and Nicolini, D. 2011. "Challenges to Learning From Clinical Adverse Events: A Study of Root Cause Analysis in Practice." In *A Socio-cultural Perspective on Patient Safety*, edited by E. Rowley and J. Waring. Farnham: Ashgate Publishing Limited.

Metaxiotis, K., Ergazakis, K. and Psarras, J. 2005. "Exploring the World of Knowledge Management: Agreements and Disagreements in the Academic/Practitioner Community." *Journal of Knowledge Management*, 9(2), 6–18.

Milton, N. 2010. *The Lessons Learned Handbook: Practical Approaches to Learning from Experience*. Oxford: Chandos.

Mitton, C., Adair, C.E., McKenzie, E., Patten, S.B. and Perry, B.W. 2007. "Knowledge Transfer and Exchange: Review and Synthesis of the Literature." *Milbank Quarterly*, 85(4), 729–68.

Morath, J.M. 1998. *The Quality Advantage: A Strategic Guide for Health Care Leaders*. Hoboken, NJ. John Wiley & Sons, Inc.

Morath, J.M., and Turnbull, J.E. 2005. *To Do No Harm: Ensuring Patient Safety in Health Care Organizations*. San Francisco, CA: Jossey-Bass.

Moore, M.F. 2006. "Embedded in Systems Engineering." *Information Outlook*, 10(5), 180.

Moorman, C. and Miner, A.S. 1998. "Organizational Improvisation and Organizational Memory." *Academy of Management Review*, 23(4), 698–723.

Mulvaney, S.A., Bickman, L., Giuse, N.B., Lambert, E.W., Sathe, N.A. and Jerome, R.N. 2008. "A Randomized Effectiveness Trial of a Clinical Informatics Consult Service: Impact on Evidence-Based Decision-Making and Knowledge Implementation." *Journal of the American Medical Informatics Association*, 15(2), 203–11.

National Patient Safety Foundation. 2010. *Unmet Needs: Teaching Physicians to Provide Safe Patient Care*. Boston, MA: Lucian Leape Institute at the National Patient Safety Foundation.

National Quality Forum. 2010. *Safe Practices for Better Healthcare – 2010 Update*. Washington, DC: National Quality Forum.

National Reporting and Learning Service (NRLS). *Alerts*. Available at: http://www.nrls.npsa.nhs.uk/resources/type/alerts/

Nelson, E.C., Batalden, P.B., Homa, K., Godfrey, M.M., Campbell, C., Headrick, L.A., Huber, T.P., Mohr, J.J. and Wasson, J.H. 2003. "Microsystems in Health Care: Part 2 – Creating a Rich Information Environment." *Joint Commission Journal on Quality and Safety*, 29(1), 5–15.

Nelson, E.C., Batalden, P.B., Huber, T.P., Mohr, J.J., Godfrey, M.M., Headrick, L.A. and Wasson, J.H. 2002. "Microsystems in Healthcare: Part I – Learning from High-Performing Front-Line Clinical Units." *Joint Commission Journal on Quality Improvement*, 28(9), 472–93.

NHS Scotland. 2011. *Knowledge into Action Test of Change Projects: Discussion Paper for Steering Group*. Available at: http://www.knowledge.scot.nhs.uk/media/CLT/ResourceUploads/4004386/20111021%20Knowledge%20into%20Action%20Test%20of%20Change%20Projects%20v0.1.doc.

NHS Wales. 2010. *Learning to Use Patient Stories*. Cardiff: NHS Wales. Available at: http://www.wales.nhs.uk/sites3/Documents/781/T4I%20(6)%20Learning%20to%20use%20Patient%20stories%20(Feb%202011)%20Web.pdf

Nicolini, D., Powell, J., Conville, P. and Martinez-Solano, L. 2008. "Managing Knowledge in the Healthcare Sector. A Review." *International Journal of Management Reviews*, 10(3), 245–63.

Nonaka, I. and Takeuchi, H. 1995. *The Knowledge-Creating Company*. New York, NY: Oxford University Press.

Oborn, E., Barrett, M. and Racko, G. 2010. *Knowledge Translation in Healthcare: A Review of the Literature*. University of Cambridge: Judge Business School. Available at: http://www.jbs.cam.ac.uk/research/working_papers/2010/wp1005.pdf [accessed September 30, 2011].

Office of Environmental Information/Office of Information Collection. 2009. *Terminology Services Glossary*. Available at: http://iaspub.epa.gov/sor_internet/registry/termreg/home/overview/home.do

Ong, M.S. and Coiera, E. 2011. "A Systematic Review of Failures in Handoff Communication During Intrahospital Transfers." *Joint Commission Journal on Quality and Safety*, 37(6), 274–84.

Orzano, A.J., McInerney, C.R., Scharf, D., Tallia, A.F. and Crabtree, B.F. 2008. "A Knowledge Management Model: Implications for Enhancing Quality in Health Care." *Journal of the American Society for Information Science and Technology*, 59(3), 489–505.

Orzano, A.J., McInerney, C.R., Tallia, A.F., Scharf, D. and Crabtree, B.F. 2008. "Family Medicine Practice Performance and Knowledge Management." *Healthcare Management Review*, 33(1), 21–8.

Pascale, R., Sternin, J. and Sternin, M. 2010. *The Power of Positive Deviance: How Unlikely Innovators Solve the World's Toughest Problems*. Boston, MA: Harvard Business Press.

Patterson, K.Grenny, J., Maxfield, D., McMillan, R. and Switzler, A. 2008. *Influencer: The Power to Change Anything*. New York, NY: McGraw-Hill.

Paul, D.L. 2006. "Collaborative Activities in Virtual Settings: A Knowledge Management Perspective of Telemedicine." *Journal of Management Information Systems*, 22(4), 143–76.

Paulin, D. and Suneson, K. 2012 "Knowledge Transfer, Knowledge Sharing and Knowledge Barriers – Three Blurry Terms in KM." *The Electronic Journal of Knowledge Management*, 10(1), 81–91. Available at: www.ejkm.com

Peele, A.S., Goldberg, S. and Trompeta, J.A. 2011. "Collaborative Use of the Peer Assist Model in Large Transplant Programs in the United States." *Progress in Transplantation*, 21(2), 124–30.

Perla, R.J., Bradbury, E. and Gunther-Murphy, C. 2013. "Large-Scale Improvement Initiatives in Healthcare: A Scan of the Literature." *Journal for Healthcare Quality*, 35(1), 30–40.

Perla, R.J., and Parry, G.J. 2011. "The Epistemology of Quality Improvement: It's all Greek." *BMJ Quality Safety*, 20(Suppl 1), i24–7.

Peute, L.W., Aarts, J., Bakker, P.J. and Jaspers, M.W. 2010. "Anatomy of a Failure: A Sociotechnical Evaluation of a Laboratory Physician Order Entry System Implementation." *International Journal of Medical Informatics*, 79(4), e58–70.

Plsek, P.E. and Greenhalgh, T. 2001. "The Challenge of Complexity in Health Care." *British Medical Journal*, 323(7313), 625–8.

Polanyi, M. 1958. *Personal Knowledge*. London: Routledge and Kegan Paul.

Polanyi, M. 1966. *The Tacit Dimension*. London: Routledge and Kegan Paul.

Polanyi, M. and Sen, A. 2009. *The Tacit Dimension*. Chicago, IL: University of Chicago Press; Reissue edition.

Popovich, M.J., Esfandiari, S. and Boutros, A. 2011. "A New ICU Paradigm: Intensivists as Primary Critical Care Physicians." *Cleveland Clinic Journal of Medicine*, 78(10), 697–700.

Porter, C.P., Beall, M.E., Chindlund, J.F., Corliss, R.S., Krawczyk, C.M., Tompson, S.R., Zipperer, L. 1997. *Special Libraries: A Guide for Management*, Fourth edition. Washington, DC: Special Libraries Association.

Porto, G. and Lauve, R. 2006. "Disruptive Clinician Behavior: A Persistent Threat to Patient Safety." *Patient Safety and Quality Healthcare*, 3, 16–24. Available at: http://www.psqh.com/julaug06/disruptive.html.

Powell, A.E. and Davies, H.T. 2012. "The Struggle to Improve Patient Care in the Face of Professional Boundaries." *Social Science and Medicine*, 75(5), 807–14.

Poyhonen, A. and Smedlund, A. 2004. "Assessing Intellectual Capital Creation in Regional Clusters." *Journal of Intellectual Capital*, 5(3), 351–65.

Pronovost, P. and Freischlag, J.A. 2010. "Improving Teamwork to Reduce Surgical Mortality." *Journal of the American Medical Association*, 304(15), 1721–2.

Pronovost, P. and Vohr, E. 2010. *Safe Patients, Smart Hospitals: How One Doctor's Checklist Can Help Us Change Healthcare from the Inside Out*. New York, NY: Hudson Street Press.

Pronovost, P., Needham, D., Berenholtz, S., Sinopoli, D., Chu, H., Cosgrove, S., Sexton, B., Hyzy, R., Welsh, R., Roth, G., Bander, J., Kepros, J. and Goeschel, C. 2006. "An Intervention to Decrease Catheter-Related Bloodstream Infections in the ICU." *New England Journal of Medicine*, 355(26), 2725–32.

Pronovost, P.J., Angus, D.C., Dorman, T., Robinson, K.A., Dremsizov, T.T. and Young, T.L. 2002. "Physician Staffing Patterns and Clinical Outcomes in Critically Ill Patients: A Systematic Review." *Journal of the American Medical Association*, 288(17), 2151–62.

Quality Interagency Coordination (QuIC) Task Force. 2000. National Summit on Medical Errors and Patient Safety. Available at: http://www.quic.gov/summit/index.htm

Raja, U., Mitchell, T., Day, T. and Hardin, M. 2008. "Text Mining in Healthcare: Applications and Opportunities." *Journal of Healthcare Information Management*, 22(3), 52–6.

Rangachari, P. 2008. "Knowledge Sharing Networks Related to Hospital Quality Measurement and Reporting." *Healthcare Manage Review*, 33(3), 253–63.

Rangachari, P. 2009. "Knowledge Sharing Networks in Professional Complex Systems." *Journal of Knowledge Management*, 13(3), 132–45.

Ranmuthugala, G., Cunningham, F.C., Plumb, J.J., Long, J., Georgiou, A., Westbrook, J.I. and Braithwaite, J. 2011. "A Realist Evaluation of the Role of Communities of Practice in Changing Healthcare Practice." *Implementation Science*, 6(1), 49–54.

Resar, R.K. 2006. "Making Noncatastrophic Health Care Processes Reliable: Learning to Walk before Running in Creating High-reliability Organizations." *Health Services Research*, 41(4 pt. 2), 1677–89.

Reason, J.T. 1990. *Human Error*. New York, NY: Cambridge University Press.

Reason, J.T. 1997. *Managing the Risks of Organizational Accidents*. Aldershot: Ashgate Publishing Limited.

Reinders, H. 2010. "The Importance of Tacit Knowledge in Practices of Care." *Journal of Intellectual Disability Research*, 54(Suppl. 1), 28–37.

Riege, A. 2005. "Three Dozen Knowledge-Sharing Barriers Managers Must Consider." *Journal of Knowledge Management*, 9(3), 18–35.

Robb, B.G. and Zipperer, L. 2009. "Knowledge Management in Hospitals: Drawing from Experience to Define the Librarian's Role." *Journal of Hospital Librarianship*, 9(3), 307–17.

Robinson, J.G. and Gehle, J.L. 2005. "Medical Research and the Institutional Review Board: The Librarian's Role in Human Subject Testing." *Reference Services Review*, 33(1), 20–24.

Roger, K.R. 2006. "Making Noncatastrophic Healthcare Processes Reliable: Learning to Walk before Running in Creating High-Reliability Organizations." *Health Services Research*, 41(4.2), 1677–89.

Rogers, E. 2007. "The Top 10 KM Myths." *Knowledge Management Review*, 10(2), 6–7.

Rogers, E.M. *Diffusion of Innovations*, Fifth edition. New York, NY: Free Press.

Rollins, G. 2012. "Unintended Consequences: Identifying and Mitigating Unanticipated Issues in EHR Use." *Journal of AHIMA*, 83(1), 28–32.

Romig, M., Goeschel, C., Provonost, P. and Berenholtz, S.M. 2010. "Integrating CUSP and TRIP to Improve Patient Safety." *Hospital Practice*, 38(4), 114–21.

Romiszowski, A. and Mason, R. 2004. "Computer-Mediated Communication." In *Handbook of Research on Educational Communications and Technology*, edited by D.H. Jonassen. Mahwah, NJ: Lawrence Erlbaum, 397–432.

Rowley, E., and Waring, J. 2011. *A Socio-cultural Perspective on Patient Safety*. Farnham: Ashgate Publishing Limited.

Ruben, B.D. 1993. "What Patients Remember: A Content Analysis of Critical Incidents in Health Care." *Health Communication*, 5(2), 99–112.

Russell, J., Greenhalgh, T., Boynton, P. and Rigby, M. 2004. "Soft Networks for Bridging the Gap Between Research and Practice: Illuminative Evaluation of CHAIN." *British Medical Journal*, 328(7449), 1–6.

Sackett, D.L., Rosenberg, W.M., Gray, J.A., Haynes, R.B. and Richardson, W.S. 1996. "Evidence Based Medicine: What It Is and What It Isn't. *British Medical Journal*, 312(7023), 71–2.

Sandy, L.G. 2002. "Homeostasis Without Reserve – The Risk of Health System Collapse." *New England Journal of Medicine*, 347(24), 1971–5.

Savoia, E., Agboola, F. and Biddinger, P.D. 2012. "Use of After Action Reports (AARs) to Promote Organizational and Systems Learning in Emergency Preparedness." *International Journal of Environmental Research and Public Health*, 9(8), 2949–63.

Sawyer, R.K. 2000. "Improvisational Cultures: Collaborative Emergence and Creativity in Improvisation." *Mind, Culture, and Activity*, 7(3), 180–85.

Schaafsma, F., Verbeek, J., Hulshof, C. and van Dijk, F. 2005. "Caution Required when Relying on a Colleague's Advice: A Comparison Between Professional Advice and Evidence from the Literature." *BMC Health Services Research*, 31(5), 59.

Scharkow, M. 2011. "Online Content Analysis Using Supervised Machine Learning: An Empirical Evaluation." Paper presented at the 2011 ICA Conference, Boston, May.

Schein, E. 1999. *The Corporate Culture Survival Guide*. San Francisco, CA: Jossey-Bass.

Schein, E. 2004. *Organizational Culture and Leadership*. San Francisco, CA: Jossey-Bass.

Schilling, L., Dearing, J.W., Staley, P., Harvey, P., Fahey, L. and Kuruppu, F. 2011. "Kaiser Permanente's Performance Improvement System, Part 4: Creating a Learning Organization." *Joint Commission Journal on Quality and Safety*, 37(12), 532–43.

Schmidt, E., Goldhaber-Fiebert, S.N., Ho, L.A., McDonald, K.M. 2103. "Simulation Exercises as a Patient Safety Strategy: A Systematic Review." *Annals of Internal Medicine*, 158(5 Pt 2), 426–32.

Schön, D. 1983. *The Reflective Practitioner, How Professionals Think In Action*. New York, NY: Basic Books.

Schwartz, D.G. 2006. *Encyclopedia of Knowledge Management*, IGI Global. [electronic]

Scott, S.D., Hirschinger, L.E., Cox, K.R., McCoig, M., Hahn-Cover, K., Epperly, K.M., Phillips, E.C. and Hall, L.W. 2010. "Caring for Our Own: Deploying a Systemwide Second Victim Rapid Response Team." *Joint Commission Journal on Quality and Patient Safety*, 36(5), 233–40.

Seager, L., Smith, D.W., Patel, A., Brunt, H. and Brennan, P.A. 2012. "Applying Aviation Factors to Oral and Maxillofacial Surgery: The Human Element." *British Journal of Oral and Maxillofacial Surgery*, 51(1), 9.

Seaman, J.T. Jr and Smith, G.D. 2012 "Your Company's History as a Leadership Tool." *Harvard Business Review*, 90(12), December, 44–52, 133.

Senge, P.M. 1990. *The Fifth Discipline*. New York, NY: Random House.

Senge, P.M. Kleiner, A.R., Roberts, C., Ross, R.B. and Smith, B.J. 1994. *The Fifth Discipline: The Art and Practice of the Learning Organization*. New York, NY: Doubleday/Currency.

Shulman, R., Singer, M., Goldstone, J. and Bellingan, G. 2005. "Medication Errors: A Prospective Cohort Study of Hand-Written and Computerized Physician Order Entry in the Intensive Care Unit." *Critical Care*, 9(5), R516–21.

Sibinga, E.M. and Wu, A.W. 2010. "Clinician Mindfulness and Patient Safety." *Journal of the American Medical Association*, 304(22), 2532–3.

Sinkowitz-Cochran, R.L., Garcia-Williams, A., Hackbarth, A.D., Zell, B., Baker, G.R., McCannon, C.J., Beltrami, E.M., Jernigan, J.A., McDonald, L.C. and Goldmann, D.A. 2012. "Evaluation of Organizational Culture Among Different Levels of Healthcare Staff Participating in the Institute for Healthcare Improvement's 100,000 Lives Campaign." *Infection Control and Hospital Epidemiology*, 33(2), 135–43.

Smith, M., Saunders, R., Stuckhardt, L. and McGinnis, J.M. (eds). 2012. Committee on the Learning Health Care System in America, Institute of Medicine. *Best Care at Lower Cost: The Path to Continuously Learning Health Care in America*. Washington, DC: National Academies Press.

Snowden, D. 2002. "Complex Acts of Knowing: Paradox and Descriptive Self-Awareness." *Journal of Knowledge Management*, 6(2), 100–111.

Sollenberger, J.F. and Holloway, R.G. 2013. "The Evolving Role and Value of Lbirarians and Libraries in Health Care." *Journal of the American Medical Assoication*, 310(12), 1231–2.

Sorensen, A.V. and Bernard, S.L. 2012. "Accelerating What Works: Using Qualitative Research Methods in Developing a Change Package for a Learning Collaborative." *Joint Commission Journal on Quality and Patient Safety*, 38(2), 89–95.

Spear, S. 2010. *Chasing the Rabbit*. New York, NY: McGraw Hill.

Spolin, V. 1963. *Improvisation for the Theater: A Handbook of Teaching and Directing Techniques*. Evanston, IL: Northwestern University Press.

Stamatoplos, A. 2009. "Improvisational Theater as a Tool for Enhancing Cooperation in Academic Libraries." Presented at the ACRL Fourteenth National Conference, Seattle, WA, March 12–15.

Stewart, T.A. 2007. *The Wealth of Knowledge: Intellectual Capital and the Twenty-first Century Organization*. New York, NY: Random House Inc.

Stoller, J.K. 2013. "Electronic Siloing: An Unintended Consequence of the Electronic Health Record." *Cleveland Clinic Journal of Medicine*, 80(7), July, 406–9.

Sullivan, T.M., Ohkubo, S., Rinehart, W. and Storey, J.D. 2010. "From Research to Policy and Practice: A Logic Model to Measure the Impact of Knowledge Management for Health Programs." *Knowledge Management for Development Journal*, 6(1), 53–69.

Swensen, S.J. and Dilling, J. 2011. "Technology Management." In *Engineering a Learning Healthcare System: A Look at the Future: Workshop Summary*, edited by C. Grossmann, W.A. Goolsby, L. Olsen and J.M. McGinnis. Washington, DC: The National Academies Press, 250–55.

Swinglehurst, D., Greenlaugh, T., Russell, J. and Myall, M. 2011. "Receptionist Input to Quality and Safety in Repeat Prescribing in UK General Practice: Ethnographic Case Study." *British Medical Journal*, 343, d6788.

Tagliaventi, M.R. and Mattarelli, E. 2006. "The Role of Networks of Practice, Value Sharing and Operational Proximity in Knowledge Flows Between Professional Groups." *Human Relations*, 59(3), 291–319.

Timmel, J., Kent, P.S., Holzmueller, C.G., Paine, L., Schulick, R.D. and Pronovost, P.J. 2010. "Impact of the Comprehensive Unit-Based Safety Program (CUSP) on Safety Culture in a Surgical Inpatient Unit." *Joint Commission Journal on Quality and Patient Safety*, 36(6), 252–60.

Titscher, S., Meyer, M., Wodak, R. and Vetter, E. 2000. *Methods of Text and Discourse Analysis*. London: Sage Publications.

Tompson, S.R. and Zipperer, L. 2011. "Systems Thinking for Success." In *Best Practices in Corporate Libraries*, edited by M. Porter and S. Kelsey. Santa Barbara, CA: CLIO Press, 129–50.

Treadwell, J.R., Lucas, S., Tsou, A.Y. 2013. "Surgical Checklists: A Systematic Review of Impacts and Implementation." *British Medical Journal – Quality and Safety*, August 6 [Epub ahead of print].

Tucker, A. and Edmondson, A. 2003. "Why Hospitals Don't Learn from Failures: Organizational and Psychological Dynamics that Inhibit System Change." *California Management Review*, 45(2), 55–72.

Tucker, A.L. and Spear, S.J. 2006. "Operational Failures and Interruptions in Hospital Nursing." *Health Services Research*, 41(3.1), 643–62.

Turner, B.M. 1976. "The Organizational and Intraorganizational Development of Disasters." *Administrative Sciences Quarterly*, 21(3), 378–97.

Uhlig, P.N., Brown, J., Nason, A.K., Camelio, A., and Kendall, E. 2002. "John M. Eisenberg Patient Safety Awards. System innovation: Concord Hospital." *The Joint Commission Journal on Quality Improvement*, 28(12), 666–72.

Valaitis, R.K., Akhtar-Danesh, N., Brooks, F., Binks, S. and Semogas, D. 2011. "Online Communities of Practice as a Communication Resource for Community Health Nurses Working with Homeless Persons." *Journal of Advanced Nursing*, 67(6), 1273–84.

Van Deventer, M.J. 2002. "Measuring Intellectual Capital." In *Introducing Intellectual Capital Management in an Information Support Services Environment*. Thesis, University of Pretoria, Soutrh Africa. Available at: http://www.docstoc.com/docs/74466512/Chapter-4-Measuring-intellectual-capital [accessed October 28, 2013].

Vaughan, D. 1996. *The Challenger Launch Decision: Risky Technology, Culture, and Deviance at NASA*. Chicago, IL: University of Chicago Press.

Vera, D. and Crossan, M. 2004. "Theatrical Improvisation: Lessons for Organizations." *Organization Studies*, 25(5), 727–50.

VHA Patient Safety Center of Inquiry (118M). "Safety Huddle." US Department of Veterans Affairs. Available at: http://www.visn8.va.gov/PatientSafetyCenter/safePtHandling/safetyhuddle_021110.pdf

Wachter, R.M. 2010. "Patient Safety at Ten: Unmistakable Progress, Troubling Gaps." *Health Affairs*, 29(91), 165–73.

Wachter, R.M. and Pronovost, P.J. 2006. "The 100,000 Lives Campaign: A Scientific and Policy Review" [with IHI reply: Berwick DM, Hackbarth AD, McCannon CJ]. *Joint Commission Journal on Quality and Patient Safety*, 32(11), 621–7, 628–33.

Walshe, K. and Offen, N. 2001. "A Very Public Failure: Lessons for Quality Improvement in Healthcare Organisations from the Bristol Royal Infirmary." *Quality in Health Care*, 10(4), 250–56.

Walton, J.M. and Steinert, Y. 2010. "Patterns of Interaction During Rounds: Implications for Work-Based Learning." *Medical Education*, 44(6), 550–58.

Waring, J.J. and Bishop, S. 2012. "'Water Cooler' Learning: Knowledge Sharing at the Clinical 'Backstage' and its Contribution to Patient Safety." *Journal of Health Organization and Management*, 24(4), 325–42.

Waterfield, J. 2010. "Is Pharmacy a Knowledge-Based Profession?" *American Journal of Pharmaceutical Education*, 74(3), 50.

Watson, K. 2011. "Serious Play: Teaching Medical Skills with Improvisational Theater Techniques." *Academic Medicine*, 86(10), 1260–65.

Weberg, D. 2012. "Complexity Leadership: A Healthcare Imperative." *Nursing Forum*,14(4), 268–77.

Weick, K.E. 1993. "The Collapse of Sensemaking in Organizations: The Mann Gulch Disaster." *Administrative Science Quarterly*, 38(4), 628–52.

Weick, K.E. 1995. *Sensemaking in Organizations*. Thousand Oaks, CA: Sage Publications.

Weick, K.E. 1996. "Drop Your Tools: An Allegory for Organizational Studies." *Administrative Science Quarterly*, 41(2), 301–3.

Weick, K.E. 2001. "Improvisation as a Mindset for or Organizational Analysis." In *Organizational Improvisation*, by K.N. Kamoche, M.P. Cunha and J.V. Cunha. New York, NY: Routledge, 49–69.

Weick, K.E. and Sutcliffe, K.M. 2001. *Managing the Unexpected*. San Francisco; CA: Jossey-Bass.

Weick, K.E. and Sutcliffe, K.M. 2003. "Hospitals as Cultures of Entrapment: A Re-Analysis of the Bristol Royal Infirmary." *California Management Review*, 45(2), 73–84.

Weick, K.E. and Sutcliffe, K.M. 2007. *Managing the Unexpected: Assuring High Performance in an Age of Complexity*, 2nd edition. San Francisco, CA: Jossey Bass.

Wenger, E. 2000. "Communities of Practice and Social Learning Systems." *Organization*, 7(2), 225–46.

Wenger, E. 2004. "Knowledge Management as a Doughnut: Shaping your Knowledge Strategy through Communities of Practice." *Ivey Business Journal*. Available at: http://www.knowledgeboard.com/download/1890/Knowledge-management-as-a-doughnut.pdf [accessed December 31, 2011].

Wheaton, K. 2009. "Making the Transformation to Sharing Knowledge." *Information Outlook*, 13(6), 21–4.

White, C.L. 2011. "Nurse Champions: A Key Role in Bridging the Gap Between Research and Practice." *Journal of Emergency Nursing*, 37(4), 386–7.

Wickramasinghe, N., Bali, R.K., Lehaney, B., Schaffer, J. and Gibbons, M.C. 2009. *Healthcare Knowledge Management Primer*. New York, NY: Routledge.

Wiig, K. 2004. *People-Focused Knowledge Management: How Effective Decision Making Leads to Corporate Success*. Oxford: Elsevier.

Williams, L. and Bagian, J. 2014. "Humans and EI&K Seeking: Factors Influencing Reliability." In *Patient Safety: Perspectives on Evidence, Information and Knowledge Transfer*, edited by L. Zipperer. Farnham: Gower.

Willis, C.D., Mitton, C., Gordon, J. and Best, A. 2012. "System Tools for System Change." *BMJ Quality and Safety*, 21(3), 250–62.

Wilson, T.D. 2002. "The Nonsense of 'Knowledge Management.'" *Information Research*, 8(1). Available at: http://informationr.net/ir/8-1/paper144.html.

Wilson, T.D. 2005. "The Nonsense of Knowledge Management Revisited." In *Introducing Information Management An Information Research Reader*, edited by E. Maceviciute and T.D. Wilson. London: Facet, 151–64.

Wu, A.W. 2000. "Medical Error: The Second Victim." *British Medical Journal*, 320, 726–7.

Wu, Y. and Li, Y. 2008. "Research on the Model of Knowledge Audit." Paper presented at the Wireless Communications, Networking and Mobile Computing Fourth International Conference.

Wyatt, J.C. 2001. "Management of Explicit and Tacit Knowledge." *Journal of the Royal Society of Medicine*, 94(1), 6–9.

Yanow, D. 2001. "Learning in and from Improvising: Lessons from Theater for Organizational Learning." *Reflections*, 2(4), 58–65.

Youngberg, B.J. (ed.) 2011. *Principles of Risk Management and Patient Safety*. Sudbery, MA: Jones Bartlett.

Zack, M., McKeen, J. and Singh, S. 2009. "Knowledge Management and Organizational Performance: An Exploratory Analysis." *Journal of Knowledge Management*, 13(6), 392–409.

Zimmerman, B., Lindberg, C., and Plsek, P.E. 1998. *Edgeware: Insights from Complexity Science for Healthcare Leaders*. Irving, TX: VHA.

Zipperer, L. 2004. "Clinicians, Librarians and Patient Safety: Opportunities for Partnership." *Quality and Safety in Health Care*, 13(3), 218–22.

Zipperer, L. 2011. "Knowledge Services." In *The Medical Library Association Guide to Managing Health Care Libraries*, 2nd edition, edited by M.M. Bandy and R.F. Dudden. New York, NY: Neal-Schuman, 313–17.

Zipperer, L. and Amori, G. 2011. "Knowledge Management: An Innovative Risk Management Strategy." *Journal of Healthcare Risk Management*, 30(4), 8–14.

Zipperer, L. and Steward, B. 2013. "KM Workshop Materials." Chicago, IL. February 8, 2013.

Zipperer, L. and Sykes, J. 2009. "Engaging as Partners in Patient Safety: The Experience of Librarians." *Patient Safety and Quality Healthcare*, 6, 28–30, 32–3.

Zipperer, L., Gluck, J. and Anderson, S. 2002. "Knowledge Maps for Patient Safety." *Journal of Hospital Librarianship*, 2(4), 17–35.

Glossary

After Action Reviews
"... short, structured review meetings, conducted to draw out lessons from a task or activity. After action reviews are useful for helping individuals and teams gain immediate performance feedback, and to identify and carry forward lessons for immediate application" (Milton 2010: 54).

Authority Gradient
"Refers to the balance of decision-making power or the steepness of command hierarchy in a given situation. Members of a crew or organization with a domineering, overbearing, or dictatorial team leader experience a steep authority gradient. Expressing concerns, questioning, or even simply clarifying instructions would require considerable determination on the part of team members who perceive their input as devalued or frankly unwelcome. Most teams require some degree of authority gradient; otherwise roles are blurred and decisions cannot be made in a timely fashion. However, effective team leaders consciously establish a command hierarchy appropriate to the training and experience of team members. Authority gradients may occur even when the notion of a team is less well defined"[1] (AHRQ PSNet).

Boundary Spanners
These are individuals who have ties both within the organization and external to their work environment others may not possess (Chuang, Jason and Morgan 2011).

Champions
An individual who "provides direction and inspires, encourages, promotes and creates trust in the process, and in the future. In return, everyone in [involved in the practice/project/initiative] needs to trust, respect, and communicate

---

1   Adapted with permission from AHRQ Patient Safety Network: Shojania, K.G., Wachter, R.M. and Hartman, E.E. *AHRQ Patient Safety Network Glossary*. Available at: http://psnet.ahrq.gov/glossary.aspx.

effectively with the champion. Champions must provide a combination of control and flexibility to create the highest likelihood of ... success" (Lorenzi et al. 2009: e-print page 7).

Clinical Microsystem
"... a small group of people who work together on a regular basis to provide care to discrete subpopulations of patients. It has clinical and business aims, linked processes, and a shared information environment, and it produces performance outcomes. Microsystems evolve over time and are often embedded in larger organizations" (Nelson et al. 2002: 474).

Collaboration Software
"Software that allows people to work together on the same documents and projects over local and remote networks. Also called 'social software,' collaborative software embraces the communications systems as well, including e-mail, videoconferencing, instant messaging and chat" (Office of Environmental Information/Office of Information Collection 2009: n.p.).

Complex Adaptive System
"A complex, nonlinear, interactive system that has the ability to adapt to a change environment" (Zimmerman, Lindberg, and Plsek 1998: 263).

Complexity
"A description of phenomenon demonstrated in systems characterized by nonlinear interactive components, emergent phenomena continuous and discontinuous change and unpredictable outcomes." The term is used to "characterize systems that behave in ways that are different than simple, linear and equilibrium based-systems" (Lindberg, Nash and Lindberg 2008: 271–2).

Culture of Safety/Safety Culture
"The concept of safety culture originated outside health care, in studies of high reliability organizations, organizations that consistently minimize adverse events despite carrying out intrinsically complex and hazardous work. High reliability organizations maintain a commitment to safety at all levels, from frontline providers to managers and executives. This commitment establishes a 'culture of safety' that encompasses these key features:

- acknowledgment of the high-risk nature of an organization's activities and the determination to achieve consistently safe operations;

- a blame-free environment where individuals are able to report errors or near misses without fear of reprimand or punishment;

- encouragement of collaboration across ranks and disciplines to seek solutions to patient safety problems; and

- organizational commitment of resources to address safety concerns"[2] (AHRQ PSNet).

Deep Tacit
"Collectively shared beliefs, mental models, and values that determine what individuals view as important and even what they define as relevant knowledge. This knowledge is the most difficult to access, and is usually transferred unconsciously through a set of practices that are unique to every organization" (DeLong 2004: 84).

Early Adopters
Opinion leaders in organizations that generate support for innovations. Early adopters are "respected by their peers and is the embodiment of successful, discrete use of new ideas. ... The early adopter decreases uncertainty about a new idea by adopting it" (Rogers 2003).

Evidence-based Medicine (EBM)
"The conscientious explicit and judicious use of current best evidence in making decisions about the care of individual patients" (Sackett et al. 1996: 71). It is referred to as evidence-based practice to expand its use in non-medical doctor (i.e. nursing) and allied health arenas.

Executive Walkarounds
A structured process designed to facilitate management and frontline staff two-way discussions about safety. The results from those conversations are captured, analyzed, prioritized, and acted upon (Frankel et al. 2003).

Great Catch
Also referred to as near misses, close calls or good catches. An event or situation that might have resulted in an accident, injury or illness but did not, either by change or through timely intervention (Quality Interagency Coordination

---

2   Adapted with permission from AHRQ Patient Safety Network: Ranji, S., Wachter, R.M. and Hartman, E.E. *Patient Safety Primer: Medication Errors.* AHRQ Patient Safety Network. Available at: http://psnet.ahrq.gov/primer.aspx?primerID=5 [Updated October 2012].

Task Force 2000); Given that "near misses are valuable tools for learning about systems vulnerability and resilience" (Morath and Turnbull 2005: 268) they are presented as learning opportunities, hence the use of the "great or good catch."

Huddles/Safety Huddles
Safety huddles are based on after action review (AAR), a highly successful method of knowledge sharing that is used in high reliability organizations. They are built on structured methods of making "tacit knowledge explicit" among team members, thus usable next time a similar situation is faced (VHA Patient Safety Center of Inquiry n.d.: n.p.).

Informaticist
Informaticists are those schooled in Informatics – "the interdisciplinary study of the design, use, applications and implications of information technology. It goes beyond technical design, to focus on the relationship between information system design and use in real-world settings. These investigations lead to new forms of system architecture, new approaches to system design and development, new means of information system implementation and deployment as well as new models of interaction between technology and social, cultural and organizational settings."[3]

Informationist
An extended role for clinical librarians. "Informationists are cross-trained in reference library skills and the essentials of specific biomedical disciplines. They work as full-time members of clinical and some research teams while maintaining formal relationships with their home libraries. They search the literature in response to questions, critically appraise the findings, and summarize them in concise written reports" (Davidoff and Miglus 2011: 1906).

Intellectual Capital
"Knowledge (that can be converted into value or profit) and skills that lead to a competitive edge in the marketplace" (Wickramasinghe et al. 2009: 188).

Knowledge Acquisition
Describes the "practices, processes and routines used to move knowledge into a state where it is kept available for future use" (Delong 2004: 23).

---

3   See http://www.informatics.uci.edu/about/

Knowledge Intensive Organization
A "knowledge-intensive" organization refers to organizations where most work is of an intellectual nature and where well-educated, qualified employees form the major part of the workforce. (Alvesson 2000, 2001) as cited by Hurley and Green (2005).

Knowledge Retention
The act of building "corporate memory" through knowledge acquisition, translation of tacit knowledge into explicit form (i.e. evidence or information) and behaviors and processes that enable its access and use once represented in concrete fashion (DeLong, 2004). It enables the knowledge to stay within the organization rather than departing with knowledge workers when they leave.

Knowledge Sharing
"An exchange of knowledge between two individuals: one who communicates knowledge and one who assimilates it. In knowledge sharing, the focus is on human capital and the interaction of individuals. Strictly speaking, knowledge can never be shared. Because it exists in a context; the receiver interprets it in the light of his or her own background" (Paulin and Suneson 2012: 83; quoting *Encyclopedia of Knowledge Management*, Schwartz 2006).

Knowledge Transfer
"The focused, unidirectional communication of knowledge between individuals, groups, or organizations such that the recipient of knowledge (a) has a cognitive understanding, (b) has the ability to apply the knowledge, or (c) applies the knowledge" (Paulin and Suneson 2012: 83; quoting *Encyclopedia of Knowledge Management*, Schwartz 2006).

Knowledge Translation
Knowledge translation represents a process for improving communication between the producers and consumers of knowledge to increase the application of research-based knowledge in practical forms (Lane and Flagg 2010).

Knowledge Worker
Employees that have "high degrees of expertise, education or experience and the primary purpose of their jobs involved the creation, distribution of application of knowledge. Knowledge workers think for a living" (Davenport 2005: 10).

Learning Culture
A culture that values observation, reflecting, creating and acting (Reason 1997).

Lessons Learned
"Knowledge or understanding gained by experience that has a significant impact for an organization. The experience may be either positive or negative" (Milton 2010: 14).

Local Knowledge
"Knowledge which the actors themselves process and which is subject to little extraneous influence. ... a dynamic process of acquisition and integration of contextual information and experience" (Antweiler 1998: 472).

Machine Learning
"Machine learning is an artificial intelligence (AI) discipline geared toward the technological development of human knowledge. Machine learning allows computers to handle new situations via analysis, self-training, observation and experience" (see http://www.techopedia.com/definition/8181/machine-learning).

Near Misses
An event or situation that might have resulted in an accident, injury or illness but did not, either by change or through timely intervention (Quality Interagency Coordination Task Force 2000). Sometimes referred to as "close calls" or good catches, "Near misses are valuable tools for learning about systems vulnerability and resilience" (Morath and Turnbull 2005: 268).

Non-individual Knowledge
Knowledge that resides in social relationships (Tagliventi and Mattarelli 2006).

Normalization of Deviance
This expression describes the gradual shift in what is regarded as normal after repeated exposures to "deviant behavior" (behavior straying from correct [or safe] operating procedure) (Vaughan 1996). Corners get cut, safety checks bypassed, and alarms ignored or turned off, and these behaviors become *normal* – not just common, but stripped of their significance as warnings of impending danger. ... Providers in the system become inured to malfunction. In such a system, what should be regarded as a major warning of impending danger is ignored as a normal operating procedure[4] (AHRQ PSNet).

---

4   Adapted with permission from AHRQ Patient Safety Network: Shojania, K.G., Wachter, R.M. and Hartman, E.E. *AHRQ Patient Safety Network Glossary*. Available at: http://psnet.ahrq.gov/glossary.aspx.

Ontologies

"An ontology is a controlled vocabulary that seeks to show how certain terms are related to one another" (HERO Glossary).

Peer Assist

A peer assist is a meeting where the project team invites people with relevant knowledge and experience to come and share their lessons (written and unwritten) with a team. Dixon (2000) discusses as well (Milton 2010: 124).

Positive Deviants/Positive Deviance

Positive deviants are individuals who adopt innovative approaches to deeply imbedded problems and are able to create change through harnessing improvements through their behavior and actions. "Postive deviance leverages modifications moving away from the norm in a social system to generate positive change" (Lindberg, Nash and Lindberg 2008).

Production Pressure

"Represents the pressure to put quantity of output – for a product or a service – ahead of safety. Production pressure refers to delivery of services – the pressure to run hospitals at 100 percent capacity, with each bed filled with the sickest possible patients who are discharged at the first sign that they are stable, or the pressure to leave no operating room unused and to keep moving through the schedule for each room as fast as possible. Production pressure produces an organizational culture in which frontline personnel (and often managers) are reluctant to suggest any course of action that compromises productivity, even temporarily"[5] (AHRQ PSNet).

Reflective Practice

Conscious effort to learning through the process of doing – whether mundane or unique activities. "A practitioner's reflection can serve as a corrective to over learning. Through reflection he can surface and criticize the tacit understandings that have grown up around the repetitive experiences of a specialized practice and can make new sense of the situations of uncertain or uniqueness which he may allow himself to experience" (Schön 1983: 61). It differs in nature from learning through reading and didactic presentation.

---

5   Adapted with permission from AHRQ Patient Safety Network: Shojania, K.G., Wachter, R.M. and Hartman, E.E. *AHRQ Patient Safety Network Glossary.* Available at: http://psnet.ahrq.gov/ glossary.aspx.

Second Victim
The clinician or healthcare worker adversely affected by medical error and near miss. Negative impacts could affect physical and psychological health and professional relationships (Wu 2000).

Sensemaking
"An action at the team or organizational level to "make sense" out of information to understand the environment, generate knowledge and make decisions. It is an important element of interpreting high-risk events by responding to what is happening in real time"[6] (AHRQ PSNet).

Situation-Background-Assessment-Recommendations (SBAR)
"An acronym for Situation, Background, Assessment, Recommendation, this structured communication technique is used to standardize communication between two or more people (Haig, Sutton, and Whittington 2006), thereby promoting a focus on teamwork rather than individual expertise. It helps set the expectation within a conversation that specific, relevant, and critical informational elements are going to be communicated every time a patient is discussed" (Frush, Leonard, and Frankel 2013: 60).

Special Librarianship
"A distinct area of librarianship that differs from pubic, school or academic libraries. "The mission of special libraries is to provide focused [resources] to a defined group of users on an ongoing basis to further the mission and goals of their parent organization. ... special libraries are oriented to a single subject or range of subjects determined by the field or activity and interests of the libraries parent organization" (Porter et al. 1997: 2).

Systems Thinking
"A way to view the world, including organizations, from a broad perspective that includes structures, patterns, and events rather than simply the events themselves. ... Systems thinking helps [one] to perceive the whole, the elements of which continually affect each other over time and operating ideally toward a common purpose." (Tompson and Zipperer, 2009: 129). Systems thinking has been defined as one of the five elements of a learning organization as popularized by Peter Senge (1990).

---

6   Adapted with permission from AHRQ Patient Safety Network: Shojania, K.G., Wachter, R.M. and Hartman, E.E. *AHRQ Patient Safety Network Glossary*. Available at: http://psnet.ahrq.gov/glossary.aspx.

Tag Cloud

"A tag cloud is a stylized way of visually representing occurrences of words used to described tags. The most popular topics are normally highlighted in a larger, bolder font. Visitors to a blog or site using a tag cloud are able to easily see the most popular tags within the page – making it easy to discern the topics covered in one quick look. Also called a weighted list."[7] For example, Tagul was used to create the clouds used in this text, see Figure 1.1 and 7.1.[8]

Unintended Consequences

Responses to changes in systems (technological or otherwise) that were unanticipated. Often acerbated by technologies (like electronic medical records in healthcare) they negatively affect the workplace through activating communication patterns, generating errors, affecting the power structure and workflow. They can remain latent until the system fails (Rollins 2012).

Wagon Wheel Concept

A diagramming technique that "provides a quick and easy snapshot of team communications. The goal of the method is to identify the main communication channels existing for each position on the team and the nature of those communications" (Klinger and Hahn 2003: 21).

Wicked Question

"Wicked questions do not have an obvious answer. … They are questions that articulate the embedded and often contradictory assumptions we hold about an issue, context or organization" (Zimmerman, Lindberg, and Plsek 2001: 151).

Wiki

"An application that is collaborative in nature, where anyone can add, delete, or edit content and the page's history is viewable to everyone" (HERO Glossary).

---

7   See http://www.webopedia.com/TERM/T/tag_cloud.html
8   See http://tagul.com

Appendix 1

Investing in Knowledge Management: Internal Vs. External Investment

Author/diagramer: Michael F. Moore, MLS

Based on the work of Peter Senge

Emphasizing external information dissemination at the expense of internal knowledge sharing can work against an organization. A typical scenario is a health system that devotes resources to developing an attractive, public website but does not develop a useful intranet to boost employees' access to information.

Scenario

THE PROBLEM

A healthcare company missed a deadline for a funding application due to lack of access to critical information needed to complete the proposal. The board later discovered that several employees had relevant experience with the subject matter and could have contributed to the project had their experience been identified and appropriately used.

THE PLAN IN THEORY

The board recognized the need to manage long-term employee knowledge so it could be more accessible. A plan was crafted to improve internal knowledge management (KM).

THE PLAN IN PRACTICE

- The company hired a communications specialist as their knowledge manager.

- The KM plan was launched by examining internal resources, but quickly shifted to an emphasis on external marketing of evidence. Resources were directed to external, not internal, information distribution.

- The organization's culture and mental models about knowledge sharing were not examined. Internal KM was deemed less significant, and a generic tool was used to gather and share expertise.

- The generic KM tool was introduced without building support among users. Employees were neither required, nor encouraged, to use it.

- Managers created and applied metrics based on the external KM initiative. No metrics were developed to measure success of internal improvement; thus, its impact was not tracked.

- Staff members saw no value in contributing to the internal KM tool.

- Over time, opportunity was lost because the value of internal KM was not articulated, measured or rewarded. The original problem of lack of internal knowledge awareness arose again.

Symbols in the Causal Loop Diagram

Symbol	Name	Represents	Description
Text	Boxes	Links	Descriptions of specific activities that contribute to the loop.
⟹	Arrows	Loops	Circles of causality among links where every element is both cause and effect.
⟍○	Snowball	Reinforcing loops	Loops that grow or shrink at an ever-increasing rate: virtuous or vicious.
▲	See-Saw	Balancing loops	Loops that grow or shrink within limits, maintaining stability, and achieving equilibrium.
+/−	Plus and Minus signs	Effects	Positive or negative effects of a given link: effects change depending on what part of the story is represented.

Building a Causal Loop Diagram

Using the "Seven Steps for Breaking through Organizational Gridlock" from Senge et al. (1994), *The Fifth Discipline Fieldbook: Strategies and Tools for Building a Learning Organization*. New York, NY: Doubleday/Currency, 169–72.

STEP 1: IDENTIFY THE SYMPTOMS OF THE PROBLEM

- Healthcare company board problem: Critically needed employee knowledge is inaccessible; business opportunities are missed.

- Internal program problem: Knowledge sharing discourages wider participation.

STEP 2: MAP ALL QUICK FIXES

- Investing in external, not internal, information distribution

- Hiring a tactician rather than a strategist to facilitate a team approach.

- Emphasizing external marketing.

- Using generic technology for internal KM without building community support among those expected to contribute to and use it.

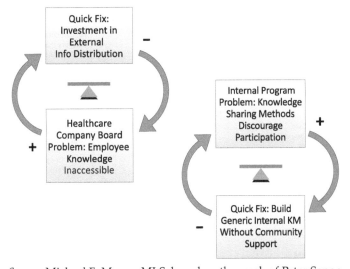

Source: Michael F. Moore, MLS, based on the work of Peter Senge.

STEP 3: IDENTIFY UNDESIRABLE IMPACTS

- Investing in external information distribution leads to a lack of investment in internal KM, which worsens the organization and internal program problems.

- Use of a generic technology solution for internal KM fails to generate participation by employees.

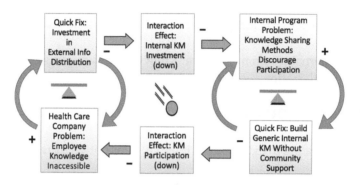

STEP 4: IDENTIFY FUNDAMENTAL SOLUTIONS

- Healthcare company board problem: Investing more fully in internal KM.

- Internal program problem: Exploring KM mental models and building a vision that encourages KM participation.

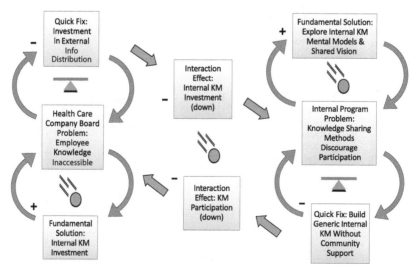

STEP 5: MAP SIDE EFFECTS OF QUICK FIXES

- External information distribution: More tangible feedback from external standards, leading to more external information distribution investment.

- External information distribution: Success is measured by external participation, thus leading to more external information distribution investment.

- Generic solution for internal KM: Staff unwilling to invest additional funds into a poor solution.

- Generic solution for internal KM: People lose interest in participating in internal KM.

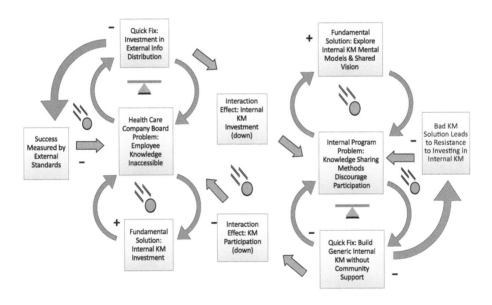

STEP 6: FIND INTERCONNECTIONS TO FUNDAMENTAL LOOPS

- With a better internal KM process (based on good KM mental models and a shared vision), participation in internal KM would increase, thus addressing board problem and showing the success of internal KM investment.

- With a better internal KM process, will the external standards still be met even though less has been invested in external KM?

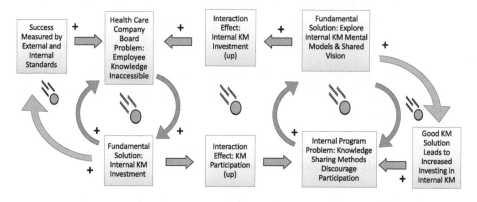

STEP 7: IDENTIFY HIGH-LEVERAGE ACTIONS

- Exploring KM mental models and shared vision to look for high-leverage opportunities to invest in internal KM processes.

Appendix 2

Interviewee Role and Type of Location

Interviewee	Type of role	Known to interviewer	Organizational characteristics from which experience was drawn (not a factor in selection)
1	Blunt end	Yes	Acute care teaching hospital
2	Blunt end	No	Multi-location system
3	Sharp end	No	Acute care teaching hospital
4	Sharp end	Yes	Acute care teaching hospital
5	Sharp end	Yes	Acute care teaching hospital
6	Blunt end	No	Acute care teaching hospital
7	Blunt end	Yes	Acute care teaching hospital
8	Sharp end	Yes	Multi-location system (patient sharp end)
9	Sharp end	No	Acute care hospital
10	Blunt-blunt end	Yes	NA
11	Blunt-blunt end	Yes	NA
12	Sharp end	No	Acute care teaching hospital
13	Blunt end	No	Multi-location system
14	Sharp end	No	Reflected on work at a hospital/currently at blunt-blunt end
15	Blunt-blunt end	No	NA
16	Blunt-blunt end	Yes	NA
17	Blunt end	Yes	Acute care hospital
18	Blunt end	Yes	Patient advocate
19	Blunt end	No	Unit administrative support/blunt end work in sharp end environment
20	Blunt end	No	Community hospital

Appendix 3

A Selection of Tacit Knowledge
Sharing Behaviors That Can Impact
Quality Aims Through Support
of Reliability as Identified by
Interviewee Experience

Quality Aims (Chasm Report 2001: 5–6)	KSharing Behaviors	HRO Element Support (Weick and Sutcliffe 2001)	Supportive quotes (edited for clarity)
Safe: "avoiding injuries to patients from the care that is intended to help them."	Sharing what doesn't work.	Tracks small failures.	• "It's that sense of ability to talk with someone else and get additional help that you get many expert opinions in the room and that everybody's opinion is acceptable and counts. And that's a little bit what I mean by that safety culture. You can't feel comfortable t-to trust, to open your opinion to someone if you believe you'll be ridiculed or leadership won't care that there's a safety concern" (Interview 15/290–293).
	Being accountable to share what your tacit knowledge alerts you to.		• "If you build a system and you build a culture, high reliability is going to be an end result, but those two beginning steps are very difficult first steps. But I think to get the preoccupation with 'failure to say "Whoa! That could really happen, I wonder if XX knows about that" or whoever the entity would be. To get into that dialogue takes all those other two measures to be in place for it to get there" (Interview 14/609–615).
			• "Isn't [tacit knowledge being applied] when someone calls a time out? Isn't that what's happening when a 'lower level employee' recognizes that something is not working and wants to bring it to management. They don't have any credentials to say that they've seen this happen. ... It's a leveling of the culture and recognition that everybody has their own expertise, their own knowledge, their own experience, and that is valuable to the group as a whole" (Interview 17/485–493).
	Seeks deeper understanding.	Resists oversimplification.	• "I can't just go in their take a report and say that is what happened ... I'll have them *show* me something so I can get an understanding. I cannot make the assumption that I know how they are supposed to be doing something. I am not a nurse" (Interview 12/131; 143–145).
			• "[... bringing them into the conversation] just exposes people to all the potentials that are out there, it kind of opens their eyes up to other things that maybe they don't think about in their own environment...." (Interview 20/281; 289–302).

Quality Aims (Chasm Report 2001: 5–6)	KSharing Behaviors	HRO Element Support (Weick and Sutcliffe 2001)	Supportive quotes (edited for clarity)
Safe (Continued)		Remains sensitive to operations.	• "We've had situations over the years [reminding all staff that], if someone's not listening to you, that they have a responsibility to do so. Generally if you talk to people, they knew something was wrong, but it's how they communicate what's wrong so that someone else recognizes its a problem [that is key]. So I talk to them about that, and encourage them, if you have a question and someone is not listening to you, you need to call someone else." (Interview 12/412–425).
	Mentoring/shadowing.	Maintains capabilities for resilience.	• "An associate that was having a little difficulty and they kind of learned by seeing and just being there again. It was kind of like being 'present' because I can explain them all kinds of things. I can pull out the policy on disciplinary action, but to me it means nothing until they've actually experienced it. And not just one, but a couple to get it under their belts. They don't get that from a book. They don't get that from policy and procedure. They have to be part of that and they learn as they're doing it" (Interview 20/55–68).
	Consults with other to gather knowledge beyond records and books. Facilitates a culture that encourages tacit knowledge sharing.	Takes advantage of shifting locations of expertise.	• "It was an environment that was created in the NICU where you could talk to others, you could get their support, you could do what you felt was right without any kind of, you know, I'm going against this doctor. He is in charge of the NICU, [with the teams help] we were able to get this baby the help it needed … we intervened immediately and the baby did fine … it was, I think, teamwork at its best and it was that whole environment where you are free and comfortable to consult with other people, to put your heads together, you know what I mean? And to intervene for this baby … I mean these babies could die really quick. It felt really good to be in an environment like that (Interview 3/192–202).
Effective: providing services based on evidence to those who could benefit and to not provide services that patients would not benefit from.	Encourages surfacing of concerns.	Tracks small failures.	• "Some of the little nuggets that we've picked up [doing Leadership Safety rounds] over the last three years, we would not have picked up until something bad happened … Often with errors, especially catastrophic, there's always those that will say "Yeah, well, we've actually known about this for a long time, but didn't have a way to share that'" (Interview 2/252–266). • "They were so appreciative that they were actually getting feedback and I think that is so important with sharing the knowledge. We can't do it once and then we walk away because people want that reinforcement or feedback that something's changing" (Interview 18/482–485).

Quality Aims (Chasm Report 2001: 5–6)	KSharing Behaviors	HRO Element Support (Weick and Sutcliffe 2001)	Supportive quotes (edited for clarity)
Effective (Continued)	Sees value in context.	Resists oversimplification.	• "If you're not appropriately appreciative of the experience base that other people have that causes them to see information with nuances that they can't explain very well to you, but that color their perception of the situation in ways that are value added. You are not going to effectively engage with people as a productive team member" (Interview 16/150–156). • "... could a supervisor really supervise work if they sit in their office all day? They have to be out there at least some of the time observing practices and mentoring people through those risks that they may not be identifying ..." (Interview 11/351–354).
	Appreciates team/collaborative involvement.		• "We spent two days at that [collaborative] series doing different activities and looking at different things and all of a sudden, you had one of those light bulb moments come on, and it's like, 'This is where I'm going wrong.' I was like, 'It's much bigger than this. I've been missing the point ...' It was just powerful being in that room and I don't think anybody said that, but it was just hearing everybody say things and then me putting things together looking at what our experience had been and looking 'I've got to change this and I've got to go a different direction'" (Interview 20/108–124).
	Sharing of experience through mentoring/coaching/ observation.	Remains sensitive to operations.	• "[Tacit] knowledge" gives me "something to hang [the facts] on and when there's a story involved, when there is a bit of history that you share with me about a similar encounter ... I am then able to find someplace to hang this on to make it easier to retrieve it" (Interview 9/40–44). • "It's hard to tell a story about errors that you were involved in, but it's important [for students] to realize these things happen" (Interview 12/74–75). • "I had heard of ['nurses eating their young'] but until someone actually walked me through and provided me with examples of things that happened, I was like, 'I had no idea.' I then knew I needed to think about this differently now. 'How am I going to teach in that environment, then if it's just nurses?' [The experience] showed me the importance of how deleterious this interaction could be to patient safety if I'm not communicating with that in mind" (Interview 18/136–150).

Quality Aims (Chasm Report 2001: 5–6)	KSharing Behaviors	HRO Element Support (Weick and Sutcliffe 2001)	Supportive quotes (edited for clarity)
Effective (Continued)	Sees value in context/peer orientation in situ.	Maintains capabilities for resilience.	• "I feel that we're so regimented and we only know how to solve the problems with what we know. That knowledge of looking differently and solving a problem, again I'm not sure that we could write it down, but it's something that if you can impart that to folks, it can make them much more effective in doing some of the changes that we expect of them" (Interview 10/153–157). • "You have to see it through the other person's eyes. We send patients [to ambulatory-type settings] all the time, but I've really not spent a lot of time in them. I'm pretty healthy, so even as a patient I haven't been in an office practice that much. But just being [with a 'transition to home' team] and breaking down those silos and talking about what their work is like has made our work better and our learning better because we've seen the bigger picture" (Interview 20/201–212).
		Takes advantage of shifting locations of expertise.	• "None of us are as smart as all of us" (Interview 9/341). • "It was truly tacit knowledge as he [an organizational leader] never said the word, but the learned experience and the learned concept that came out that [exchange] was very important to me" (Interview 15/74–76). • "Informal leaders sometimes are stronger influencers than the C-suite to some staff. You have to know who those informal leaders are. If you worked in the trenches, you know who those people are. They have to be part of a transition. They have to be recognized because there's sometimes a huge disconnect between the C-suite and the management level individuals" (Interview 14/366–372).
Patient-centered: providing care that is respectful and addresses patient needs, preferences and values and that is guided by those principles	Solicits insights from others.	Tracks small failures.	• "I think what patients have been screaming for was to be a partner in their care. They acknowledge that they do not have a medical or nursing degree, but they do know either themselves or their family member well and they thought that they had something to contribute to the care process. I don't think we do that enough yet when we do it, it's extremely valuable" (13/343–349).

Quality Aims (Chasm Report 2001: 5–6)	KSharing Behaviors	HRO Element Support (Weick and Sutcliffe 2001)	Supportive quotes (edited for clarity)
Patient-centered (Continued)	Sees value in listening as a skill and professional responsibility.	Resists oversimplification.	• "Until I asked [my patient] 'what is it you want?' I didn't really understand what I was doing for him" (Interview 9/87–88). • "I think that the best blunt end staff choose to have interactions and conversations in ways so the experiences of the patient, of the families, of the frontline caregivers are truly accessed and woven into the tacit knowledge of the blunt end at every level" (Interview 5/420–423). • "So the two of us [patient and family member], when we're together [with the care team] really gained and gleaned a lot of their unspoken knowledge of the direction that things were going to go in" (Interview 8/553–555). • "If we hear the way a patient is feeling about something, or what makes them feel cared for, the individual patient's experience is no something that you can easily transfer from one to another" (Interview 7/550–560).
	Sharing of experience through mentoring/coaching/ observation.	Remains sensitive to operations.	• "I gave them a tour of the OR. They were terrified, they didn't want to go in, but I wanted them to see the environment. Once they did, they seemed to appreciate it and their attitudes changed and they became much more supportive and responsive and also met some people, which helped a lot. …" (Interview 6/707–717). • "First, we all got together and we realized we had a problem, but when we heard it from the patients, and actually put it in their perspective, everybody was on board. And ironically, when we went to the physicians with what we heard at the focus group they're like, 'This is really good stuff. We hadn't thought of this either" (Interview 20/429–436).
	Teamwork.	Maintains capabilities for resilience.	• "One of the reasons that I always, when I am rounding, I try to make sure that I've got the nurse with me at the bedside because I want to make sure that we're communicating well. When the nurse and I both hear the same thing from the patient or the patient and the nurse both hear the same things from me then I know that I've got an ally who's going to reinforce my plan with the patient or the nurse can help facilitate a conversation that the patient may have mentioned to them, but they may be a little bit awkward, feel a little bit awkward by bringing it up with me. But I also think that it's an opportunity for the nurse and I to learn from one another. (Interview 9/275–283).
		Takes advantage of shifting locations of expertise.	• "So that creativity or that piece of work that the patients bring in, may feel threatening, but if we use it, it probably will make our work a lot easier and probably get rid of things that we think are value added, but patients have no feeling that it's value added" (Interview 10/386–389).

Index

Note: Page numbers in **bold** indicate figures.